Barbarian seas

Late Rome to Islam

Published by Periplus Publishing London Ltd
Publisher: Danièle Juncqua Naveau
Series consultant: Dr Sean Kingsley
Managing editor: Nick Easterbrook
Assistant editor: Jenny Finch
Production manager: Sophie Chéry
Production assistants: Arvind Shah, Ludovic Pellé
Picture research: Jane Lowry

Reprographics: Periplus Publishing London Ltd
Printed and bound in Italy by Graphicom

ISBN: 1-902699-57-2

Barbarian seas

Late Rome to Islam

Sean Kingsley

Periplus

London

Acknowledgements

In the preparation of this book, the author and Periplus Publishing London Ltd would like to thank numerous people and institutions for generously offering their time and assistance: Krzysztof Babraj, George Bass, Carlo Beltrame, David Blackman, William Bowden, Rupert Chapman III, Felicity Cobbing, Richard Hodges, Robert Hohlfelder, Luc Long, Marlia Mango, Carol Meyer, Claude Santamaria, Robert R. Stieglitz, Hanna Szymanska, Giuliano Volpe, Shelley Wachsmann, David Whitehouse, Ivan Mirnik and Ante Rendic-Miocevic. Special thanks are extended to: Peter Clayton for his very generous support and supply of photographs; to Juliet Frankel and the Kingsley clan for shoulders to lean on.

Marine archaeology is a laborious and often thankless business. Years of advanced planning are required to organise an excavation, and for every month spent exploring a shipwreck at least one year is needed after the fieldwork to painstakingly process finds and research results. Thus, we are indebted to the numerous marine archaeologists who have contributed to this volume, whose hundreds of hours spent in the silent waters of the Mediterranean, meticulously recording and reconstructing ancient ships, form the backbone of this encyclopaedia:

Professor Frederick van Doorninck Jr, Institute of Nautical Archaeology, Texas A & M University;

Frederick M. Hocker, Project Director, Vasa Research, National Maritime Museums of Sweden;

Jean-Pierre Joncheray;

Dr Yaacov Kahanov, the Leon Recanati Institute for Maritime Studies, University of Haifa;

Dr Anna Marguerite McCann, Archaeological Director, Skerki Bank Project, Visiting Scholar, Massachusetts Institute of Technology;

Dr Stefano Medas, Istituto Italiano di Archeologia e Etnologia Navale, Venezia, Università di Bologna, Facoltà di Conservazione dei Beni Culturali, Ravenna;

Dr Rubens D'Oriano, Soprintendenza per i Beni Archeologici delle provincie di Sassari e Nuoro;

Professor Gianfranco Purpura, Department of the History of Law, University of Palermo;

Dr Edoardo Riccardi;

Dr Cheryl Ward, Department of Anthropology, Florida State University;

Sean Kingsley,
London, 2004

Contents

Introduction

...the enjoyment of almost every object that can afford pleasure to the different tastes and tempers of mankind may be procured by the possession of wealth. In the pillage of Rome a just preference was given to gold and jewels, which contain the greatest value in the smallest compass and weight, but, after these portable riches had been removed by the more diligent robbers, the palaces of Rome were rudely stripped of their splendid and costly furniture. The sideboards of massy plate, and the variegated wardrobes of silk and purple, were irregularly piled in the wagons that always followed the march of a Gothic army. The most exquisite works of art were roughly handled or wantonly destroyed: many a statue was melted for the sake of the precious materials and many a vase, in the division of the spoil, was shivered into fragments by the stroke of a battleaxe. The acquisition of riches served only to stimulate the avarice of the rapacious barbarians, who proceeded by threats, by blows, and by tortures, to force from their prisoners the confession of hidden treasure.

Edward Gibbon, *The History of the Decline and Fall of the Roman Empire* (1776).

The decline and fall of the Roman Empire, as regaled above by the great historian Edward Gibbon describing the third siege and sack of Rome by the Goths on 24 August, AD 410, is one of the most evocative themes of history. It is a heavyweight intellectual debate that has challenged some of the greatest minds of the 18th to 21st centuries. Literally hundreds of books and articles have grappled with the question: did Rome fall and, if so, when and with what consequences?

The birth of archaeology in the 19th and early 20th centuries should have gone a long way to settling the debate, but to the excavators of Rome, Lepcis Magna and almost every major ancient city of the Roman Empire, the ruins of the 4th to 10th centuries were unappealing. In the imagination of the early archaeologist, coloured by the rose-tinted view of classical authors, Rome symbolised the zenith of cultural achievement and was an epic civilisation, bursting with monumental architecture and the finest art.

The Later Roman Empire, by contrast, was considered a grubby era lacking in finesse and unworthy of study. Consequently, early archaeologists usually hacked these upper archaeological levels away without record, eager to reach the eternal treasures of the Roman age. The two periods were judged historically incompatible, rather like the gaping cultural divide between the USA today and the quaint backwaters of 18th-century America.

All this has now changed. The study of Late Antiquity (4th–8th centuries AD) is riding the crest of a wave, as scientific archaeology makes up for the sins of its fathers, realising that in many regions Roman forms of government, town planning and trade flourished as late as the 7th century. This is particularly true for the East Mediterranean after the foundation of Constantinople in the early 4th century, where pick, spade and sophisticated magnetometry have found hundreds of villages and towns built just as carefully as in the age of Rome.

Most eastern cities even expanded beyond the confines of the Roman fortifications as population levels swelled. The Late Antique mosaics of Syria, Jordan and Israel are amongst the finest to survive from classical antiquity, and the tonnes of pottery, glass and marble excavated from these ruins have fostered a new respect for the huge volume of traffic that continued to ply the Mediterranean Sea.

The current fascination with the crucial role played by economies in motivating and sustaining Mediterranean communities is reflected in two new and monumental books: *The Economic History of Byzantium. From the Seventh through the Fifteenth Century* (Dumbarton Oaks, Washington, 2002) and *Origins of the European Economy. Communications and Commerce AD 300–900* by Michael McCormick (Cambridge University Press, 2002). In these new histories, shipwrecks and trade are pivotal in attempts to reconstruct a period still occupied by barbarians, but that new research has shown to be culturally multi-coloured rather than steeped in darkness.

In many ways, marine archaeologists arrived at the same conclusion four decades earlier. In 1960, Gerhard Kapitän and P. Gargallo surveyed a fascinating prefabricated cargo of marbles at Marzamemi, Sicily, pre-ordered for a Byzantine church. In 1962, Alain Visquis found the hull and cargo of a unique 9th-century Saracen wreck at Agay, off southern France. From 1961–64, George Bass and Frederick van Doorninck fully excavated a Byzantine ship that had struck the island of Yassi Ada, Turkey, in AD 625/6 with a cargo of 900 amphorae of wine collected from an ecclesiastical estate.

The imperial pleasure barges and decadent shipments of Roman marble columns and luxury statues may have become a thing of the past, but in diet, dress and culture, Late Antiquity followed the same ideals and dreams as the Eternal City. Since society was more egalitarian than that of Rome, the lords of Late Antiquity – Byzantines, Christians, Vandals, Arabs – had greater access to the fruits of the empire.

Today, marine archaeologists have found 222 shipwrecks dating between the 4th and 10th centuries, 92 of which have come to light in the last 12 years. These new discoveries are the focus of this encyclopaedia, which explains just how wrong history was to judge Late Antiquity as a dark age. Instead, the maritime genius of the period is exposed in all its glory in one volume for the first time. The empire may have been divided and barbarians may have been howling at its creaking gates, but the period was nothing less than revolutionary for seafaring.

BRITANNIA I

Londinium

GERMANIA II

BELGICA II

LUGDUNENSIS II

LUGDUNENSIS III

LUGDUNENSIS SENONIA

BELGICA I

GERMANIA I

RAETIA II

NORICUM RIPENSE

PANNONIA I

VALLIA

MAXIMA SEQUANORUM

NORICUM MEDITER-RANEUM

SAVIA

AQUITANICA II

AQUITANICA I

LUGDUNENSIS

ALPES POENINAE

RAETIA I

PANNC

AEMILIA

VENETIA ET HISTRIA

DALMATIA

VIENNENSIS

ALPES COTTIAE

LIGURIA

FLAMINIA ET PICENUM

Ravenna

NOVEM POPULI

NARBONENSIS I

NARBON-ENSIS II

ALPES MARITIMAE

Pisa

TUSCIA ET UMBRIA

PICENUM SUBURBI-CARIUM

Salona

GALLAECIA

TARRACONENSIS

Marseille

CORSICA

ROMA

VALERIA

SAMNIUM

APULIA ET CALABRIA

Rome

CAMPANIA

Tarraco

SARDINIA

Naples

LUCANIA ET BRUTTII

CARTHAGINIENSIS

BALEARES

BAETICA

Carthago Novo

SICILIA

Carthage

TINGITANIA

MAURETANIA CAESARIENSIS

MAURETANIA SITIFENSIS

NUMIDIA

AFRICA

BYZACENA

Sabratha

Oea

Lepcis Magna

Late Roman provinces and coastal cities after the early 4th century AD

TRIPOLITANIA

© Periplus Publishing London Ltd

SCYTHIA

Chersonesus

Tomis

ESIA I

DACIA
RIPENSIS

DACIA
MEDITER-
RANEA

DARDANIA

MOESIA II

THRACIA

HAEMI-
MONTUS

RHODOPE

EUROPA

Heraclea

Constantinople

Ionopolis

Sinope

PAPHLAGONIA

HELLENO-
PONTUS

PONTUS
POLEMONIACUS

HONORIAS

GALATIA

ARMENIA I

AL-
A

EPIRUS
NOVA

MACEDONIA

Thessalonica

THESSALIA

EPIRUS
VETUS

olis

HELLES-
PONTUS

BITHYNIA

PHRYGIA
SALUTARIS

PHRYGIA
PACATIANA

CAPPADOCIA II

CAPPADOCIA I

ARMENIA II

MESOPOTAMIA

OSRHOENE

Smyrna

LYDIA

ASIA

PISIDIA

LYCAONIA

CILICIA

CILICIA
II

EUPHRATENSIS

Ephesus

CARIA

PAMPHYLIA

ISAURIA

Tarsus

Antioch

ACHAEA

Anthedon

Athens

Corinth

LYCIA

Side

Seleucia

Laodicea

SYRIA

SYRIA SALUTARIS

Aperlae

Myra

INSULAE

Salamis

Tripolis

PHOENICE

PHOENICE
LIBANENSIS

CRETA

Paphos

CYPRUS

Beirut

Sidon

Tyre

PALAESTINA II

Ptolemais

Caesarea

Dor

ARABIA

Alexandria

Pelusium

PALAESTINA I

Ashkelon

Gaza

Ptolemais

enice

Marea

AEGYPTUS

AUGUST-
AMNICA

PALAESTINA
SALUTARIS

LIBYA
SUPERIOR

LIBYA INFERIOR

Aqaba

Myos Hormos

Detail from a relief on the obelisk of Theodosius in Istanbul, showing kneeling barbarians appeasing the Byzantine emperor with gifts.

I. Winds of change

As the end of the world approaches, many things menace us which never existed before: inversions of the climate, horrors from the heavens and storms contrary to the season, wars, famine, plagues, in some places earthquakes...

Pope Gregory the Great to an Anglo-Saxon king, June AD 601.

Following three centuries of relative political, religious and economic stability, the Roman Empire entered the eye of a storm in the late 4th century AD. In the space of 100 years, many of the provinces that Rome had spilt so much blood to conquer were lost. From the 4th to 8th centuries AD, winds of change blew new peoples on to the political map – Abbasids, Avars, Byzantines, Goths, Lombards, Umayyads and Venetians – who introduced new forms of culture and communication. Late Antiquity was to be a period of unprecedented ferment across the Mediterranean, when society was dramatically transformed. As the tide of history started to turn, the old and the new were intermixed. Classical civilisation was now laced with unknown institutions, from the Christian Church to mediaeval feudalism in the West, and the first exotic scents of an Oriental Islam in the East.

In theory, the military threats to the borders of the empire would be expected to have played havoc with the old, established sea-lanes of *mare nostrum*. Between the early 5th century AD and the second half of the 6th century, the western Mediterranean fragmented into a maze of independent barbarian kingdoms. In AD 383 the Altar of Victory – symbol of military omnipotence – was removed from the Senate in Rome. In the year AD 405 the Rhine froze over, enabling thousands of Germanic migrants to spill into the Empire, ushering in a Dark Age.

Five years later Alaric the Goth sacked Rome. By the 440s Gaul and its key waterways were annexed from the empire to the Visigoths. Worse was to follow: in AD 442 the Vandals under King Gaiseric became masters of the North African provinces of Proconsularis, Byzacena, Tripolitania and Eastern Numidia and their massively wealthy resources of oil and wheat. Rome's vital breadbasket, which had fed the empire for centuries, was gone. The economic impact was as if the oil fields of modern Saudi Arabia suddenly ran dry. Finally, in 476 the last Roman emperor of the West was removed from office by the Germanic general, Odovacer. By a twist of fate, this emperor was called Romulus (Augustulus). Thus, the legendary founder of Rome and the last warrior of the empire shared the same name.

Following the devastating effects of the Gothic War (535–54), Italy hardly had time to draw breath before the Lombard incursions into the north of the

Porphyry statue of the Late Roman emperors and deputies standing opposite each other as a reflection of the division of the empire in the 4th century. From Constantinople, now in St Mark's Cathedral, Venice.

Photo: Peter Clayton

peninsula from 568–9. In the same decade, the partition of the Frankish kingdoms left the great commercial entrepôt of Marseille out on a limb as a final bastion of a once-great trading empire.

By the 5th century AD, Rome was but a forlorn shadow of its heyday, stripped of its gleaming marble revetments and of its outspoken rabble, which declined in size from 800,000 to 350,000 people after the raid of 410, to 100,000 around 500, and to fewer than 30,000 in the 7th century. Archaeological fieldwork conducted in South Etruria confirms the same picture of abandonment across the countryside: by AD 400, 50% of early Roman Imperial sites were unoccupied. Citizens now took for granted city buildings lying in ruins, and in these times of great economic insecurity turned to rich and powerful landowners, toiling fields under their protection and spawning European feudalism. As the 5th century priest Salvian of Marseille wrote, "Those who are accepted on to the estates of the rich are transformed like the pigs of Circe… those considered to be free are turned into slaves."

Land and sea transport undoubtedly suffered from these disruptions. In the 5th century, the *cursus publicus*, that great network of Roman roads with reliable way stations (*mansiones*) spaced as close as 16km apart, started to go into wrack and ruin in the West. Milestones, left unattended, fell down and were overgrown. By the late 4th century the western section of the Via Egnatia, a major communication artery of the empire running crosswise through the Balkans and linking the Adriatic and Aegean with Rome and Constantinople, was lost to the Visigoths. Disruption remained a constant theme as the Danube frontier was besieged by the Avars in the 6th century and by the Bulgars a century later. Transport between the Danube basin, Thessalonika and the Golden Gates of Constantinople was fraught with danger.

Nowhere in the western Mediterranean is the scale of change at port cities so clear as at the UNESCO World Heritage Site of Butrint in Albania, where 10 years of excavations conducted by the Institute of World Archaeology of the University of East Anglia have revealed a vivid picture of stagnation. The

Mosaic in the Roman estate of Diaporit at Butrint, Albania. The floor was cut into during Late Antiquity to insert wooden posts to support fishermen's huts.

Photo: Institute of World Archaeology, University of East Anglia.

city's Triconch Palace, once an opulent Late Roman town house boasting baths and mosaics, lost all its glory around the mid-5th century, when its elaborate floors were violated by wooden posts to support a shanty village of fishermen's huts. The very heart of *romanitas* (being Roman) had been rudely ripped away.

It is testimony to the deep-rooted and enduring legacy of Rome that in many ways traditional forms of trade and shipping did manage to continue, in some places as late as the mid-7th century AD. For as Old Rome fell, Constantinople – or New Rome – was emerging as an imperial capital on the northern shores of the eastern Mediterranean. The seeds of change were sown by the Emperor Diocletian (284–305), who – with the wisdom of Solomon – resolved the bloody dilemma of imperial succession to the throne by dividing the empire between the West and East. This sweeping reform of dual divide and rule became permanent under Constantine I the Great (306–337).

Constantine founded Constantinople as a deliberate replacement for Rome. Inaugurated on 11 May 330, New Rome was given all the trappings of its grand western forefather, from a senate to a hippodrome. Indeed, it was to here that Constantine's son, Arcadius, shipped the Altar of Victory from Rome. The establishment of a welfare state system was to transform the sleepy backwaters of the eastern Mediterranean into heavily sailed seas.

Built at a point of huge geographic, strategic, political and economic importance, the new Early Byzantine Empire ruled from Constantinople was to dominate communication between the Aegean, Black Sea, Near East, Asia and Europe, in some cases for up to 1,000 years. The peak period of prosperity, artistic and economic, spanned the reigns of the Emperor Anastasius (491–518), who upon his death left the treasury with a surplus of 320,000lbs of gold, and Justinian (527–565), who greedily set about spending this windfall as quickly

A mosaic floor in the Triconch Palace at Butrint, Albania. A kiln for making ships' iron nails was built over the floor in Late Antiquity, badly burning the mosaic.

Photo: Institute of World Archaeology, University of East Anglia

The well sheltered maritime waterways of Constantinople. From the Nuremberg Chronicle by Hartmann Schedel (1440–1514) 1493 (woodblock), German School (15th century). Stapleton Collection.

© The Bridgeman Art Library

as possible. Even as late as the 940s, when Liutprand of Cremona visited Constantinople, the splendour of New Rome continued to astonish. The emperor's audience hall boasted a golden throne with an 'automata' of singing birds, roaring lions, and a mechanical contraption that lifted up the throne before a visitor could arise from the position of prostration.

At the same time, society was experiencing an equally sweeping religious transformation with the emergence of Christianity, which, following the Edict of Milan in AD 313, became the official state religion in 381. The profound impact of this spiritual awakening on Late Antique society, town planning and even maritime trade cannot be underestimated. Wealthy landowners no longer expressed social and political prestige amongst peers by competing for civic pride, laying out horrendous sums of money for the construction of endless statues, bathhouses or theatres. As the once strictly linear streets of the empire's towns were encroached upon by shops and houses (creating the beginnings of mediaeval village lanes in the West and the winding alleys of the Arab *souk* in the East), instead the upper classes diverted their wealth into generous donations to churches and later monasteries in the form of silver plates, mosaic floors, marble columns and money.

Christianity superimposed itself on the divine pantheon of Rome, in numerous cases building churches on the foundations of former pagan temples from around AD 450. Pampered by emperors and the rich and famous, the Church very rapidly became a landowner of incredible proportion and wealth, owning orchards, fleets of ships, ports, and even lending credit to merchants. During a visit to Jerusalem, the Empress Eudocia is reputed to have spent the enormous sum of 20,480lbs of gold on church construction (about 1,500,500 pieces of gold) at a time when two gold pieces could sustain one person for a year. The silver-leaf revetment of the imperial church of Hagia Sophia in Constantinople alone would have required an outlay of 40,000 pounds of silver. It was not uncommon for cities like Umm el-Jimal in Jordan to boast 15 churches.

In contrast to the West, the 5th to mid-7th centuries were a Golden Age in the eastern Mediterranean, when exciting new markets emerged, former swamps, languishing fields and the desert landscapes of Syria's limestone massif and Palestine's Negev were reclaimed. As commerce thrived, Mediterranean society underwent a period of unprecedented social mobility. This was a world in which historical texts tell us that the son of a sausage maker could rise to become a consul. As Theodoret succinctly explained in the later 4th century AD, "some men prefer a sailor's career, some a soldier's; some become athletes, some farmers; some ply one trade, some another."

Yet everyday life in the eastern provinces was far from utopian; the Byzantine State had its own 'barbarian' horde seething at the gates of the empire. The Slavs were a continuous menace, attacking Thessalonika in 586, 604, 615, 682, and the Peloponnese after 582. Even more troublesome for the East were the Sasanians of Persia (inhabiting modern Iran). Throughout the 5th century and as late as 562 the Byzantine State begrudgingly paid them incredible sums to 'buy' the peace: 11,000lbs of gold in 532; and 30,000 gold coins annually for a 50-year peace treaty in 561.

A 1st century AD monumental porphyry marble statue reused in the 5th century Byzantine esplanade at Caesarea, Israel.

Photo: Peter Clayton

The imperial Byzantine Church of Hagia Sophia, built as the new Cathedral of Constantinople by the Emperor Justinian between 532 and 537.

Photo: Peter Clayton

Yet this tentative peace never held, and in AD 617 Alexandria fell to the Persians. One year later the annual shipment of wheat to the poor of Constantinople (see Chapter 2) ceased forever, thus ending a long-lived system of free dole redistributions to major Mediterranean cities going back 650 years. Less than two decades later Umayyad Arabs fell on a financially and militarily exhausted empire. The Battle of Yarmuk waged in Palestine in AD 636 opened the way for Syria, Palestine, Armenia and Egypt with all its wealth to fall to the Arabs. By the late 7th century North Africa was lost, and by 711 the conquest of Gibraltar exposed Spain to the Arabs. Although the Umayyad caliphate unsuccessfully besieged Constantinople in 678 and 718, the Byzantine Empire's domination of the Mediterranean was shattered. By the end of the 7th century, the Byzantine Empire was greatly reduced in size, under constant attack, and deprived of some three-quarters of its former tax revenues.

While the pages of history lay the blame for the death of an empire on the hammer blow of 7th-century war, modern research suggests the seeds of decline were sown just under 200 years earlier. For in AD 541, deadly black rats transmitted the bubonic plague throughout the Mediterranean. More appropriately for maritime historians, ships carried this deadly cargo. First appearing in Egypt in autumn 541, the plague struck Alexandria, Gaza, Antioch and Syria the following year, reaching the Balkans and the West in 543. As the plague raged in Constantinople for four months, 10,000 people died daily. In Palestine, the terrified population claimed that headless Ethiopian sailors in brass

Multi-coloured mosaic floor in the Byzantine Church of Petra, Jordan, decorated with scenes of wild animals, fruit and vegetation. Built in the mid- to late 5th century AD.

Photo: Peter Clayton

ships could be seen spreading disease along the beaches. The bubonic plague of AD 542 was history's first great pandemic and, with a mortality rate of 78%, may have wiped out as much as one-third of the Mediterranean's population. It would be another 206 years before the plague finally burnt itself out.

Coupled with a series of terrible earthquakes that toppled the coastal cities of the Near East between Tripoli and Tyre in the first half of the 6th century, it is not hard to imagine how an emaciated state and society were relatively easy pickings for Sasanians and Umayyads. Yet, just as facsimiles of Roman society endured into the Byzantine State, so did the empires of the Umayyads (AD 638–750) and the Abbasids (AD 750–1099) imitate some of the winning formulas of Old and New Rome. This took the form of regular tax imposition, the maintenance of roads and milestones in the late 7th and 8th centuries, and the minting of Arab-Byzantine coins in order to partake of the profits of a trading empire. Just how long traces of classical antiquity endured in the Early Islamic world is hotly debated and, as we shall see (Chapters 3, 4, 6), underwater archaeology is today one of the most reliable scientific sources for grappling with this problem.

The great earthquake of Beirut

Within one decade of the outbreak of the bubonic plague in the eastern Mediterranean, the Near East suffered the additional calamity of extremely violent earthquakes in AD 550/1. Vivid accounts preserved in the writings of various historians describe how the traumatised population may have felt that the end of the world was nigh. John Malalas chronicled the "tremendous earthquake" that shook the coastal cities of Tyre, Sidon, Beirut, Tripolis, and as far south as Ptolemais in northern Palestine. Particularly poignant is an unusually complete account recorded by John of Ephesus:

But we have decided to report for posterity a terrible disaster and a great and remarkable portent which happened in the city of Beirut in Phoenicia during the earthquake which destroyed the cities. For in the terrible confusion, when the sea at God's will had retreated and withdrawn from Beirut... for a distance of nearly two miles, the dreadful depths of the sea became visible. Suddenly wonderful, varied and amazing sights could be seen – sunken ships full of different cargoes...

For the inhabitants of the cities and towns on the coast immediately rushed into the sea on a bold and determined impulse, to steal with wicked avarice the huge overturned treasures which were at the bottom of the sea – an impulse which cost them their lives. Therefore when many thousands of people, rushing into the depths of the sea on a deadly impulse, had begun to take the treasures and remove them quickly... then a tremendous surge of the sea, rushing up unobserved to return to its original depth, overwhelmed and consumed in the depths of its eddying waters all those wretched people... like Pharaoh, they went down to the depths and were drowned, as it is written, like stones...

Those who had lingered on the edge of the shore in these places... fled to the shore... But after they had escaped, as if from hunters, a violent earthquake took place which overturned houses in the cities, especially Beirut. The houses as they fell crushed those who had escaped from the sea, and so nobody survived. For with the sea rising up against them from behind and the earthquake bringing down the city in front of them because of their evil greed, they were caught between two disasters... Therefore those who had sought wealth were delivered up to total destruction and lost their lives, and their bodies were found floating on the waves like rubbish. Then in the rubble of the destroyed city, at God's command, fire broke out and for almost two months the flames burned and flared up among the ruins, till even the stones were burnt and turned to lime. Then the Lord sent down rain from heaven for three days and nights, and so the fire burning in Beirut was put out. Any who had been saved from the sea's return and the collapse of the city, lay in the city wounded and injured and consumed by thirst, since the city's aqueduct had been destroyed.

John of Ephesus (485.20–23) translated in E. Jeffreys, M. Jeffreys and R. Scott, *The Chronicle of John Malalas* (Melboune, 1986).

What is certain, however, is that with the decline of the Umayyad caliphate and the emergence of the Abbasids, the maritime flavour of the Mediterranean changed dramatically. Classical civilisation dating back to 5th century BC Athens was gone forever, to be replaced by mediaevalism in the West and Islam in the East, clearing the way for new types of trade patterns and seafaring that were to ebb and flow into the Ottoman period. In theory, the Byzantine Empire imposed an embargo on commerce with the Arab world, whose Mediterranean maritime tradition, in any case, was almost nonexistent (no ships are recorded as accompanying the siege of Palestine in AD 636). According to the historian, al Baladhuri, the Arabs had no shipyards before their construction in Egypt in 669.

Christianity, the Early Byzantine Empire's tool of religious propaganda, which had united the eastern Mediterranean in the 5th–7th centuries, now started to crumble. Thus, in the later 820s a fleet of 10 Venetian ships arrived in Alexandria and stole the relics of St Mark for Venice, having smuggled them out of the port in a basket covered with cabbage leaves and pork. Christ was on the retreat. Despite this, from the later 8th century, pilgrim traffic no longer stopped at Constantinople on the way to Jerusalem, but now sailed via Arab Egypt, a sure sign of the reversal of power in the eastern Mediterranean. Meanwhile, the wealth of the Byzantine Empire continued to haemorrhage to 'barbarians' as Constantinople shopped for peace: in AD 768 Constantine V sent 2,500 silk garments to the Slavs to ransom prisoners seized on the Greek islands. A few years later his daughter-in-law, the Empress Irene, paid Harun al-Rashid almost 140,000 gold coins a year for seven years' peace.

Instead of Syrians and cargoes of wine, oil and Roman types of pottery, the character and protagonists of maritime trade were also very different. Many of the recorded merchants of the mid-8th to mid-9th centuries were slave traders, and a legendary slave market in Rome catered directly for the markets of the Arab world. At much the same time, Viking fleets had now sailed on to the pages of history and, in AD 859–62, could be seen raiding Morocco and rowing along the Riviera, wreaking havoc at Gallic sites such as Arles. *Mare nostrum* and its legacy were by now distant memories, forgotten like the very shipwrecks that for centuries had foundered by their hundreds across the waters of the Mediterranean.

II. The fat of the land:
Late Antiquity's economic portfolio

Despite the web of catastrophe and strain that beset the world of Late Antiquity, it was a testimony to the human spirit that maritime trade found a way not only to survive, but also to thrive. Few of the quays and breakwaters of the great Roman ports of Ostia, Marseille and Carthage were kept in a good state of repair (see Chapter 6) and, instead, a more flexible and natural approach to seafaring evolved, which was to prove no less than a nautical revolution for merchant entrepreneurs (see Chapter 4).

This new drive was largely a vision of the eastern Mediterranean. Although western merchants and 'European' cargoes can be traced amongst historical texts and shipwrecked cargoes of the period, the hallmark of eastern merchants and state policies predominates. Between the 4th and 6th centuries the *navicularii* of Spain, Gaul, Italy, Sardinia and Africa disappear from the pages of history. The power base had shifted as Near Eastern merchants dominated maritime trade, crowding harbours and bringing a strongly oriental flavour to port cities by the late 4th century AD. Thus, according to St Jerome, "The Syrians have, up to the present day, an innate tendency for trade. Their love of profit takes them all over the world, even in these times when the Roman world has been invaded. Their passion for trade pushes them in the search for wealth among swords and into the killing of the innocent, and to flee from poverty, coming face to face with danger… they are businessmen and the most greedy of mortals."

Trade and the welfare state

Swift to exploit markets in lands newly conquered by barbarian rulers, the rise of the eastern merchant was in many ways a direct consequence of new state policies. Since the 2nd century BC, Rome had taxed its provinces 'in kind', compelling landowners to contribute wheat, oil, wine, clothing and pork to the imperial treasury. Part of this enormous wealth was then distributed free to the populace of Rome as a dole for the poor, a rabble notoriously prone to disorder if not continuously appeased. Cunningly, Rome deliberately over-taxed the provinces, enabling oil, in particular, to be sold on commercially to Gaul and Spain. For this purpose the state ran 2,300 olive-oil shops, *mensae oleariae*, across the city.

The procurement of grain and olive oil for what was known as the *annona civica* required a chain of hundreds of merchants and ships. In its heyday, no less than 120,000 tonnes of grain was annually imported into Rome from North Africa, which would have required 800 sea-crossings in a type of ship capable of holding 340 tonnes of cargo. Despite the decline in the size of its

Oceanus holding a ship on a mosaic in the southern aisle of the Byzantine Church at Petra, Jordan. Built in the mid- to late 5th century AD. Maritime imagery reflects the importance of the sea in exporting local produce, a key source of wealth.

Photo: Peter Clayton

population, 120,000 people still received free grain in the first quarter of the 5th century, with 33,600 tonnes being imported in AD 452 and 6,300 tonnes around AD 530.

Free daily handouts of olive oil were also an integral part of Rome's welfare state, with North Africa supplanting Baetica in Spain as the prime supplier during the 3rd century. The epicentre of olive cultivation was the Sahel region of Tunisia, which boasted an estimated 10 million olive trees in antiquity, and the countryside around Lepcis Magna in Libya may have produced 20 million litres of exportable oil yearly, the equivalent of 350,000 full amphorae. Not surprisingly, the waters of southern France, Italy and the Balkans are littered with shipwrecks containing thousands of North African amphorae, mostly from Tunisia.

This policy of importing staple agricultural produce as tax for free or subsidised redistribution was immediately adopted by Constantinople upon its foundation. The preserved writings of John Malalas inform us that in AD 330 the Emperor Constantine "distributed largesse in Constantinople to the [citizens of Byzantium]; these were reed tokens for perpetual daily bread distribution. He called the loaves 'palatine' because they were given out in the palace. He set aside wine, meat and garments with each loaf and set aside revenues for them from his own resources; he called the loaves 'politikoi' (civil)."

The logistics involved in this system were again enormous. In both the 5th and 6th centuries some 80,000 people received free bread in Constantinople annually, milled in the city's 20 state bakeries until *circa* 618, when the source of the wheat, Egypt, was lost to the Arabs. For just under 300 years, some 31,200 tonnes was shipped annually by the state up the Nile to Alexandria for shipment to New Rome. If transported in merchant vessels of 50-tonne capacity, this suggests that 624 shipments must have been needed each year.

Although wheat comprised the mainstay of daily nutrition in the Late Antique world, olive oil was equally essential for dipping food into and for lighting and cleaning. The State certainly taxed the provinces of Palestine, Syria and Cyprus for shipments of oil because a section of the Theodosian Code, an official law book published across the empire, confirmed that in AD 408 "the regulation of Your magnificence shall remain fixed with regard to the measure of oil, so that eighteen scruples shall be retained from each sextarius and distributed to the benefit of certain orders, in accordance with your regulated arrangement... This measure is established as a fixed benefit for the guilds designated by your recommendation, and we trust that it will not be tampered with by the fraud of any person hereafter."

Whether wine was also an integral part of the state's taxation for free distribution remains a mystery. Certainly in the West subsidised wine from Italian vineyards was offered to select parts of the population at a discounted price of one-quarter market value. One edict of AD 346 from the Theodosian Code confirms that in "accordance with the statute of My brother Constantius, all the landholders of Italy shall provide the wine which is customarily furnished for use as cellar supplies." There is, however, little reason to suspect that Constantinople did other than follow the model of Rome, and huge deposits of wine amphorae originating in Gaza and Ashkelon, excavated in recent years in the port city of Beirut in Lebanon, certainly reveal a pattern of large-scale shipments northwards towards the capital.

Constantinople did not represent the whole picture, because sectors of the population in other large cities – Carthage, Alexandria, Antioch and Thessalonica – also enjoyed free or subsidised grain. Imperial officials and employees were similarly entitled to free rations, which could be considerable: at times in the late 4th century, Carthage took delivery of single consignments of between 36,000 and 99,000 litres of oil.

The wheels of war

As if the haemorrhage of large parts of farmers' wheat, olive and grape crops to the state as tax was not bad enough, the pursuit of war often created a further layer of economic oppression on the peasants of Late Antiquity. The Early Byzantine army could be a voracious monster, comprising around 645,000 soldiers during the reign of Constantine I and at least 150,000 soldiers in the 6th century, when the West was lost.

According to some estimates, the military war machine consumed well over half the total annual state budget. Other scholars, however, believe that the total expense of the Byzantine army during the reign of Justinian was 2.4 million gold coins (*solidi*), about one-sixth of the state's entire annual revenue. This more liberal figure dovetails better with evidence from Egypt, where about 20,000 soldiers were garrisoned, using up under 10% of Egypt's total provincial economic output.

Papyri from 6th-century Egypt show that during peacetime daily military food rations consisted of the equivalent of 1.4kg of bread, 1kg of meat, 1.1 litres of wine, and 0.07 litres of oil. In AD 360, soldiers on active service received biscuit for two days out of three and bread on the third day, ordinary wine one day and sour wine the next, and pork for one day out of three, with mutton on the other two days.

Military rations were originally supposed to be received through tax demanded from farmers in the form of crops. But by the early 5th century the system was in disarray as the Byzantine government could no longer prevent soldiers illegally commandeering extra taxation, ranging from horses to wine. Consequently, a prohibition against this behaviour was issued in Syria, Palestine and Egypt in AD 409. From now on soldiers were to be paid in coin and were personally responsible for buying foodstuffs. In times of war, however, estate and farm produce was commonly demanded, and the Yassi Ada shipwreck of AD 625/6 may have carried just such a military cargo.

Wine and oil

The emergence of the Early Byzantine Empire in the East, governed from Constantinople, was a powerful catalyst which kick-started the maritime economy of this half of the eastern Mediterranean. Both the *annona civica* and *annona militaris* – agricultural produce secured by the state by taxing the provinces – imposed law and order over vast regions, creating new sea-lanes that were heavily criss-crossed.

Late Antique taxation is traditionally seen as a brutally oppressive evil of the age, but in reality it had the effect of forming a society of specialised agricultural and industrial producers: in order to meet annual tax demands, peasants and landowners simply had to farm more efficiently. By the early 5th century AD, most farmers were pleasantly surprised to find themselves with surplus produce after the payment of tax, which they could dispose of as they wished for profit. Investment in land and agriculture was the safest and most common form of economic investment, and Egyptian papyri of the 6th century AD inform us that agricultural production created 20 times more revenue than industry.

The extensive web of village and estate oil and wine presses densely clustered across Egypt, Palestine, Cyprus and Syria dates from the early 5th to the mid-7th century AD. Unlike today, wine was not simply drunk for pleasure in the world of Late Antiquity. Rather, it was an essential form of nutrition, providing an estimated one-quarter of an individual's daily caloric intake and about one-third of the body's iron levels. Current research suggests that men required between 146 and 182 litres of undiluted wine annually and women about half that amount. Hence the huge demands on the humble grape, which rapidly became the king of commercial crops.

Geographically, the southernmost cluster of Mediterranean wine presses are 12 rock-cut treading basins at Ikhmindi in southern Egypt and Meinarti in northern Sudan. These seem to relate to the Nubian-Egyptian wine trade of 550–750, when the king and officials of Dongola annually received (among other commodities) 1,300 *kanyr* of wine in exchange for 400 slaves.

Foundations of a wine press in the 4th- to 5th-century AD Jewish village of Sumaqa in the Carmel Mountains, Israel.

Photo: Sean Kingsley

The heart of the wine trade, however, was Palestine, where a staggering 900 wine presses have been documented, mainly north of Jerusalem (but with some large presses in the Negev desert cities). Although Palestinian soils were immensely suitable for grape cultivation, it is very possible that the rapid rise of the wine industry here was boosted, at least in part, by religious ideology in the form of the invention of the concept of the Holy Land. For the fledgling Christian Church, the grape, vineyard and the wine press symbolised specific biblical imagery, primarily wine as a symbol of Christ's blood, but also Christ and the True Vine. Similarly, the vineyard symbolised the image of the people of Israel or the Church. Thus, for Gregory the Great (AD 604) the wine press was the Passion itself in which Christ was crushed. As churches sprang up throughout the Mediterranean, the association of viticulture with Christianity may well have been a prime reason for the grape's popularity. After all, who could resist sipping on wine from the land of the Bible, where the figures of the Old Testament and later Jesus and the Apostles once trod?

A 5th- to 6th-century AD oil press at el-Bara (ancient Kaper Pera) in the Limestone Massif of Syria. This isolated region exported olive oil throughout the Mediterranean.

Photo: Marlia Mango

A 4th- to 5th-century AD oil press mill in a Samaritan estate at Rakit in the Carmel Mountains, Israel.

Photo: Sean Kingsley

Alongside the nutritional value of wine and its recreational role, it also had an important medicinal function. In the 7th century AD, Alexander Tralles recommended Laodicean wine from Syria for kidney ailments. Light white Ashkelon wine from Palestine was also prescribed to treat stomach ache, quartan fever, colic, liver disease and eye infection.

A vast swath of land stretching from Jerusalem in Palestine into northern Syria was the eastern empire's olive oil heartland. An individual needed about 20kg of this essential product in antiquity for food, lighting, cosmetics and industrial use. Circular rotary olive crushers and large, standing orthostats from this industry have been found by archaeologists littering fields between the Holy Land and Greece. The Jewish historian Josephus Flavius tells us that Palestine's Galilee was already "a special home of the olive" in the early 1st century AD, and archaeologists have recorded 365 Late Antique oil press installations in Israel, of which 128 cluster around 58 rural settlements in the western and Lower Golan.

The farmers of northern Syria were equally specialist in olive oil cultivation, and 245 presses are known from 45 villages in the hinterland east of Antioch. Despite the problems of overland transport in these dizzy highlands, rising up to 600m above sea level, oil export was one of the principal mainstays of the Syrian economy. In total, estimates of the scale of this industry in the combined territories of Antioch and Apamea suggest that 8,000 presses may have seen a hive of activity in the 5th and 6th centuries. One of the most important maritime containers of Late Antiquity, an amphora form known as Late Roman 1 (LR1, see p. 43), undoubtedly originated in Syria, where it was probably specifically designed to hold olive oil (before its shape was imitated all along the coasts of south-east Turkey, Rhodes, Cyprus and parts of Egypt).

Industry

Although a more risky form of capital investment than agriculture, large-scale industry continued to thrive throughout the Mediterranean in Late Antiquity. Once again, the general pattern is one of gradual decline in the West accompanied by a surge in the East from the 5th century onwards. If oil and wine cultivation was largely the realm of the peasant farmer (often under the employ of rich landowners), then most industry was predominantly an urban activity. From Alexandria to Constantinople, papyrus, purple dye, cloth, silk, gold, copper, marble, fish and glass were piled on to ships.

In recent years, archaeologists have unearthed subtle traces of other produce, which travelled across distant seas to satisfy the demands of Byzantine consumers. Writing preserved on papyri of the 5th and 6th centuries reveals a particular appetite in Egypt for Gazan pickled fish. Selected species were also farmed in artificial *vivaria*, purpose-built plastered tanks that have been excavated on estates at Ashkelon and Tell Tanninim in Israel, just north of the port of Caesarea.

Fishing was undoubtedly a primary industry of Egypt's economy, and

An early 7th-century AD artificial fishpond at Tell Tanninim, Israel. Stairs lead on to a floor surrounded by amphorae deliberately broken and plastered into edges to replicate fish breeding nests. Excavated by the Tanninim Archaeological Project (1996-99), directed by Robert R. Stieglitz (Rutgers University, Newark).

Photo: Sean Kingsley and courtesy of Robert Stieglitz (Rutgers University, Newark)

The 5th–6th-century AD gold mine at Bir Umm Fawakhir in the eastern Egyptian desert.

Photo: Carol Meyer

although the archaeological evidence from the province is surprisingly thin, archaeologists were pleasantly surprised to find Nilotic fresh-water mussels, *Aspatharia rubens*, in excavations at the city of Sepphoris in the Galilee. Red Sea parrot fish bones also crop up in the towns of the Negev desert, such as Eboda and Rehovot. Hundreds of fish bones from both Mediterranean and Red Sea species examined at the military fort of Upper Zohar in the Negev must have been transported at least 85km overland into this most arid of climates.

Such meagre but important archaeological traces leave no doubt that Byzantine merchants never hesitated to go where market forces dictated. As cargoes of fish within amphorae on shipwrecks in the western Mediterranean prove, North Africa similarly continued to be exploited for its abundant natural resources in Late Antiquity. The lively scenes of all manner of marine life – realistic and fantastic – decorating the floors of hundreds of North Africa's Roman mosaics, confirm the wealth of its fishing grounds.

Whilst one-tenth of British and Spanish ironworks closed in Late Antiquity, the early 5th-century AD Illyrian furnaces of the Danube hinterland remained in use, with some individual mines producing a million tonnes of slag. Dark, hot and claustrophobic, mines were highly unpleasant places to work, and it was *ad metalla* that convicts were condemned into the 6th century. With the decline of the West, exploited miners needed little excuse to escape these hardships, even going over to mine for the Goths under more comfortable working conditions.

Further east, the iron and copper mines of Macedonia thrived, while Thessalonica's factories supplied the army. The devout hermits of mountainous Caesarea in Asia Minor paid their taxes in local Cappadocian iron, and single mines of the 5th to 7th centuries in the Taurus mountain have scarred the modern landscape with slag heaps of 600,000 tonnes or more. The ports of Cilicia received customs dues on local lead and tin in the 5th and 6th centuries.

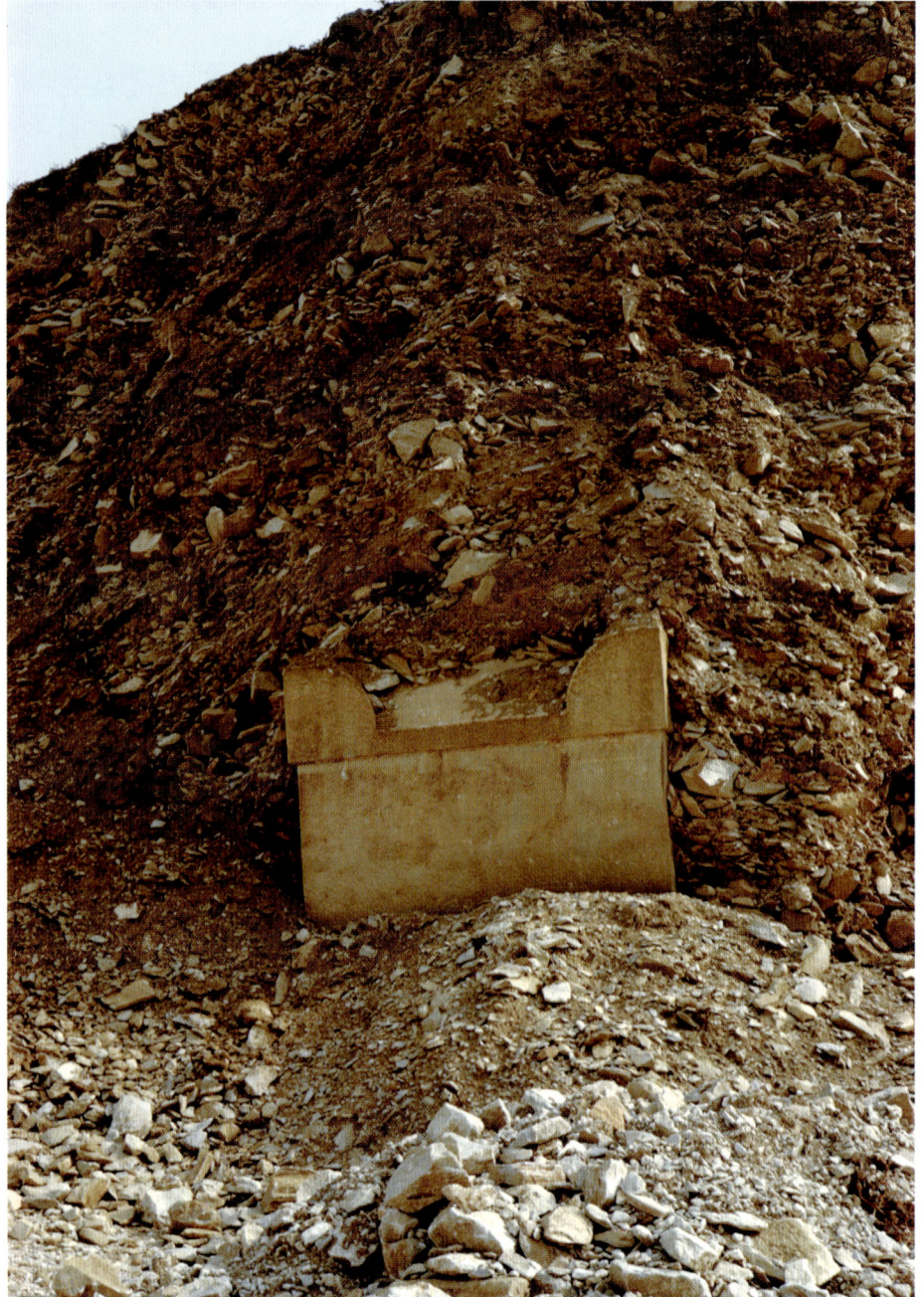

A sarcophagus abandoned in the Byzantine quarries on the island of Proconnesos, Turkey, the most valuable Mediterranean source of marble in Late Antiquity.

Photo: Marlia Mango

In the 4ᵗʰ century, the copper mines of Phainon in Nabataea – dating far back in history to the Chalcolithic period (4000 BC) – still continued, although the Troodos massif of Cyprus was now the major centre of the region's copper industry. It was most probably from here that the city district of copper workers in Constantinople imported its raw material.

With the fall of the West, Constantinople seems to have taken serious measures to keep a grip on gold and silver processing, which lay at the very heart of the empire's economy. Miners continued to work the ancient silver mines of Greek Laurion in the 5ᵗʰ and 6ᵗʰ centuries, a time when Armenia's gold mines also flourished. Thracian Pangaios and Attic Sounion supplied some of the 40,000lbs of silver that adorned the imperial Church of Hagia Sophia in Constantinople.

In an attempt to prevent the loss of gold mines to barbarians in areas such as the Balkans, the Byzantine state seems to have deliberately opened new mining towns closer to home. Just such a remarkable imperial venture has been explored by Carol Meyer at Bir Umm Fawakhir in the eastern desert of Egypt on behalf of the Oriental Institute of the University of Chicago. Here, amongst mountainous ridges and desert landscapes fed by natural water wells, but largely suitable only for camels, sheep, goat and Bedouin, is a remarkably dense cluster of more than 200 buildings. With a population of around 1,000 people, some 2–3g of gold was painstakingly extracted from one tonne of ore in the 5th and 6th centuries. As gold became an increasingly scarcer resource, mines offering such low yields now simply had to be exploited.

More visible amongst the modern ruins of ancient sites are the marbles whose export sustained a terrific quantity of maritime traffic in Late Antiquity. As in the case of mining, while the West's marble quarries collapsed in the early 5th century, eastern operations continued unabated and intensified into the 6th century. Processed slabs were transported by sea, in the form of sculpted Constantinopolitan capitals reaching Ravenna and the odd column and base stowed as extra saleable 'ballast' amongst primary cargoes on ships like Tantura A near Dor and the Megadim wreck, both off Israel. Larger shipments include the church architecture on the 6th-century Marzamemi wreck that foundered off Sicily with a 76-tonne cargo of prefabricated fixtures for a Justinianic church.

The most famous Late Antique marbles were quarried over a period of 250 years from AD 320 near the harbour town of Saraylar on the northern shore of Marmara Island. Here, the ancient, rugged face of the Proconnesian marble industry scars an area of more than 40km² – consisting of largely open yards from independent, privately-owned workshops. The ambitions of this industry are still evident at the site today, in the form of a gigantic 4.45m diameter column drum, which was only partly quarried during the reign of Theodosius

A Mediaeval glass factory at Tyre in Lebanon. In the foreground are the remains of two tank furnaces.

Photo: David Whitehouse

before the quarries went out of use in the 6th century. Proconnesian products reached Marseille, Milan, Rome, Antioch, Jerusalem, Alexandria and Morocco. It was also from Marmara that 28 of the huge bases on the Marzamemi ship wrecked off Sicily in the second quarter of the 6th century originated.

More enigmatic is the fragile matter of glass. Certainly, Egypt, Palestine, Transjordan, Phoenicia, Cilicia, Sardis and Constantinople all specialised in glass blowing to produce windowpanes, hanging lamps, and domestic wares such as dishes and bottles. Surviving workshops are relatively rare and, other than in Alexandria, the best evidence is from Israel, where manufacture was common in Palaestina Prima and Secunda, between the Galilee and central coastal area. The Jewish town of Beth She'arim in the Galilee was renowned for its glassworks from the 4th century onwards, and the massive scale of production is today fossilised by a 9-tonne glass slab still lying inside a melting-tank.

A slab of comparable size has been excavated in the city of Apollonia (Israel), where the demand for wood to fuel furnaces for the glass industry destroyed the region's wooded landscape. The largest production centre in the Mediterranean known at present has been excavated at coastal Bet Eli'ezer, some 8km south of Caesarea. The 17 single-use, 7th-century glass kilns consisted of twin firing furnaces and a rectangular melting chamber, each capable of producing 8–10 tonnes of glass in a single firing.

Stone punches for stamping 4th- to 7th-century AD Tunisian pottery bowls and plates (African red-slip wares) with fish, hens and elaborate Christian crosses.

After Mackensen, *Journal of Roman Archaeology* 11 (1998), figs. 8.13, 8.15 and 9.1, 3

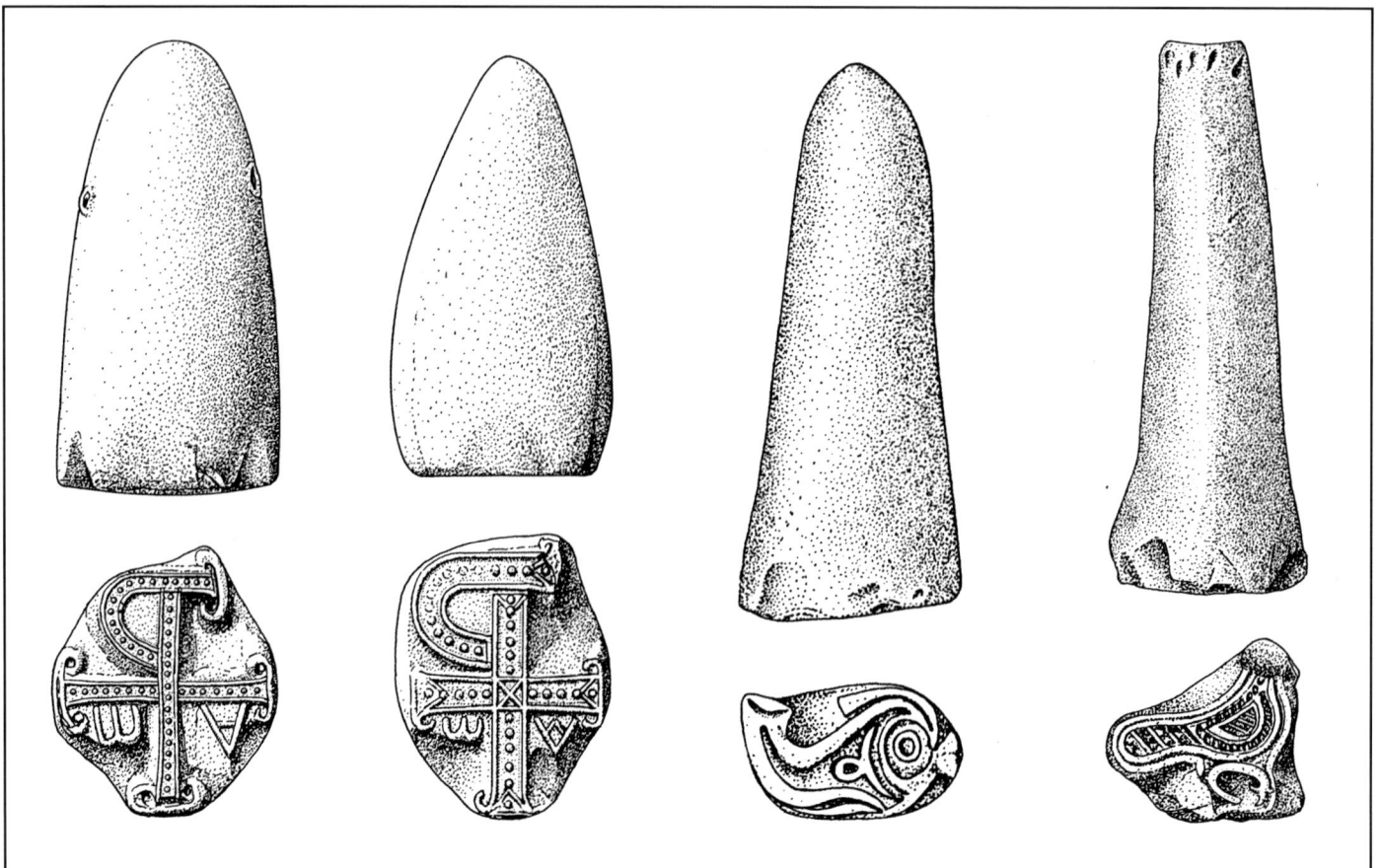

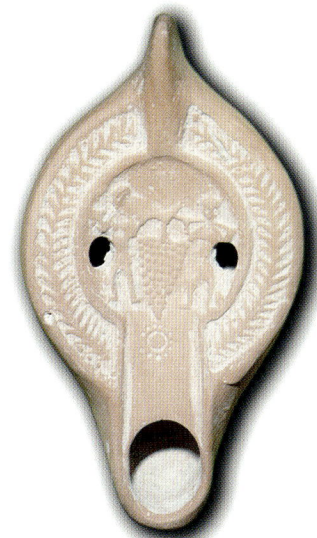

Although much of Egypt and Palestine's glass was no doubt destined for local town houses, concentrations of jettisoned glass ingots along the coast of Israel leave little doubt that ships also exported raw glass. But how far did it travel? Constantinopolitan purple glass certainly reached as far east as the Chinese tombs of Guyuan *circa* 569, while glass bleached in imitation of Indian rock crystal was one of the ancient world's most highly prized materials. Marine archaeologists still eagerly await the discovery of a glass cargo on a Late Antique Mediterranean shipwreck.

The most mundane type of product manufactured in massive quantities for export was pottery: oil lamps, bowls and, most exhaustively, amphorae. The best evidence for export of the former two categories is African red-slip ware, which was manufactured on dozens of late 4th- to 7th-century estates and villas in central Tunisia, between Bordj el Djerbi to the north and Djilmi, located about 180km south of Carthage.

Above left: Tunisian fine-ware oil lamp stamped with the Chi Rho symbol of Christ, 4th–5th century AD.

Photo: Peter Clayton.

Above right: African red-slip oil lamps from Tunisia were often decorated with popular biblical motifs, such as the 'Great Grapes of Canaan' that depict Joshua's two spies. Top: lamp mould, stone. Below: oil lamp, terracotta.

Photo: Peter Clayton

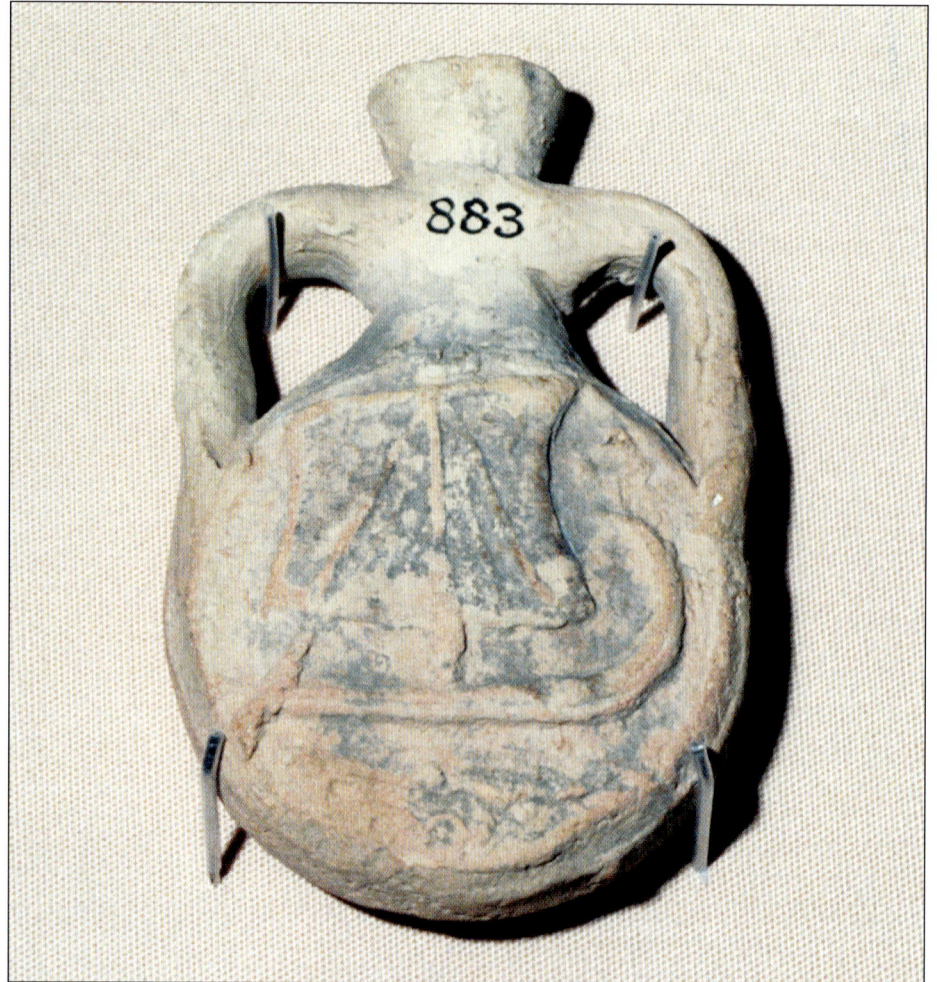

St Menas flask in the British Museum. Manufactured around the Christian pilgrimage site of Abu Mena in Egypt, the flask depicts a sailing ship. Containers filled with holy oil made ideal gifts for zealous pilgrims.

© The British Museum – photo: Peter Clayton

African red-slip plates often depicted well-known Biblical stories, such as Noah's Ark (above) and Jonah being flung overboard to the whale (left). Terracotta fragments from Tunisia, 4th–5th centuries AD.

Photos: Peter Clayton

Unlike the contemporary fine-ware bowls and plates manufactured in Phocaea in western Turkey and northern Cyprus, which had a very limited array of stamped bases, African red-slip wares were famous for their dazzling array of stamped decoration ranging from biblical figures, saints and lions, to simple crosses. These could be purchased in fairs or markets throughout the Byzantine Empire or even pre-ordered: a trader's terracotta sample 'pad' from Tunisia, stamped with a page of designs, was clearly available to itinerant merchants for taking orders. Incidentally, pattern books were equally common for clients to choose scenes for mosaics.

By far the most important pottery product manufactured in Late Antiquity was the amphora. Again, with the rise of mercantile fortunes in the eastern Mediterranean a new range of amphorae evolved in Egypt, Palestine, Syria, the Aegean and North Africa. Interestingly, each region possessed its own unique style of jar, a feature that is of great use to marine archaeologists in dating amphorae and identifying their areas of production. The debate about what each style contained continues to rage, and shipwrecks have become by far the most important source for researching this subject because contents and residues are frequently preserved underwater. Scenes on mosaics from Jordan and Israel show that jars and produce were easily transported by camel overland to ports. However, as kilns dotted along the Nile, Lake Mareotis in Egypt, at Ashkelon in Israel and at Paphos, Cyprus, show, building amphora workshops and kilns alongside port cities was more efficient and therefore most common.

Making a purchase

One of the major economic achievements of the Roman Empire that united distant communities throughout the provinces was the imposition of a single monetary system. The same coin could buy you bread and wine whether you were shopping in Rome, London or Alexandria. Such ease of purchase simplified commerce. While extreme changes challenged the fabric of society across the empire between the 4th and 7th centuries, the state deliberately ensured monetary stability that retained a stable base for merchants. Thus, when an archdeacon from Marseille stole oil and fish sauce from a merchant, it was in *solidi* (4,000) that he was fined. Egyptian papyri again inform us that not just the army, but also peasants, stonemasons, unskilled workmen, and grape pickers were all paid in gold coins. As John Chrysostom wrote in the Early Byzantine period, "The use of coin welds together our whole life, and is the basis of all our transactions. Whenever anything is to be bought or sold, we do it all through coins."

As the coinage of the early Roman empire disappeared under the currency crises and inflation of the second half of the 4th century, the *solidus* emerged as the dominant coin under the reforms of Diocletian (284–305) and Constantine I the Great (306–337). The Late Antique system involved a 4.55 gold *solidus* (Greek *nomisma*) and various denominations in silver, billon (debased silver)

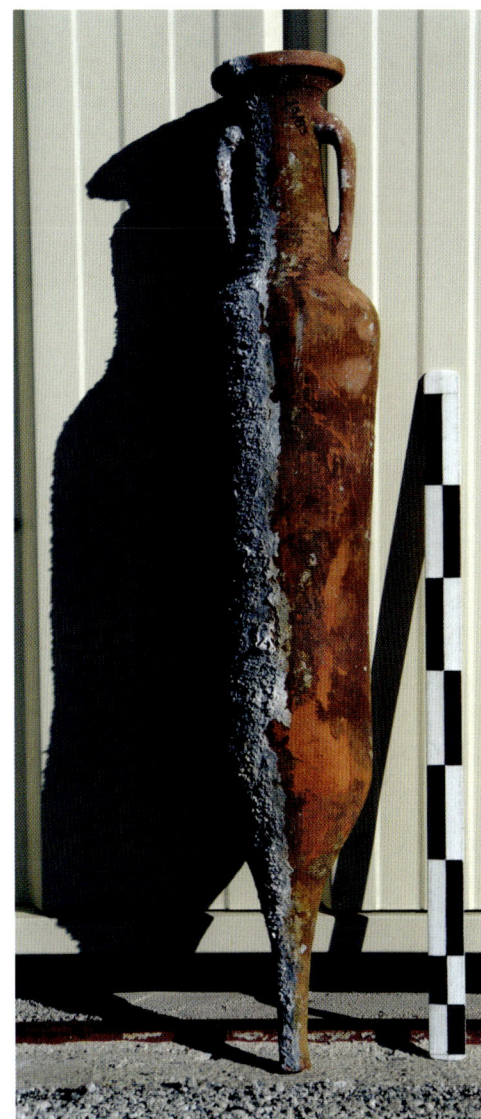

A *spatheia*-type amphora of Tunisian origin from the Dramont E ship wrecked off southern France between AD 425 and 455.

Photo: Claude Santamaria

25

Obverse and reverse of a gold *solidus* of
Anastasius I (AD 491–518).

Photo: Peter Clayton

Obverse and reverse of a gold *solidus* of
Justinian II (AD 685–695).

Photo: Peter Clayton

Obverse and reverse of a late 7th-century
AD Arab-Byzantine gold *solidus*, with
Arabic inscription.

Photo: Peter Clayton

Obverse and reverse of a gold *solidus* of
Heraclius (AD 610–641).

Photo: Peter Clayton.

and bronze known as a half *solidus* (*semissis*), one-third *solidus* (*tremissis*), and a *follis* (40 *nummi*, at about 7,200 *nummi* to the *solidus*). Gold issues were minted at Ravenna, Carthage and Constantinople, and bore the formal mint mark CONOB, an abbreviation of *Constantinopolis* (CON) and *obryzum* (OB), refined gold.

Interestingly, even though many provinces had fallen to 'barbarians', the conquerors were quick to follow the monetary model of the Byzantine state in the late 5th and early 6th centuries, imitating the coins of Constantinople. In design, their *solidi* depicted the Byzantine emperor's name, bust and 'Victory' carrying a cross. Some 'pseudo-imperial' Western coins often incorrectly struck the abbreviation of Constantinople's mint with COMOB or COHOB (instead of the correct CON or CONOB). The rulers of Provence in France continued to produce pseudo-imperial coins until AD 613 and, thereafter, issued *solidi* in their own names, now carrying mint marks of Western cities like Vienne and Marseille.

In this transparent system of monetary imitation, we see a desperate, deliberate attempt to welcome in merchants and exotic produce from distant provinces, whilst at the same time politically keeping the Byzantine state at arm's length. Much as today, the development of common markets was in the interest of everyone, and it was this spirit of cooperation that enabled ships with strangely exotic cargoes to penetrate the dark waters of the Mediterranean.

Fraudulent payment was an ever-present concern for merchants of Late Antiquity, which resulted in the creation of a complex system of standardised checks and balances. The desire for nobody to be taken for a ride resulted in the Mediterranean-wide adoption of the bronze/brass steelyard, a weighing device based on a fulcrum mechanism. Suspended from a hook, an amphora or sack of wheat could be suspended from a secondary hook, while a counter-balance weight (plain or decorated) was slid down the length of a long beam. When a horizontal balance was achieved, the weight of the merchandise could be read in Greek letters off the beam. Steelyards are common discoveries in Late Antique cities, often inscribed in Greek with an owner's name or Christian proclamations, and are similarly common on shipwrecks. One example from the shops of Scythopolis in Israel was inscribed in both Greek and Arabic, clear evidence of an imitation of Byzantine trade models in the Early Islamic world.

Artist's impression of the bronze Colossus of Rhodes bestriding the Roman harbour mouth at Rhodes. In AD 654 it was allegedly sold, pulled down and taken away on 900 camels. Engraving by Maerten van Heemskerck, 1568.

Photo: Peter Clayton

COLOSSVS SOLIS.

The end of classical antiquity

Late Antiquity marks the period when traditional Mediterranean forms of classical civilisation came to a rude and abrupt end. As we have seen for the West, war and decline did not necessarily curtail the endeavours of the merchant. In fact, long-distance trade seems to have been almost the last form of traditional culture to collapse.

Yet the mid- to late 7th century was undoubtedly a period of great transition and upheaval, when the echoing memory and use of classical forms of trade finally vanished from the tired shores of the Mediterranean. The pottery kilns that had fired millions of clay amphorae, and held the masses of agricultural produce that marine archaeologists find on shipwrecks, were abandoned, as were the wine presses of Palestine. Scientific analyses of atmospheric pollution, derived from metal production and deposited as stratified and dateable layers within Swiss peat bogs, show a strong decline in industry at this time. After a peak in the Roman period, the lowest levels in lead mining cluster around AD 648. No longer did Rome's mines beat to the sound of hammer and pick, and the dwindling fires of the great furnaces were extinguished.

The rarity of metals is verified by the tale of a Jewish merchant from Emesa who, in AD 654, is alleged to have bought the bronze Colossus of Rhodes from an Arab conqueror, and carried it away on 900 camels. Thus, the very character of antiquity was eroded as this 33m-high statue, one of the wonders of the ancient world, ceased to grace the mouth of one of the Mediterranean's great Roman harbours. A few years later, in 663, the Byzantine Empire rudely stripped Rome of its metal statues and of the roof of the Pantheon. Although Egyptian papyrus was still being unloaded on the docks of Marseille as late as 675, it was no longer a cheap product used by everyone for making string, lamp wicks and for wrapping groceries and writing letters, but had become a luxury item for the aristocracy.

As the shadows gathered over classical shipping and trade, the breadbasket of the empire started to change dramatically. Islam's traditional prohibition against the drinking of alcohol essentially killed off the Mediterranean's elaborate millennia-old wine trade, and in its place evolved wicker basket weaving, soap and wax manufacture. The fruit of the Roman Empire had gone rotten.

III. Shipwrecks:
the devil and the deep blue sea

Let's find out whose fault it is that a man's life is entrusted to a thin plank hull, why people risk the dangers of the sea. Isn't it because of greed that the sailor's shout curses the deep sea as the storm crashes over him? No, never would a seaman have entrusted himself to a ship unless the passion for trading had spurred the desire for sailing. And then a man is borne off by the waves so he can quadruple his money: they export gold so they can import perjury with falsehood.

Valerian of Cimiez, *Homilia* 20, 7, PL, 52.754.B-C;
circa mid-5th century AD.

Life on the ocean wave

Even though the quest for profit was one primary force driving maritime trade in Late Antiquity, labelling sailors and merchants greedy would be a simplistic injustice. People participated in maritime industries for a whole host of reasons. Professional positions were more often than not hereditary, with entire families perhaps working in the same field and following a long family line that had set down roots at a coastal harbour town, alongside recognisable neighbourly faces, for many decades. The tales of the sea – sad and romantic – and worries about whether fathers and sons would return from dangerous sea voyages, or whether livelihoods invested in cargoes or merchant vessels would be scuppered by storms, only brought such communities closer together.

Mercantile communities enjoyed strong social bonds and many sailors and

Silver and gold *patera* dish from Cap Chenoua, Algeria (between Tipasa and Cherchel), decorated with a maritime fishing scene. 6th to early 7th century AD. Louvre Museum, Bj 1983.

© Photo RMN – M. Beck-Coppola

29

Mainz

Port Berteau

St Gervais B

Dramont E/F

La Batéguier

Ravenna

Olib A

Zdrija

Grazel B

Pisa

Port Vendres A

La Palud and
Héliopolis A

Le Scole A

Pian di Spille

Sud
Lavezzi A

Fiumicin

Olbia

Favaritx

Filicudi Por
Cefalu

Cabrera A

Isis

Triscina C

Femmina Morta a
Pantano Longari

Mangub

Mediterranean shipwrecks
4th to 10th centuries AD

ilba and
Morovnick

Sobra and Mljet A

Budva

Bar

Acque Chiare

Pomorie

Sinop

Ekinlik Adasi

Ayios Stephanos
Delphinian
Prasso

Gümsülük

Mandalya Gulf C

Kerne Gulf

racuse B / C

arzamemi

Yassi Ada

Iskandil Burnu

Datça

Bozburun

Dhia B

Cape
Andreas

Cape Kiti

Ginosar B

Dor and
Caesarea

Alexandria

Jezirat Faraun

Mouths of *spatheia*-type North African amphorae as found on the Dramont F shipwreck of *circa* AD 400 off southern France, lightly covered with marine vegetation.

Photo: Jean-Pierre Joncheray

merchants were plebeians, who actually scraped the most basic of livings and led a humble existence. Even at the wealthier end of commerce, a man could be launched as a leading merchant at Alexandria with 50lbs of gold (3,600 *solidi*). This may sound a fortune, but the great merchants of the same city were worth 70–275lbs of gold, both of which pale in comparison to the fortunes of the elite land magnates, who enjoyed annual incomes of 1,500 to 4,000lbs of gold from their agricultural estates.

During the 4th and early 5th centuries, the economic conditions of maritime communities were oppressed by the Late Roman Empire, which imposed harsh legislation to protect its own interests: namely the continued and unhindered supply of tax in kind (the *annona civica*). Being ensnared in the compulsory cycle of government tax shipment was in many ways an impediment to private commerce.

Even though a complex hierarchy of sailor, sea captain (*magister*), harbour porter, shipper (*navicularius*), merchant (*mercator*), investor and ship owner from lower, middle and upper classes rubbed shoulders in Late Antiquity, at its roots seafaring was conservative. Various historical texts enable a colourful picture of the age to be reconstructed. First and foremost, the shipping season was almost completely conditioned by the weather. Between November and March the Mediterranean was largely considered closed, *mare clausum*. The government restricted shipments of its precious grain and oil from Africa to between 13 April and 15 October. During the naval siege of Constantinople, between AD 674 and 678, warfare adhered to the official state line, again ceasing between these months.

The *Rhodian Sea Law*, an official seafarers' handbook written and updated between AD 600 and 800, allowed greater flexibility, stipulating that the sea should be closed between 7 November and 7 March. This extra two-month window of opportunity undoubtedly applied to private shipping, where weather-beaten and wise sea captains could read seasonal fluctuations in the weather.

Even though there is no doubt that many itinerant merchants made a living hawking their goods from port to port in a relatively random and relaxed way, the big business of the day was highly organised, meticulously regulated by contract and law, and carefully scheduled. One end of the ladder of trade is gleaned from a letter of Bishop Synesius of Cyrene in North Africa, who wrote to his brother along the coast in the port of Ptolemais after hearing that the Athenian cloth merchant had made his annual call, asking him to buy him three Attic cloaks.

Alongside this itinerant trade, with ships turning up in ports unannounced and to their own commercial rhythms, are the complicated contracts drawn up between farmers, merchants, sea captains and purchasers. These must have been enforced throughout the Mediterranean, but it is mainly thanks to the scraps of text preserved on papyri from Egypt that insights into this fascinating organisation are available. Thus, sales of wine were concluded before delivery by ship, and often even while the grapes were still on the vine. (The buyer technically became the wine owner when it was in the fermentation tanks following pressing.) Contracts also guaranteed that the wine to be delivered had to be of good quality; if the product had turned mouldy when the buyer took receipt, the seller was financially liable.

The legalities of the wine trade are clear from another Egyptian contract: "…total: 150 jars of wine, which I will deliver to you at the time of the vintage,

A modern storm in the South Bay at Dor, Israel, recreates the precise setting which witnessed numerous shipwreck disasters around these islands in the 6th and 7th centuries AD.

Photo: Sean Kingsley

in the month of Mesore [25 July to 23 August] in the coming happy third indiction in new must, of fine quality and tasty, by the measure of the monastery of Apa Apollos. You, however, will supply the containers, new ones. If the wine is found to be sour, or off, or smells by the feast of Thyris in the month of Phamenoth [26 March] of the present third indiction, I agree to exchange it for a good wine, pledging for this debt all my property…This deed is valid and guaranteed…I have given my consent."

Shippers were equally legally bound to safeguard cargoes from damage. One 5th-century papyrus contains a formal contract agreement for the transport of cargo from the harbour of Oxyrhynchus to Alexandria: "…the great… to Aurelius N.N. from the city of Oxyrhynchus… fifteen the freight thereof being golden… on condition that I will transport the cargo to the most illustrious (city of) Alexandria and will deliver it to you unadulterated, pure and undamaged by any nautical damage… and that I receive at the moment of the unloading from you… eight talents of the freight-contract…" If a sea captain failed to maintain his vessel with adequate numbers of anchors, with dunnage to protect a cargo from wave buffeting, or even if he entered a port of call that was not pre-arranged, a contract could become null and void.

The same binding legal framework applied to people hiring ships. The Rhodian Sea Law contains a revealing passage that explains how in such cases "…the contract to be binding must be in writing and subscribed by the parties, otherwise it is void. Let them also write penalties if they wish. If they do not write penalties, and there is a breach, either by the captain or by the hirer – if the

Shipwreck statistics

In 1992, Dr A.J. Parker's landmark publication, *Ancient Shipwrecks of the Mediterranean and the Roman Provinces* (Oxford), catalogued 1,200 wrecks, of which 130 dated to Late Antiquity (4th to 10th centuries). Underwater exploration since then has revealed a further 92 shipwrecks, updating the corpus to 222 sites. The principal new areas of investigation are Croatia (26 sites), Israel (25) and Bulgaria (16). Whilst most of Dr Parker's ships were clustered off France and Italy, this new research has resulted in a new top five hot spots: Croatia (37), Israel (32), France (29), Sicily (27), Bulgaria (21), with Turkey close behind (20).

Amphorae of West Mediterranean provenance are known from 57 shipwrecks and the most common cargo form are North African amphorae holding oil and fish (41 sites). Spanish jars follow a distant second (15). Amphorae of East Mediterranean provenance occur on 37 shipwrecks, with Palestinian cargoes best represented (9 sites).

Other primary cargoes include sets of marble architecture (Marzamemi B, Sicily; Hahotrim, Israel; Ekinlik Adasi, Turkey), roof tiles (6 sites), and 11 metal cargoes. These include a group of bronze lamps, censers, pitchers, bowls and a steelyard from Plemmirio A (4th–5th centuries; Sicily), hundreds of bronze plates, keys, chains, candelabra, statuettes, balances and coins from the Syrian shipwreck at Favaritx, carrying Christian liturgical objects (*c*. AD 450–600, Minorca), and a bronze consignment of female statue fragments, animal terminals for furniture, boar's tusk decoration, pendants, dishes, pots from Mateille A (*c*. AD 315, France).

Other consignments recorded include coins, North African bowls and lamps, roof tiles, water pipes, glass, millstones, and terracotta sarcophagi. Wooden hulls are preserved in various states on 46 shipwrecks.

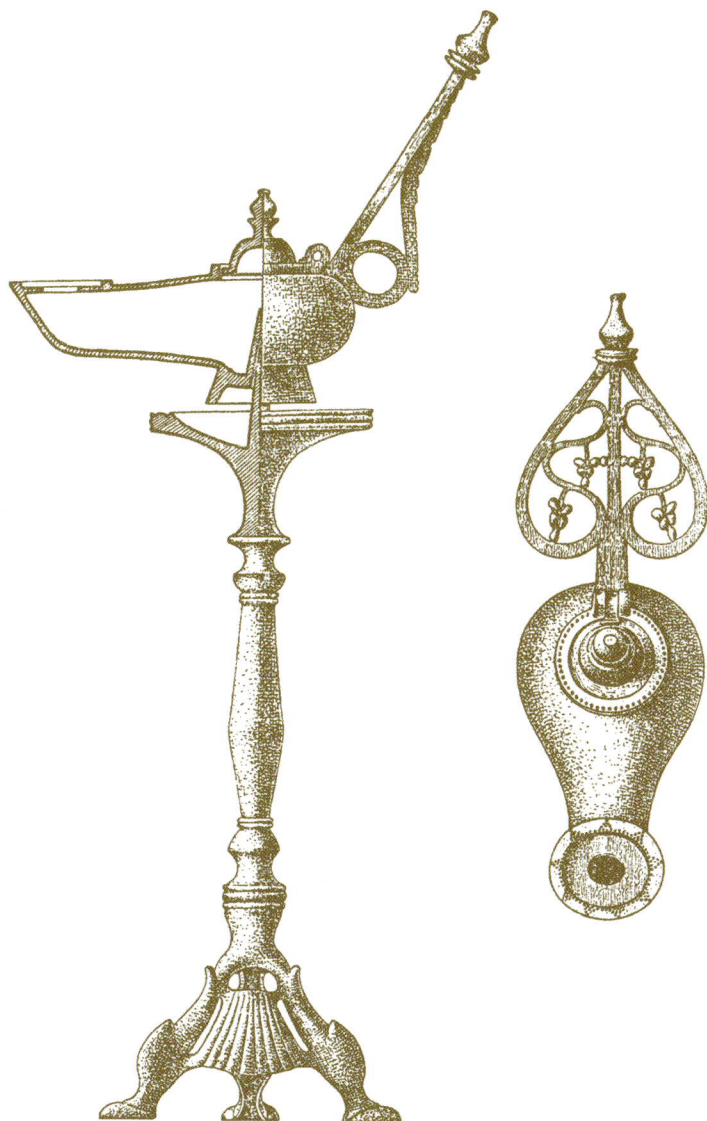

Bronze oil-lamp and stand from the Plemmyrion A shipwreck off Sicily; 4th–5th century AD.

After Kapitän and Fallico, *Bolletino d'Arte* 52 (1967), figs. 7, 9–10

hirer provides the goods…let him give the half of the freight to the captain. If the captain commits a breach, let him give the half-freight to the merchant."

The rise of Christianity was accompanied by the appearance of new types of religious periodic markets (the *panegyris*) and regional and inter-regional fairs (*mercatus* or *nundinae*), often linked to the birthdays of saints. For merchants, these were opportunities not to be missed. Not surprisingly, numerous major fairs were located at port cities and were tailored to the sailing seasons. Many of these lured merchants with the promise of tax-free trade, and catered for both the rich and those of more humble means.

The ancient writer Ammianus Marcellinus described a fair at Batnae in northern Mesopotamia, along the Roman/Persian frontier, in AD 354 as "filled with wealthy traders when, at the yearly festival, near the beginning of the month of September, a great crowd of every condition gathers for the fair, to traffic in the wares sent from India and China, and in other articles that are regularly brought here in great abundance by land and sea." Choricius described the fair of St Sergius at Gaza in southern Palestine as an egalitarian affair, where

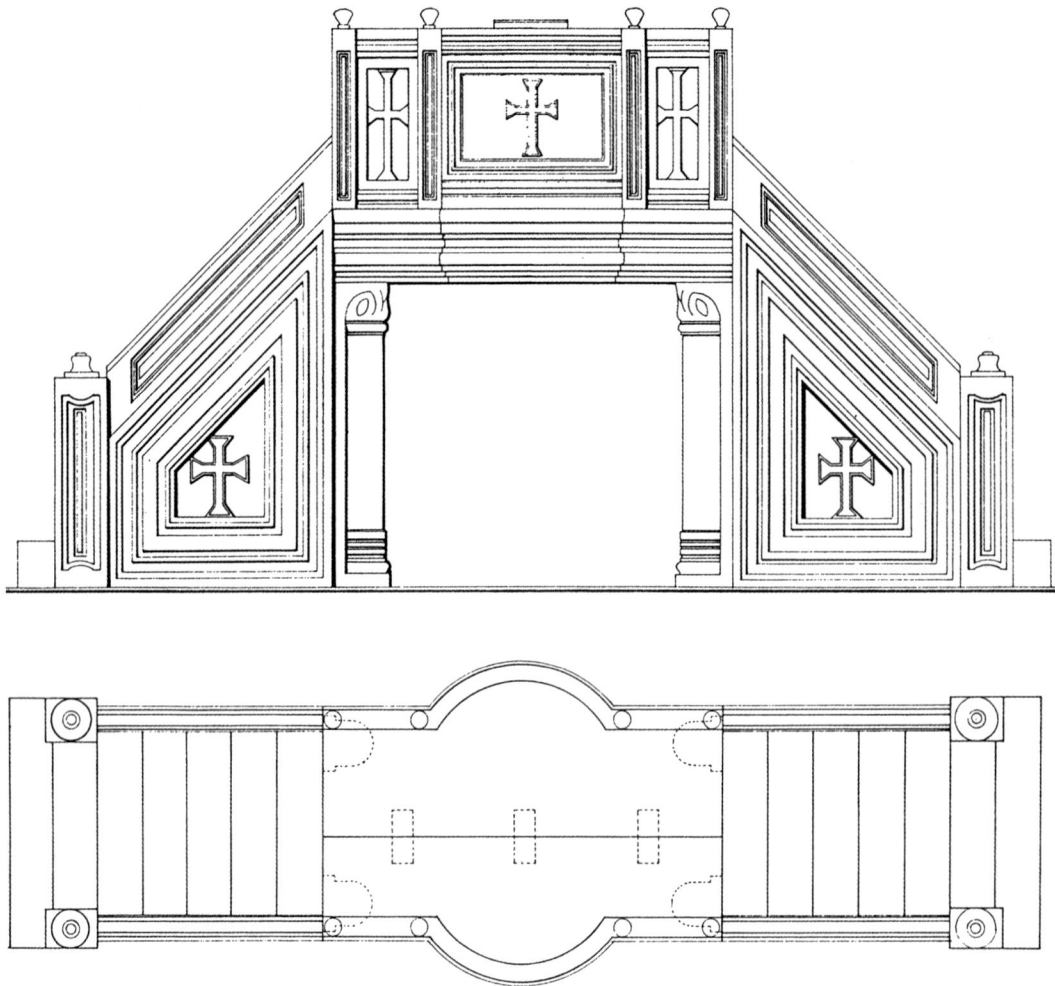

Prefabricated marble masonry for a church *ambo* recovered from the Marzamemi B shipwreck, Sicily; AD 500–540.

From Kapitän, G., 'The Church Wreck off Marzamemi', *Archaeology* 22 (1969), 130

the temporary booths set up rather like a modern town market were "copiously laden with merchandise both for the rich and for those of moderate means." In addition to being known well in advance to merchants and sea captains, dates of tax-free fairs were also publicised in pilgrims' guidebooks, which, for example, listed the markets at harbour towns such as Aegae in Cilicia (south-east Turkey), held annually over a period of 40 days in the mid-6th century.

Why merchandise travelled by sea rather than overland was a simple matter of cost and efficiency. Camels and donkeys could travel at a person's walking rate, while oxen were capable of no more than an equally pedestrian 3.2km per hour. A letter written by Theodore of Stoudios in AD 797 demonstrates that horses could cover about 40km in two days (but were completely unsuitable for the mass transport of heavy produce).

Ships of antiquity sailed at speeds of 3.4–6.2 knots in good conditions and 1.5–3.3 knots under unfavourable winds. More important than speed, of course, was the absence of awkward hills and rivers to traverse and the ability of merchant vessels to accommodate heavy freight. For large-scale, long-distance commodity movement, there simply was no realistic alternative. Compared with overland transport, the cost of maritime trade was between 17 and 22 times cheaper.

Various accounts of saints' lives, religious texts and other histories chronicle the length of sea voyages. In the 5th century, Mark the Deacon took 20 days to sail from Ascalon to Constantinople, but only 10 days to return (Palestine to Greece). The *Life of St Gregory of Akragas* (who died in 592) tells us that the saint took ship in his hometown in southern Sicily and sailed to Carthage (Tunisia) and then Tripolis in Phoenicia in 20 days. Porphyrios of Gaza sailed between Rhodes and Constantinople in five days, while Nikephoros Gregoras stated that merchant vessels took five days to sail from Rhodes to Alexandria and nine days from Cyprus to Crete. St Aberkios and his companions sailed from Brindisi to the Peloponnese in five days (Italy to Greece). As in the Roman period, the Mediterranean remained a small pond to experienced captains.

Shipwreck exploration

Maritime trade was infamous as a risky business, and ships wrecked with the exotic and mundane fruits of disparate lands have turned up in the most obvious and unlikely of places. In 1963, a Sicilian farmer was dismayed to find the heavy timbers of a 7th-century ship on the marshy no man's lands of Pantano Longarini that were an inconvenience to his reclamation plans. In a similar way, the 4th-century wooden hulls exposed by workmen building Fiumicino airport in Rome were wonderful reminders of the glory of the Eternal City, but hindered the development programme.

The construction of the Hilton Hotel in Mainz, Germany, was also brought to a halt in the winter of 1981–82 when bulldozers stumbled across rare Late Roman warships. The preservation of many shipwrecks is often a fight against

Aerial view of the Biblical port city of Dor, Israel, showing its fertile agricultural hinterland and offshore islets that created the best natural anchorage along the coast of Israel throughout antiquity. Nine ships foundered between the end two islets and the shore between the 6th and 9th centuries AD.

Photo: courtesy of Sean Kingsley

37

time and developers, because many of the most intact wooden hulls of the period are today land-locked in silts and not lost at sea.

Some of the most pioneering, early underwater surveys and excavations focused on Late Antique wrecks. From 1960, Gerhard Kapitän and P. Gargallo recovered an important cargo of prefabricated marble architecture from a Byzantine church, including 28 bases and 27 capitals of white Proconnesian marble quarried in Marmara near Constantinople, and an *ambo* with two staircases, from which a priest would deliver sermons. From 1962, Alain Visquis surveyed a unique 9th-century Saracen wreck at Agay off southern France, whose hull was covered with a cargo of Arab jars from Spain, basalt grinding-stones, a skeleton and the ship's boat. (A detailed analysis of the hull was resumed in the 1990s by Jean-Pierre Joncheray.)

Historically, the most important Late Antique shipwreck excavations were those conducted off Yassi Ada, Turkey, between 1961 and 1969. From 1961–64, George Bass (University Museum, the University of Pennsylvania) and Frederick van Doorninck fully excavated a Byzantine ship that struck a reef off the island of Yassi Ada in AD 625/6 and sank to depths of 32–39m. The vessel was well preserved and had been transporting three rows of about 900 amphorae (700 Aegean LR2 and 200 Syrian LR1). The well stocked galley area yielded iron carpentry tools, cooking wares, copper containers, coins, fishing equipment and 16 oil lamps. Tragedy must have struck quickly because this ship took a heavy loss and never had the chance to use its 11 iron anchors.

From 1967–69 (and again in 1974) George Bass fully excavated a late 4th- or early 5th-century 19m-long merchant vessel at depths of 36–42m off Yassi Ada. The origins of its 1,100 amphorae still remain unclear today, but the ship's stern revealed a wonderful collection of small finds (from a steelyard to plates and pitchers).

In the last two decades, modern scientific studies of hulls and cargoes have been conducted off France, Turkey and Israel. In 1993, Luc Long (DRASSM) and Giuliano Volpe (Università di Foggia) excavated an 18,000-litre cargo of North African and Eastern wine and oil amphorae covering 60–80m^2 in depths of 6–7m in the bay of La Palud off Port Cros, southern France. A unique find on this mid-6th century ship was a wooden weight box (see p. 41).

Frederick Hocker of Vasa Research, National Maritime Museums of Sweden, has fully excavated a well-preserved 9th-century merchant vessel at a depth of 30–37m off Bozburun, south-west Turkey. Excavations from 1995 uncovered a cargo of 1,200 wine amphorae from the eastern Crimea and the white oak keel and planking of the ship itself.

In stark contrast to the deep waters of Turkey, the shallow waters of Dor off the southern Carmel Mountains of Israel are currently revealing one of the most important collections of Byzantine ships ever found in the Mediterranean. Surveys conducted throughout the 1980s and 1990s by Kurt Raveh and the author recovered a collection of nearly all the types of amphorae manufactured in Late Antiquity, as well as personal belongings lost by sailors and merchants,

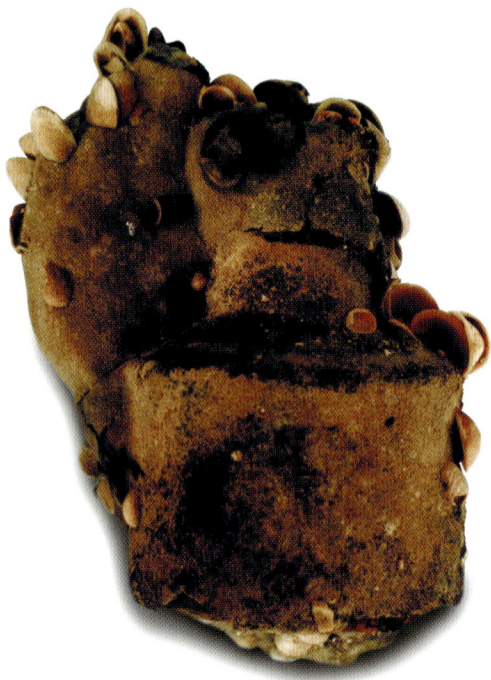

Copper pitcher from the early 7th-century AD wreck Dor A (Israel) before conservation (top, encrusted) and after conservation (below).

Photos: Sean Kingsley

including two bronze steelyards inscribed in Greek. A marble mortar and numerous copper flasks, cooking-pots, lamps and lids point to a dominance of Turkish merchants in Holy Land trade. A cargo of Palestinian wine jars on a Cypriot ship was excavated in 1999 by a team from Oxford University, Haifa University and the Nautical Archaeology Society (Portsmouth).

A joint project directed by Shelley Wachsmann (Institute of Nautical Archaeology, Texas A & M University) and Yaacov Kahanov (the Leon Recanati Institute for Maritime Studies, University of Haifa) excavated three 6th- to 9th-century ships and a cargo of Palestinian wine jars at Dor between 1994 and 1996. Tantura A represents about 25% of the hull of a small, 12m-long coaster from the 6th century, while Tantura B is a narrow 9th-century ship that may be a rare mediaeval galley. About 10m of this 30m-long Abbasid ship is preserved, as well as ropes, pottery and rigging, including a wooden roundel inscribed in Kufic script that points to Arabic ownership.

Meanwhile, an interdisciplinary team directed by Robert Ballard (Institute for Exploration) and including Cheryl Ward (Department of Anthropology, Florida State University) found four wrecks in the Black Sea in 2000 using side-scan sonar technology. These were surveyed visually using *Little Hercules*, a Remotely Operated Vehicle (ROV). Three of the wrecks lie at depths of 90–155m, are 23–25m long, and are covered with cargoes of carrot-shaped amphorae manufactured in the coastal town of Sinope, on the southern shore of the Black Sea. The fourth site is considerably deeper, lying at 320m in the anoxic (oxygen depleted) sea layer, and is a perfectly preserved 12m-long wooden ship with its mast rising 11m above the hull.

An unused white marble mortar from the shipwreck Dor F, Israel, early 7th century AD. Probably part of the cargo rather than a shipboard utensil for grinding herbs.

Photo: Sean Kingsley

Copper cooking-pot from the kitchen area of the shipwreck Dor G, Israel; early 7th century AD.

Photo: Sean Kingsley

Steelyards

The steelyard was the standard weighing device used on merchant vessels throughout Late Antiquity to guarantee accurate trade transactions. Particularly complete examples have been excavated from the Yassi Ada ship wrecked in AD 625/6, which carried eight bronze weights (and one of glass) and at least three bronze steelyards, the largest of which was 1.46m long and decorated at one end with a boar's head terminal. Its sculptural counterweight was a bust of the goddess Athena. This ship's weighing apparatus gave merchants the flexibility to weigh produce of up to 400 Roman pounds (126kg).

A pair of bronze steelyards from the Dor G shipwreck, a merchant vessel trading in Palestinian wine and wrecked off Israel between AD 600 and 640, seem to have brought bad luck to a generation of successive owners. The larger device, found in 2.2m of water, is 97cm-long and Greek letters inscribed along the beam show that it could weigh up to 160lbs. Greek inscriptions bordered by Christian crosses indicate that this steelyard had three successive owners. The earliest reads "Saviour Jesus Christ, come to the aid of Khala and

A bronze steelyard and a set of suspension chains from the shipwreck Dor G, and a marble mortar from Dor A, Israel; early 7th century AD.

Photo: courtesy of Sean Kingsley

Two bronze steelyards and a set of suspension chains used to weigh merchandise and found on the shipwreck Dor G, Israel; early 7th century AD.

Photo: Sean Kingsley

Small bronze steelyard from the shipwreck Dor G, Israel, incised with Christian crosses and Greek letters naming the object's owner as 'Psates of Rhion'; early 7th century AD.

Photo: Sean Kingsley

Artemon"; the second, "Jesus Christ, come to the aid of George son of Ision"; and the third, written on what was by then the only empty edge of the beam, "Jesus Christ, generated God, take pity on Psates of Rhion." Regrettably, this evocation fell on deaf ears, as this individual seems to have been the last merchant to operate on Dor G before she ran aground on coastal sandbanks.

A unique object from the mid-6th century wreck of La Palud, southern France, is a rectangular wooden box (now empty) that once held secure round copper or bronze weights from a merchant's balance. The designs of the weights are still preserved in the soft grain of the wood, so that a Byzantine emperor (of the period AD 527–578) staring out of the box is all that remains of the weights today.

A wooden box that once held weights for an equal-arm balance, found on the La Palud shipwreck, southern France, mid-6th century.

Photo: Philippe Foliot, CNRS-CCJ, Aix-en-Provence

41

A marine archaeologist uncovers cylindrical North African amphorae on the 4th-century AD Héliopolis A shipwreck off southern France, excavated under the direction of Jean-Pierre Joncheray. Photo courtesy of Jean-Pierre Joncheray

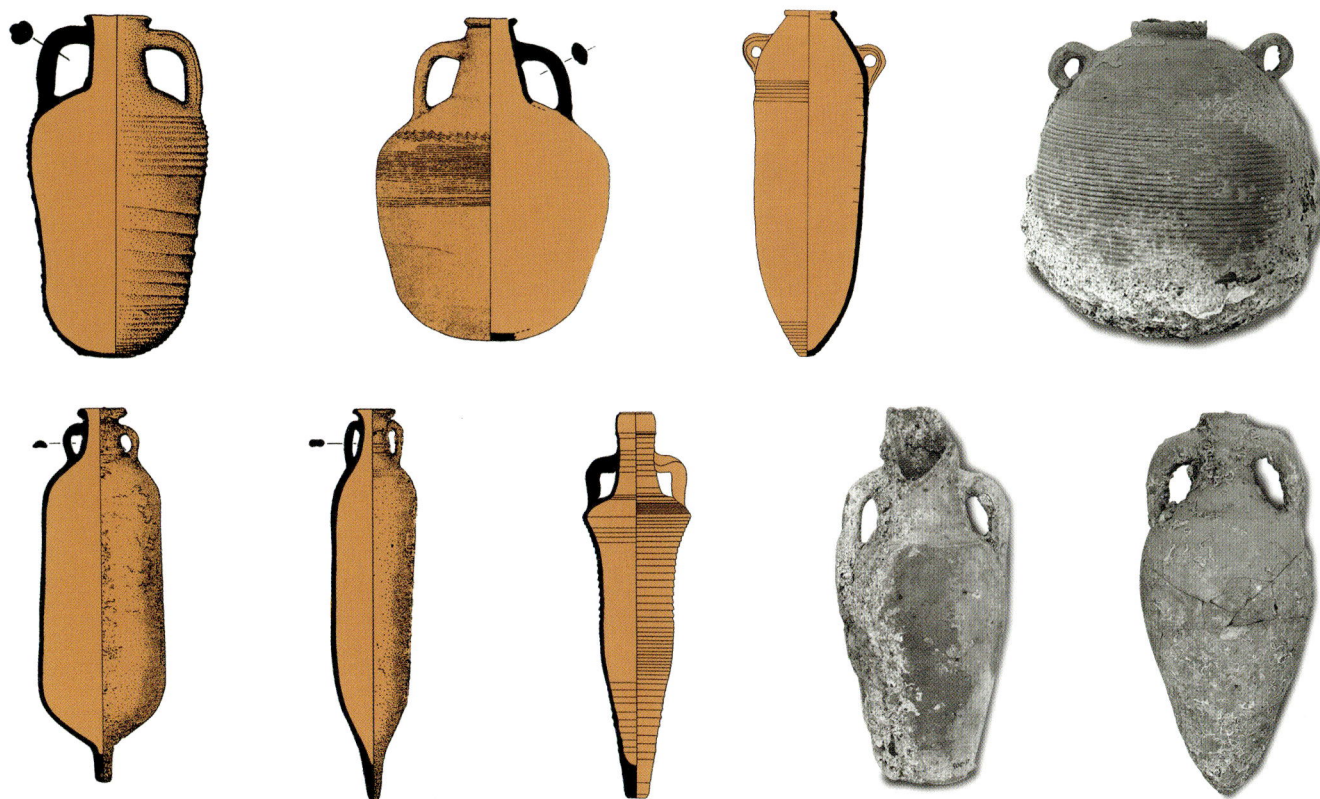

Cargoes and shipping lanes

Late Antiquity profited from the hard lessons learnt during the Roman period. Most conspicuous was the continued reliance on the amphora, a clay container with two handles set on either side of the shoulders beneath the mouth and neck. The typical Roman form of southern Gaul and Italy was a tall vessel about 1m high, characterised by an elegant long neck and correspondingly tall, slender handles. This elongated variety was dominant until the 2nd century AD, and had been designed deliberately for ease of stacking in a hull in up to four levels. Big business needed big jars.

All this changed in Late Antiquity. As independent shippers and merchants took an increasingly bigger slice of the empire's commercial action, and ship construction techniques were simplified (see Chapter 4), a new range of smaller amphorae with less liquid capacity evolved to suit the changing needs of mercantile communities. To archaeologists, these jars are a microcosm of maritime trade itself. Research into the typology (specific shapes) of these wares was pioneered during excavations in the 1970s and 1980s at the large coastal North African cities of Roman Carthage in Tunisia, Berenice in Libya and in Rome.

The excavation of shipwrecks has fine-tuned our knowledge about the origins, date and content of these wares. The most familiar product of the East Mediterranean, 'Late Roman 1' (LR1), is a short, barrel-shaped amphora about 50cm maximum height that probably originated in the Antioch region of Syria during the 4th century, where it may have been developed to transport the region's rich olive oil resources. Soon after, its production was imitated along

Amphorae are by far the most common type of cargo found on Mediterranean shipwrecks from Late Antiquity. Some of the most popular examples recovered are illustrated here, along with regions of manufacture and general dates.

Top row, left to right: 'Late Roman 1' amphora (Cyprus, Syria, south-east Turkey), 5th–7th centuries AD; 'Late Roman 2' amphora (the Aegean), 5th–7th centuries AD; 'Late Roman 4' amphora (southern Palestine), 6th–7th centuries AD; 'Late Roman 5' amphora (northern and central Palestine), 5th–7th centuries AD.

Bottom row, left to right: Tunisian amphora from the Isis shipwreck, last quarter of the 4th century AD; a *spatheia*-type amphora from Asia Minor, an imitation of a Tunisian form, from the Isis shipwreck, last quarter of the 4th century AD; 'Late Roman 7' amphora (Egyptian), 6th–7th centuries AD; amphora from Beirut, Lebanon, 6th–7th centuries AD; unusual eastern Mediterranean amphora form, 5th–7th centuries AD.

Photos: Sean Kingsley
Bottom row, two furthest right, from F: from McCann and Freed, 1994: fig. 23, no. 1, fig. 23, no. 7

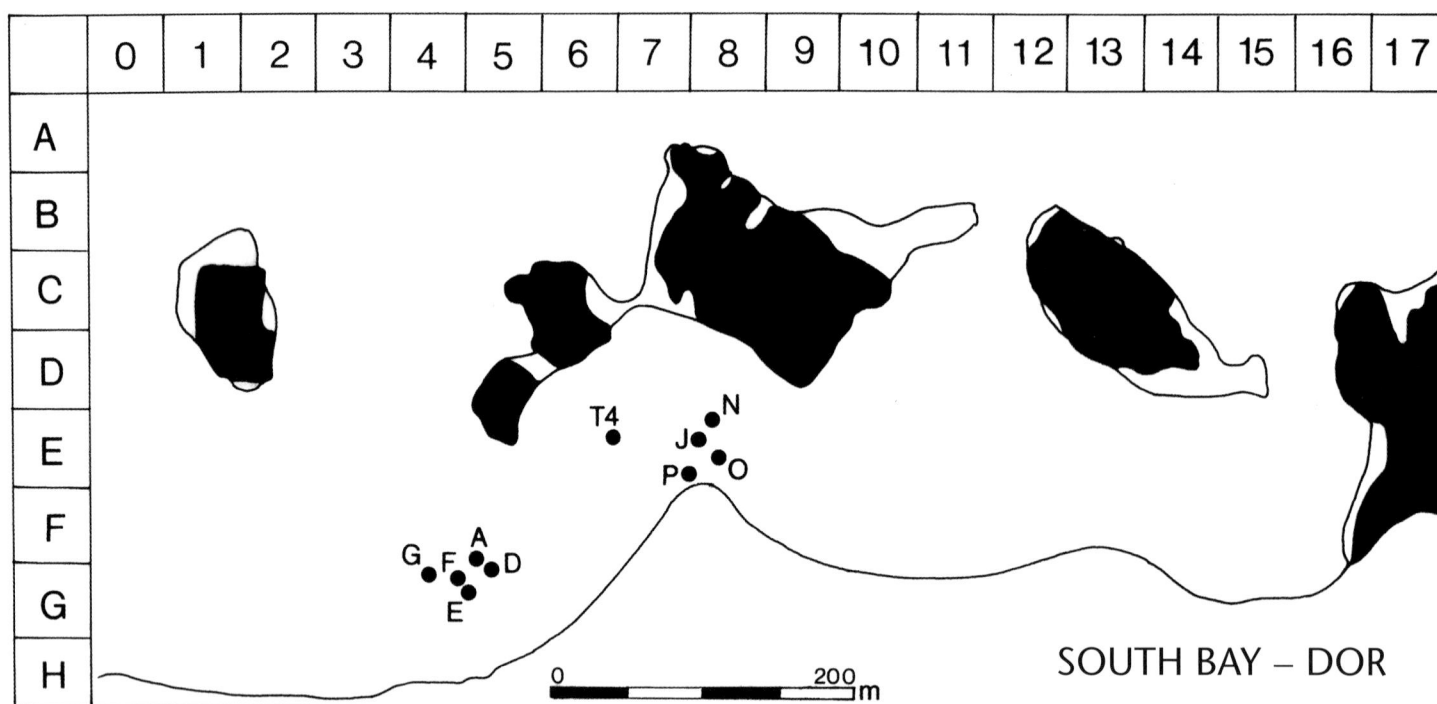

+

Map of the positions of eight Byzantine (6th–7th centuries AD) and one Abbasid shipwreck (Site O/Tantura B, early 9th century AD) found in the South Bay at Dor, Israel.

Drawing: Sean Kingsley

the coasts of south-east Turkey, south-west Cyprus, and Rhodes (with less significant manufacture later in Egypt). Early variants tend to be smaller with narrow mouth widths (seven-litre capacity), while those of the 5th and 6th centuries are taller with broader mouths of about 10cm width (19-litre capacity).

Of the 15 Mediterranean cargoes containing these amphorae, most are clustered within the eastern Mediterranean in Turkey (Yassi Ada A, Datça B), Greece (Delphinion, Ayios Stephanos), Cyprus (Cape Andreas C and E), Israel, and just outside the harbour of Alexandria. Cargo sizes are sometimes remarkable: just over 200 jars on the 7th-century Yassi Ada ship and 1,000 amphorae within a mound of 24m x 12m on the Ayios Stephanos wreck in Greece dating from the mid-6th to mid-7th centuries AD.

Four LR1 shipments have been surveyed off Croatia, and the small secondary cargo on the mid-6th-century wreck off La Palud, southern France, suggests that the further west they travelled, the smaller the consignment. Even though they may have been conceived initially for a specific region and product, the geography of manufacture and content quickly spread during the 6th and 7th centuries. Traditionally labelled an oil jar, excavations on Yassi Ada A clearly showed that in the open trading world of the first quarter of the 7th century, LR1 amphorae could contain wine just as easily as olive oil.

Organic remains of produce are often preserved underwater, but when they are not, the presence of black pitch resin lining inside jars is a good indication of a former wine content. Pliny wrote in the *Natural History* that immediately "after the rising of the Dog-star they [wine jars] should be coated with pitch, and afterwards washed with sea-water or water with salt in it, and then sprinkled with ashes of brushwood or else with potters earth..."

'Late Roman Amphora 2' (LR2) is a broad-bellied, globular container with strongly curved bow-shaped handles that was produced in the Aegean around Haleies in the north-east Peloponnese. Early variants of the 5th to first half of the 6th century incorporated distinctly splayed, funnel-shaped mouths probably designed to help receive and pour viscous olive oil. In the later 6th century, the funnel disappeared as rims became low and flat, suggesting that LR2 also lost its exclusive association with olive oil. Indeed, 1,380 grape pips were recovered from 69 (of 719 total) LR2 amphorae at Yassi Ada. In addition to the eastern cargoes at Yassi Ada and Datça (Turkey) and Prasso and Skopelos (Greece), LR2 shipments are relatively common in the West at Vendicari (Sicily) and along the northern Adriatic coast of Croatia, where seven cargoes cluster.

Two types of amphora were manufactured in Palestine. 'Late Roman Amphora 4' (LR4) is a narrow, cylindrical jar about 85cm tall, with a very short rim, small round handles and a liquid capacity of about 27 litres maximum. Dozens of kilns are scattered along the coast of southern Israel between Gaza and Ashdod. Large twin kilns from an estate in Ashkelon were excavated next to elaborate wine presses, olive oil installations, granaries and fishponds.

The second Palestinian form, 'Late Roman Amphora 5' (LR5) is a very different type of jar: only 40cm tall (22 litres) and bag-shaped with a short rim. LR5 originated in the Hellenistic era and had a long shelf life in the Roman period, before being adapted specifically for maritime trade in Late Antiquity.

A mosaic floor from the Apamea region in Syria decorated with a merchant vessel carrying local amphorae; 4th–5th century AD, Apamea Archaeological Museum.

Photo: A. Zaqzouq

Between the 5th and mid-7th centuries, rim heights were reduced from about 5cm to less than 2cm as experienced shippers realised that small rims were less likely to break during sea voyages. As with LR1 and LR2, the body walls of the LR5 amphora are densely covered with horizontal lines of ribbing and grooves that were an integral design feature to help ropes tied around jars to retain a tight grip as cargoes swayed from side to side in ships' hulls.

Palestinian jars incorporate a strange feature that is unknown on any other form of Mediterranean amphora: a 1.5cm-wide hole drilled into shoulders. Was this designed to release carbon dioxide build up from fermenting wine or to help draw off liquid when full? Probably neither, because a rabbinical passage explains that "one did not fill the jar up to the brim, but only two-thirds of the jar [did he fill], so that its fragrance spreads. One does not draw [wine] from the mouth, because of the scum, or from the bottom, because of the lees, but one pierces it and draws it from the middle of the middle-third [of the jug]." In other words, this unremarkable piece of archaeology is a rare feature designed to satisfy Jewish consumers that wine was ritually pure.

Seven wrecks along the coast of Israel at Ashkelon, Atlit, Caesarea, Dor and Givat Olga contained cargoes of Palestinian wines. Further afield, consignments of Holy Land wine were lost off southern Turkey at Kizilagac Adasi, Kekova Oludeniz and Iskandil Burnu, where a well preserved wreck contained over 300 jars. An intriguing find on this site was a freshly produced clay casserole dish still sealed to its lid in order to guarantee its ritual purity for a Jewish consumer. An LR5 amphora fished up off Corfu undoubtedly comes from a site awaiting formal discovery, and Palestinian jars reached southern France on a wreck lost off La Palud, southern France, in the mid-6th century.

Local amphorae are abundant across Byzantine settlements in Egypt, and dozens of pottery workshops along Lake Mareotis and on monasteries along the Nile are associated with wine presses. Even though hundreds of tonnes of wheat were shipped between Alexandria and Constantinople into the early 7th century, no Egyptian jars have turned up on Mediterranean shipwrecks. This anomaly is a mystery because entrepreneurs were typically quick to exploit state sea-lanes. For instance, vessels used to ship wheat between Tunisia and Rome were crammed with large quantities of North African olive oil, fish-sauce and fine-ware plates and oil lamps (such as the 250 examples on La Luque B, wrecked off France circa AD 300–325). Why Egyptian merchants failed to imitate this trade model remains an enigma.

By far the most common type of amphora recorded on Mediterranean shipwrecks originated in North Africa. The 66 shipwreck sites containing fish and oil jars from Tunisia are almost entirely clustered in the western Mediterranean. Some 14 wrecks lie off southern France, 12 off Italy (nine in

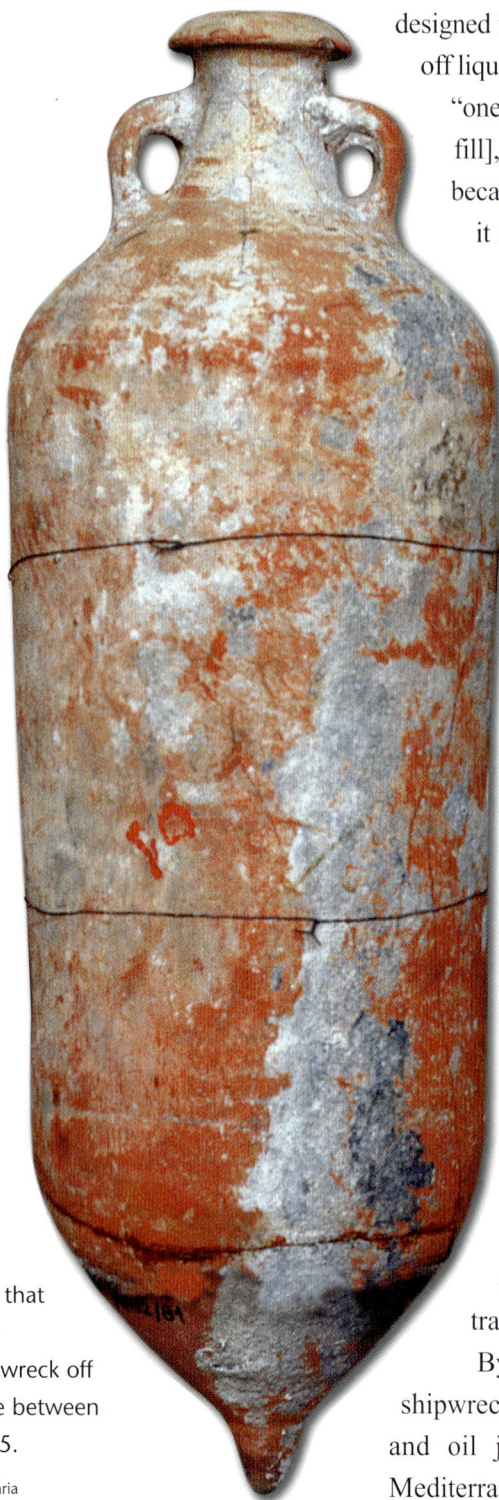

A cylindrical amphora from Tunisia, part of the main cargo that was lost on the Dramont E shipwreck off southern France between AD 425 and 455.

Photo: Claude Santamaria

Sicily), and 30 off Croatia. Less than three sites each have been recorded off Spain, Bulgaria, Montenegro, Sardinia, Libya, Algeria and Malta. Not one site is known in the East Mediterranean, clear evidence of a split in maritime trade traditions following the divide of the Roman Empire. Both the West (North Africa to the Balkans) and East (Egypt to Greece) enjoyed very different and independent spheres of commerce.

North African amphora cargoes could include as many as 1,000 examples, as on a 30m-deep wreck of *circa* AD 320–340 off Sobra in Croatia. Most jars were sealed with corks and protected in the hold by a cushioning bed of vine twigs. However, marine archaeology has strongly warned against identifying all North African amphorae as oil jars. The amphorae on the 50m-deep Cap Blanc wreck off Spain held fish-bones and scales stopped with cork disks. By the 6th century, cork stoppers had been replaced by a round sherd cut from an old amphora and sealed over a jar's mouth with plaster. (The most revealing fish cargo is the 22–25cm-long fish [*Sardina pilchardus*] of Spanish origin wrecked at Port-Vendres, France, *circa* AD 400. The amphorae rested on dunnage of heather and vine branches and were kept in position upright by wooden frames.)

Other than allusions to the Christian faith on the amphorae of Late Antiquity, such as 'God is victorious' and 'Christ God', these widely exported jars and contents were otherwise bare. By comparison, Roman variants from Italy, North Africa and Spain bore stamps or graffiti identifying the name of the shipper or merchant and contents. The disappearance of these management labels in Late Antiquity is once again evidence of a breakdown in state control over shipping and the freeing of commerce in this period.

An African red-slip plate that was one of a batch stowed as cargo on the Dramont E shipwreck off southern France, AD 425–455.

Photo: Claude Santamaria

A North African amphora from the mid-6th century La Palud shipwreck off southern France with a crude stopper in its mouth made from a broken clay jar.

Photo: Philippe Foliot, CNRS-CCJ, Aix-en-Provence

The Yassi Ada Byzantine shipwrecks

Frederick van Doorninck Jr

The 7th-century AD shipwreck

Two Byzantine shipwrecks have been excavated by expeditions of the University Museum of the University of Pennsylvania under the direction of George F. Bass off Yassi Ada, a small island in the south-eastern Aegean between the Greek island of Pserimos and the Turkish coast: a 7th-century wreck in 1961–1964, and a 4th/5th-century wreck in 1967, 1969 and 1974. Various methods of mapping deepwater wreck sites, including stereo-photogrammetry, were developed during these excavations.

The 7th-century ship, a 21m-long vessel with a capacity of about 60 tonnes, had sunk shortly after setting sail from an eastern Aegean port in AD 626, near the end of a long and devastating war between the Byzantine and Persian Empires. The date of sinking is based on 16 gold and some 50 copper coins recovered. All but one gold coin were issues of the Emperor Heraclius, and the latest copper coin had been minted in the year 625/626. The ship was carrying approximately 900 amphorae, some 700 globular jars (LR2) stacked three deep in the hold and the rest cylindrical jars (LR1) placed horizontally between the necks of the top layer. The excavators originally thought the ship had been a coastal trader involved in the transport and sale of wine. However, a recent review of the ship and its amphorae has concluded that it probably belonged to the Church and was transporting low-grade wine intended for Byzantine troops, who were soon to win a decisive victory in the heart of the Persian Empire.

The island of Yassi Ada. Photo: INA

A cylindrical cargo amphora.

Photo: INA

An inscription on a steelyard carried on board indicates that the ship's captain, Georgios, was a priest. His ship seems well suited to serve the Church. Although able to carry ample cargo, the vessel, with a slim 4:1 length-to-width ratio, sharp bow, full stern, and deep wine-glass shape, was designed for speed and carried a lateen sail. At the stern, there was a large galley complex, well equipped to prepare and serve food and drink to quite a number of passengers, often including, one supposes, churchmen.

The galley had a floor set low within the hull at a level that maximised floor space. A tile firebox with adjustable iron grill occupied the port half of the galley. The galley structure, which rose far enough above the deck to give access and adequate lighting to the interior, had a tile roof. When other openings were closed in bad weather, firebox smoke could escape through a large circular hole in one of the tiles. Although totally impractical at sea, tile roofs were sometimes used in the ancient world from Hellenistic times on to enhance a ship's appearance and status.

Utensils for the preparation and cooking of food included a mortar and pestle, 21 cooking pots, two cauldrons and a copper bake pan. A food locker contained at least 16 pantry jars. The ship's water jar stood opposite the firebox on the galley's starboard side. Serving utensils included several copper or bronze pitchers, a glass bottle, 18 ceramic pitchers and jugs, a half-dozen spouted jars with lids, and four or five settings of fine tableware, each consisting of a red-ware plate and dish, a glazed bowl and a one-handled cup. Such a well equipped facility is remarkable in an age when passengers normally provisioned themselves.

The ship was well appointed in every way. Weighing instruments consisted of the steelyard bearing Georgios' name; two smaller steelyards, one equipped with a balance pan; a set of silver-inlaid balance-pan weights; and a glass weight. The ship's tool chest contained perhaps as many as 40 tools, including axes, adzes, an awl, a bow drill and bits, billhooks (to rough trim wood), a carpenter's compass, chisels, files, gouges, hammers, knives, punches, one or more saws, and a carpenter's belt. In the boatswain's locker, just aft of the galley, there was a grapnel for the ship's boat, tools (two axes, two mattocks, two billhooks and a shovel) used when foraging for water and firewood on land, netting needles and spare lead weights for repairing fish nets, and an assortment of lead

Globular cargo amphorae. Over 800 amphorae, that had carried wine, were discovered on the shipwreck. Amphorae were the typical cargo containers of the ancient world.

Photo: INA

weights and lures for deepwater line fishing. At least eight ceramic lamps were used to illuminate the ship at night. Perhaps some of 16 unused lamps also found would have been used as dedications in churches and sanctuaries visited during the voyage. A bronze censer with open-work lid, surmounted by a cross, was probably used to sanctify both religious services and business agreements, and at meals.

The ship was carrying 11 iron anchors. They had straight arms set perpendicular to the shank, a cruciform anchor design used from the 4th to 10th centuries. Seven of the anchors were stacked on the deck midway between the bow and midships, and four bower anchors were on the bulwarks ready for use, two to either side of the anchor pile. Although the anchors had almost completely oxidised, concretions that had formed around them constituted almost perfect moulds of the anchors and made possible a close calculation of their original weights. Three of the bower anchors had each weighed about 250 Byzantine pounds (78.75kg).

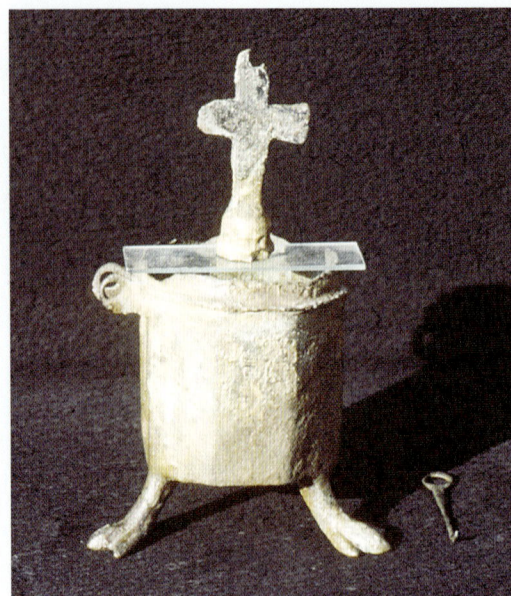

Bronze censer and cross. This incense burner suggests that Christian rituals were performed on board the ship and that its captain and/or crew were Byzantine Christians. Photo: INA

Cross-section drawing of the stern area of the Yassi Ada 7th-century ship. The hearth, here wrongly restored, took the form of a tile firebox with iron grill. Photo: INA

The other bower anchor was a best bower weighing about 350 Byzantine pounds (110.25kg). A complete set of spares with the same weights was uppermost in the anchor pile. The bottom three anchors, each weighing about 450 Byzantine pounds (141.75kg), were sheet anchors used as a last resort in storms. The bower anchors had wooden stocks when the ship sank, but there were three iron stocks available for use when greater anchor weight was desired. At least 20 separate pieces of iron were hand-forged together to make each anchor. The cross-sectional areas of shanks and arms were kept as small as possible in order to make the welds joining the pieces as strong as possible. Since the rather thin shanks often broke under stress, it was only prudent to carry a full set of spares.

Although the ship was well appointed and sported a rather elegant tile roof for the galley deckhouse, economy took precedence over appearance in her construction. Four pairs of wales girdling the sides for extra strength and the majority of timbers lining the hull interior were little more than half logs. Construction methods employed were more economical than those of just a century or two earlier. In earlier hull construction, the outer shell of hull planking was first built by edge-joining the planks together with large mortise and tenon joints fixed in place by pegs, these joints making a major contribution to hull strength; framing was then added to further strengthen the hull. In the 7th-century Yassi Ada hull, mortise and tenons were much smaller, much more widely spaced, not pegged and used only up to the waterline. Above the waterline, hull planking was fastened to already erected framing. The framing, frequently bolted to wales and keel, was now the major source of hull strength. Hull planking was no longer fastened to frames by wooden trunnels and large clench nails as in earlier times, but by light nails that barely penetrated halfway into frames. Construction costs were in these ways significantly reduced.

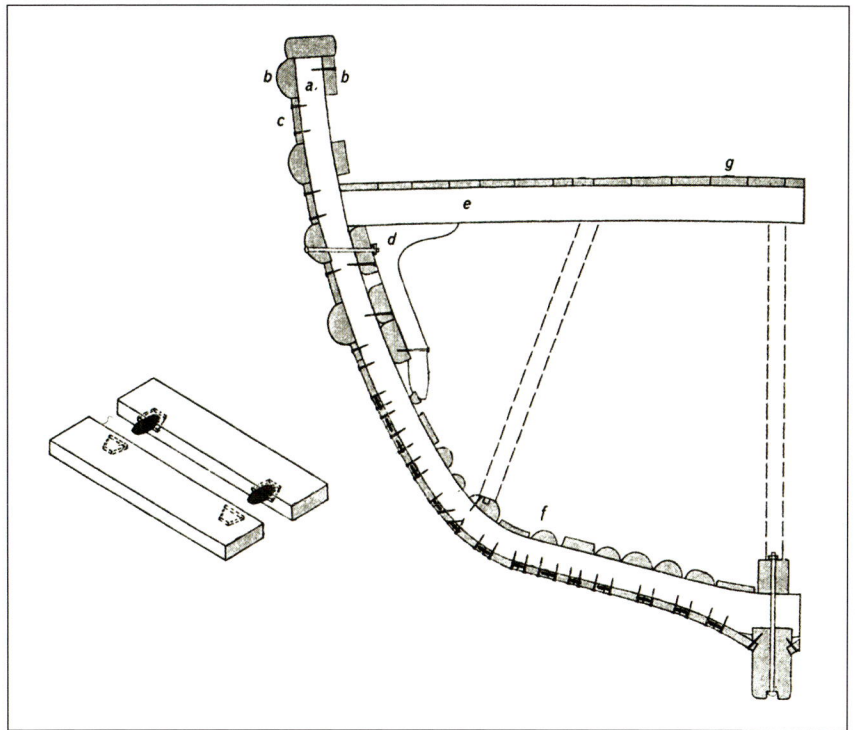

Hull section and an example of mortise and tenon plank fastening. Drawing: INA.

Reconstruction drawing of the Yassi Ada 7th-century ship being built. Drawing: INA

51

Only 110 amphorae were raised at the time of the excavation, but in the wake of the chance discovery made in 1980 of *graffiti* (carved inscriptions) hidden by marine deposits on many of the raised amphorae, an additional 570 were recovered from the seabed. The organic contents of intact amphorae were carefully examined in an effort to determine the nature of the ship's cargo. The finding of just under a dozen grape seeds (on average) in each amphora indicates that most, or all, of the amphorae had been full and were carrying low-grade wine.

Quite remarkably, a thorough cleaning of the amphorae revealed that there were 11 distinct types of cylindrical (LR1) and some 40 distinct types of globular amphorae (LR2). Furthermore, although approximately 80% of the globular jars belong to four closely related, contemporary types, the handle and neck shapes of some other globular types indicate that they had been made at least several decades prior to the ship's sinking. Some of the *graffiti* indicate that many of the recently made amphorae had earlier carried olives, possibly preserved in sweet wine, and some of these jars contained, along with grape seeds, degraded fragments of olive pits. *Graffiti* on several of the older globular jars indicate that they had once held lentils. Several dozen different marks of ownership occur on the globular amphorae; some jars had more than one owner. Many of the older jars appear to have served for some extended period of time as storage jars.

What activity would have brought together on one ship so many types of reused amphorae having so many different prior owners and varying so greatly in age? The war with Persia, then nearing its end, had been so financially costly that it became necessary for the church to lend major assistance in provisioning the army, partly through levies of produce from church-owned lands. Particularly in view of rather frequent allusions to the Christian faith among the *graffiti* on the amphorae, it seems likely that the ship's cargo of low-grade wine transported in recycled amphorae had been part of this effort.

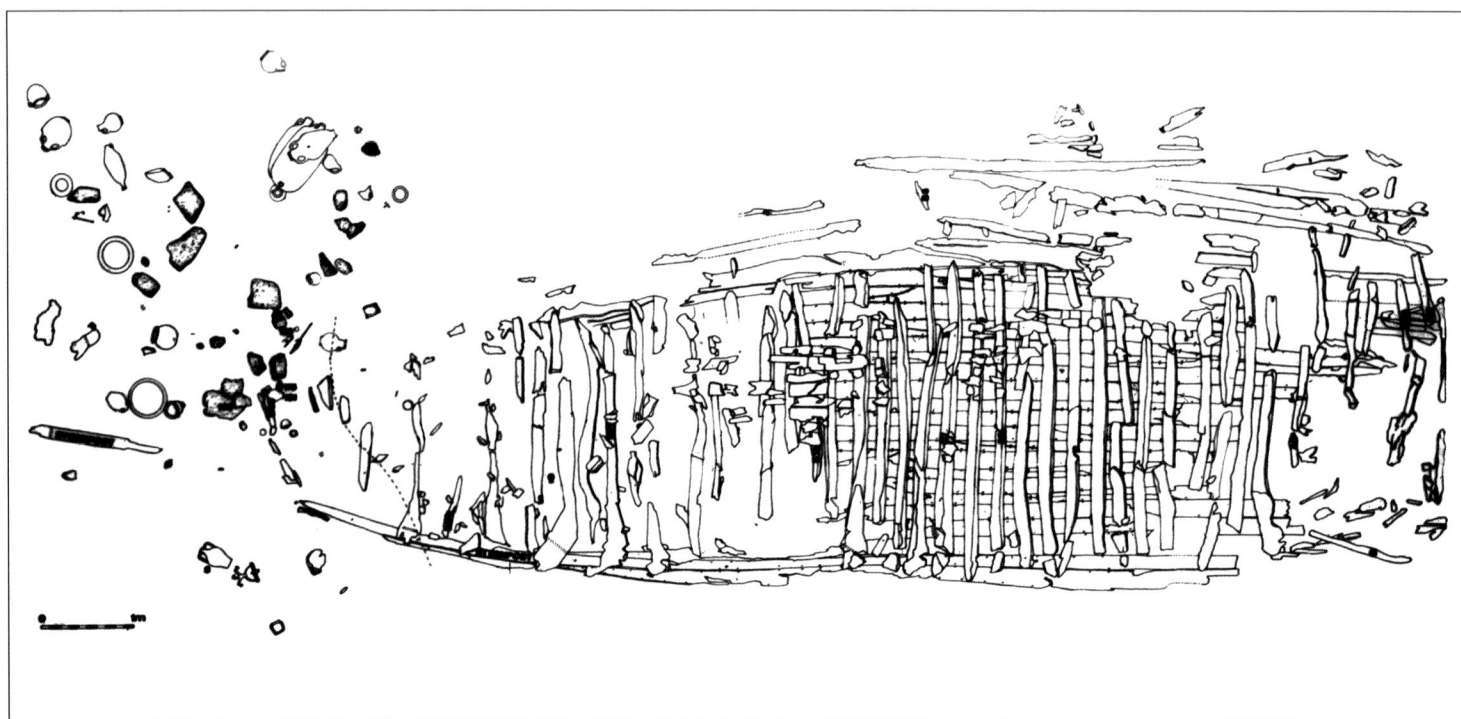

Site plan of the Yassi Ada 4th-century shipwreck. Drawing: INA

The 4th-century AD shipwreck

The late 4th- or early 5th-century Byzantine ship at Yassi Ada came to rest on the seabed at the edge of a sharp drop-off. Some portion of the ship and its contents, including any anchors remaining on the deck, undoubtedly await excavation further down the slope. Even so, the hull's port side was found extensively preserved up to the waterline within the excavated area of the wreck. The hull had an overall length of about 20m and a maximum width of just under 8m. It appears to have had the full, rounded, almost symmetrical shape of a Roman *corbita* (the most common type of Roman cargo ship), with the sternpost, keel and stem making almost equal contributions to the hull's overall length, but with the stem having a somewhat greater rake than the sternpost. Four pairs of wales girdled the hull sides between the waterline and deck level. The lower two were essentially horizontal throughout, while the upper two curved upward in the bow and stern, an arrangement sometimes seen in representations of the *corbita*.

Although traditional in shape, the hull is a harbinger of some of the developments in hull construction that we see employed in the 7th-century hull at Yassi Ada. The mortise and tenon joints used in edge-joining the hull planking, although fixed in place with pegs, were somewhat smaller, more widely spaced, and more easily assembled than they normally were in Roman hulls, and are not employed in fastening planking to keel, stem and sternpost. This lessening

George Bass examining artefacts from the 4th-century Yassi Ada shipwreck following cleaning. Photo: INA

of the contribution of mortise and tenon joints to the strength of the hull was to some degree compensated for by an increased use of iron spikes and bolts in fastening together the major non-planking elements of the hull. Trunnels alone, without clench nails, were used to fasten the framing to planking. The practice of fastening planking to already erected framing, as was done above the waterline in the 7th-century hull, finds a precursor in the midship frame, which had been erected after perhaps just five planking strakes had been installed to either side of the keel. The frame may have served to guide the shipwright in shaping the hull.

A rather spacious galley set down in the stern had a rough-stone firebox. Galley equipment included (at least) six pantry jars, a funnel, four cooking pots, 11 pitchers, a cup, a bowl, two large plates, a smaller dish, five glass vessels, a copper jug, possibly three steelyards, some copper coins, a casting net, and four lamps, one of them, signed KY, from an Athenian workshop.

The ship was carrying approximately 1,100 amphorae of three types: bag-shaped, cylindrical, and small ovoid jars. Slight evidence indicates that the bag-shaped jars contained olive oil and the other jars, wine. The cargo was probably of Aegean origin.

The Isis shipwreck, Skerki Bank

Anna Marguerite McCann

The Isis shipwreck was the first ancient wreck in the deep ocean to be found and surveyed with new robotic technology. Discovered in 1988 by Robert D. Ballard, it was documented at that time only by photography. In 1989, Ballard returned with an interdisciplinary team, including A. M. McCann (archaeological director), D. R. Yoerger (engineering director) and A. Bowen (director of the ROV Jason team). This first JASON Project focused on the Isis wreck, named after the Egyptian goddess who protected sailors and promised an afterlife. Conceived and directed by Ballard for the education of children in the sciences and archaeology, the 1989 JASON Project was also the first live, interactive television broadcast linked to an ROV (remotely operated vehicle) at work on the sea floor. Some 225,000 children and their teachers in science museums in the USA and Canada communicated directly with the team with only a half-second time-lag. Ballard and McCann returned to Skerki Bank in 1997 with a larger interdisciplinary team. They explored seven additional shipwrecks, as well as undertaking some excavation of Isis.

The Isis was found at a depth of about 800m in international waters off the north-west tip of Sicily, about 60km north-north-east of Keith Reef at Skerki Bank, a treacherous reef that lies just 1.8m below the sea's surface. The Isis site is located about 100km north of Tunis (ancient Carthage) and about 120km due west of

Location of the Late Roman Isis shipwreck and Skerki Bank with possible trading routes of the Isis, late 4th century AD.

Map: E. P. Oberlander

Selected finds from the Late Roman wreck Isis, late 4th century AD. From left to right: Table amphora (MJ89-8); amphorae (MJ89-3) (top), (MJ89-19) (below); small amphora (MJ89-7); amphoretta (MJ89-16); rotary hand quern (MJ89-40); wine jug (MJ89-18); cup (MJ89-17); lamp (MJ89-36). Photo: T. Kleindinst and J. Porteous

Trapani on the north-west coast of Sicily. The visible remains of the Late Roman ship covered an area 11.5m north-south x 9.5m east-west. The main concentration of material was in the south-west portion of this area, covering an area of 5 x 6m. The Isis site was mapped and photographed using the dual ROV *Medea/Jason* vehicle system. Selected objects were recovered with Jason's robotic arm. No digging or imaging occurred below the surface in 1989. Photo-mosaic techniques and acoustically derived bathymetric maps had not yet been developed.

Forty-eight objects were documented with 10 complete amphorae and five complete common-ware vessels recovered. Also lifted were a Roman lamp, the upper part of a cylindrical basalt millstone, sections of iron anchors, and wooden planking. A bronze coin dating to the last years of Constantius II (AD 355–361), found in a pot of pine tar used on deck for the daily maintenance of the ship, gives a *terminus post quem* for the earliest possible date of the wreck. A North African red-slip ware lamp from Carthage, datable between *circa* 375 and 425, supports this date and may also point to the ship's last port of call. Of the 10 amphorae recovered, five are large Tunisian cylindrical jars, two are from western Asia, and two probably from Calabria. They carried oil, fish sauce and wine. The common-ware pottery is largely Tunisian, while the cooking pot with pine tar originates from Pantelleria. All may be dated before AD 400, narrowing the

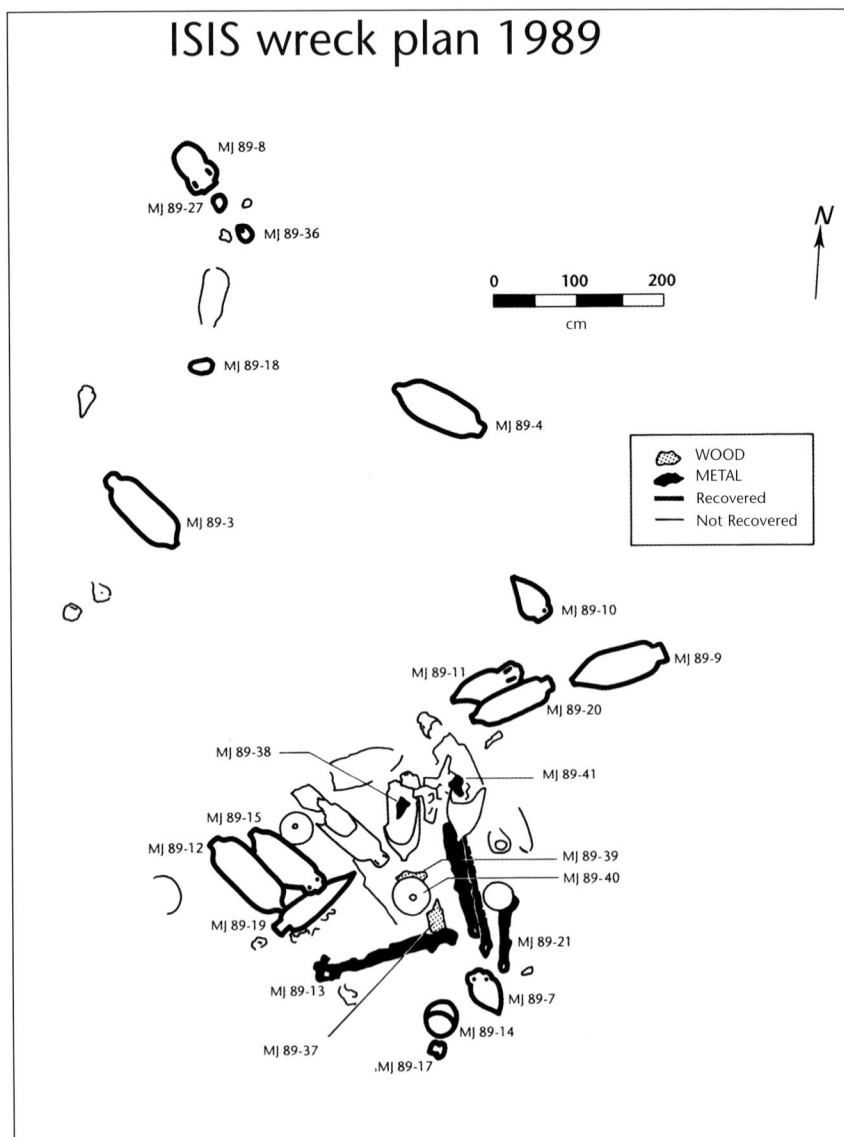

ISIS wreck plan 1989

MJ 89-8
MJ 89-27
MJ 89-36
MJ 89-18
MJ 89-4
MJ 89-3
MJ 89-10
MJ 89-9
MJ 89-11
MJ 89-20
MJ 89-38
MJ 89-41
MJ 89-15
MJ 89-12
MJ 89-39
MJ 89-40
MJ 89-19
MJ 89-21
MJ 89-13
MJ 89-7
MJ 89-37
MJ 89-14
MJ 89-17

0   100   200
cm

N

WOOD
METAL
Recovered
Not Recovered

Plan: E. P. Oberlander

probable date of the ship to the last quarter of the 4th century.

The assemblage of pottery yields two new amphora types and provides new evidence for the Late Roman date and Tunisian origin of 'Keay Type 35' jars. Some whole pieces of common-ware are also unique in their style: a small flat-bottomed table amphora from Tunisia with a tall grooved neck, and a rare miniature version of a large-sized amphora from Mauretania in North Africa. The basalt millstone from Libya with its concave hopper and protruding handles is also not a form previously known.

The Isis may also have carried a cargo of some organic substance, such as North African wheat, which disappeared along with the hull soon after the ship sank. Such a missing cargo may be represented by grains of wheat and barley found incorporated in one of the iron anchor concretions.

The vessel was built in the typical Graeco-Roman 'shell-first' method using mortise and tenon joinery. The mortises were spaced 5.5cm apart side to side, 11cm apart centre to centre, and were staggered. The mortise spacing is appropriate for a Late Roman ship of this size. Some iron and copper-alloy spikes may have been used to secure the frames and planking. The hull was constructed of pine planks held together by oak tenons (*Quercus robur* type) with some framing and decking of oak, pear and possibly Mediterranean cedar. The treenails analysed consisted of Alder buckthorn and pine. The ship was not sheathed in lead, but lead patching was observed suggesting that she was an older vessel. The original size of the ship is estimated (largely on the basis of the size of the four or more iron anchors found stacked on her deck) at 12–15m length with a beam of about 5m, yielding a carrying capacity of about 30–35 tonnes. The design of the anchors and flukes can both be paralleled on the Dramont F wreck (later 4th century AD). The Isis was probably one of the small, sturdy traders typical of the Late Roman world designed to brave the open seas between Carthage and Rome.

These finds and her location suggest that the home port of the Isis was Carthage and that she was en route to Rome. Perhaps in the more distant past she had also sailed in the eastern Mediterranean and called at ports in Italy. The Isis thus provides evidence for a new trade route over the open seas and for worldwide Mediterranean trade in Late Antiquity. The wreck is also important as one of the few documented shipwrecks from the Late Roman world.

The ROV *Jason* over the Late Roman Isis wreck, found at a depth of 800m. Photo: Quest Group Ltd

Black Sea shipping in Late Antiquity

Cheryl Ward

The Institute for Exploration recently conducted a series of surveys in the Black Sea as part of a long-term project in cooperation with several institutions and archaeologists. In 2000, maritime exploration resulted in the discovery of one of the best preserved seagoing ships from antiquity. At a depth of 320m, this ship dates to the late 5th or 6th centuries. Three other shipwreck sites marked by mounds of shipping jars were located between depths of 85 and 101m and date from the 4th to 6th centuries. These four ships are all located slightly west of Sinop in northern Turkey, along the southern shores of the Black Sea.

Maritime surveys of the Mediterranean coastline have provided data about a significant number of shipwrecks from the period of Late Antiquity, but only very scant remains of a single, small, ancient Black Sea ship have been previously reported. Residents of the Sinop region engaged in long-distance exchange as early as 4500 BC, and analyses of ceramics here and on the Crimean peninsula suggest that seaborne traffic in the region was most intense during Late Antiquity. Direct evidence for Black Sea maritime trade, so well attested by artefacts in terrestrial sites, is now directly accessible as a result of the survey efforts.

Survey methods

Using both traditional and innovative remote-sensing methods in search of deep-water archaeological shipwrecks allows nondestructive evaluation of sites in a marine environment more hostile than most, while maintaining standard archaeological approaches to site survey. Because much of the Black Sea is anoxic (oxygen-depleted), it is hostile to the biological organisms that usually destroy exposed wood in oxygenated waters. Willard Bascom recognised in 1976 that the deeper waters of the Black Sea might preserve a treasure trove of ships from antiquity, because at depths greater than 150m insufficient oxygen exists to support most familiar biological life forms. A suboxic zone in the next 20 to 50m has both low oxygen and low sulfides, and in the anoxic layer below 200m water chemistry studies consistently document relatively high concentrations of sulfides and low oxygen.

The ROV *Little Hercules*, with video and cameras, used to find and record shipwrecks in the Black Sea.

Collaborative efforts of the Institute for Exploration, the government of Turkey, the University of Pennsylvania, University of Rhode Island Graduate School of Oceanography, the Massachusetts Institute of Technology, Florida State University and the Institute of Nautical Archaeology resulted in a programme of terrestrial and marine survey focused on Sinop. The potential for wood preservation in the deep waters of the Black Sea (up to 2,210m deep), and the long occupation and central role Sinop played in regional trade, including extensive exchange with settlements on the Crimean peninsula, made this region attractive for testing several hypotheses.

Annually from 1998 to 2000, and in a final season in 2003, remote-sensing tools were used to investigate Sinop's anchorage, portions of the submerged coastline and deeper waters along suspected trade routes between Sinop, the Crimea and towards Byzantium to the west. A side-scan sonar survey of waters near Sinop harbour in 1998 produced several dozen anomalies examined through images provided by camera-carrying ROVs in 1999 that showed many of these low-relief anomalies to be colonies of large-shelled molluscs. a large, late 18th-century iron anchor, a storage jar at least 1m high, and the remains of a 19th-century steamship were also identified.

Preservation on Wreck D is extraordinarily good, and the mast (left) and stanchions here are unique examples from anywhere in the ancient world.
Photo: courtesy of the Institute for Exploration/Institute for Archaeological Oceanography-URI/GSO

In 2000, the archaeological survey focused on the survey of deep waters east and north of the promontory and investigation of the seabed about 15–30km west of Sinop. The project had several goals. We sought to discover whether human habitation sites could be identified on the ancient submerged landscape, to examine the seabed for shipwrecks, to test the hypothesis that the anoxic waters below 200m would protect shipwrecks from the expected biological attacks on organic components, and to seek data about an ancient trade route between Sinop and the Crimea indicated by terrestrial archaeological remains.

Much of the two-week survey was devoted to side-scan surveys in search of relic stream beds in the submerged landscape and shipwrecks. Once anomalous targets were identified as potential shipwrecks or habitation areas, we examined images obtained by cameras on an ROV to determine site composition. Even relatively small acoustic anomalies were identified by the DSL-120 phased-array, 120kHz side-scan sonar developed by the Woods Hole Oceanographic Institution and towed at about 40–50m above the seabed, providing returns across a swath of seabed 600m wide.

IFE developed both the optical tow sled *Argus* and the ROV *Little Hercules*, and both were operated from *Northern Horizon*, a research vessel with direct positioning capability. *Argus* carries lights and a three-chip video camera, an electronic still camera, and a 35mm colour still camera, all controlled by shipboard

Examples of the Sinopean amphorae that covered wrecks A, B and C, from the surface of shipwreck B.

Photo: courtesy of the Institute for Exploration/Institute for Archaeological Oceanography-URI/GSO

operators. A 675kHz fan-beam scanning sonar mounted directly on the tow sled *Argus* easily located acoustic targets originally identified by the DSL-120. *Little Hercules*, tethered directly to *Argus*, carries cameras capable of providing extremely high-quality images. Both vehicles worked well and provided outstanding visual images of the four shipwreck sites.

Results

Distinctive orange, carrot-shaped shipping jars from Sinop marked the location of shipwrecks A, B and C, and gave us a preliminary date of the 4th to 5th centuries for the sinking of these ships. Until we recover examples of the jars and have the opportunity to analyse them, we cannot date them more closely, nor can we predict what the ships might have been carrying to or from Sinop.

Wreck D provides a unique opportunity to examine a shipwreck from antiquity that seems to be almost entirely preserved due to the toxic nature of the deep Black Sea. Wood samples of both oak and fir were recovered from the site, and a radio-carbon date calibrated to 410–520 places the ship within the period of Late Antiquity. The presence of at least one ceramic jar visible at deck level suggests that we will have ample opportunity to learn more about this ship and its crew through sub-surface testing.

A photomosaic of part of Shipwreck B made from electronic still camera images.

Photo: courtesy of the Institute for Exploration/Institute for Archaeological Oceanography-URI/GSO

Discoveries by the Institute for Exploration's Black Sea expeditions are likely to provide new information about both technological change and trade in the Black Sea during a period of political, social and economic transition through the study of ship construction techniques and the remains of cargo. By relying on remote sensing with side-scan sonar in both shallow and deep water to detect possible archaeological sites, and investigating them with cameras mounted on ROVs, we were able to extend both our knowledge of the Black Sea and its past seafarers, and also to expand the expectations for archaeological survey in the deep sea.

60

The Bozburun Byzantine shipwreck

Frederick M. Hocker

In the late 9th century AD, a merchant ship carrying a cargo of Crimean red wine was wrecked on the south-west coast of Anatolia, near the modern Turkish town of Bozburun. The wreck contains significant evidence for the resurrection of long-distance maritime commerce after the near-collapse of the Byzantine Empire in the 7th and 8th centuries. The hull remains provide some of the earliest evidence for the arithmetical design and construction methods that later dominated seagoing ship construction in the Mediterranean. The site, located at a depth of 30–35m on a sandy slope at the base of a vertical cliff, was first surveyed by George Bass in 1973 and excavated between 1995 and 1998 by the Institute of Nautical Archaeology at Texas A&M University.

The homogenous cargo consisted of red wine, flavoured with spices and fish, carried in amphorae. The jars themselves are relatively small, poorly fired, with an average capacity of about 13 litres. Almost all are of a single type – a pear-shaped body, round bottom, a short, straight neck with thick, rolled lip and low, rounded handles. The general type is common throughout the eastern Mediterranean in the 9th and 10th centuries, although the best parallels for the Bozburun amphorae have been excavated at kiln sites in the southern Crimea.

One of three glass goblets found with a bottle (pictured overleaf).

Photo: Don Frey, courtesy of INA

Over 900 complete or nearly complete jars were recovered from an original cargo of at least 1,200 jars, stacked in at least two and probably three layers. A large portion of the lowest layer was still *in situ*, in orderly rows with the handles carefully aligned. A quarter of the jars bear *graffiti*, probably the initials of merchants, scratched into their shoulders. Two abbreviations, AN (Anastasios?) and ΓΕ (Georgios) occur in large numbers, each tightly grouped within the wreck, suggesting that individual merchants had dispatched separate consignments, even though almost all of the wine came from the same place. Six of the amphorae carried the abbreviations ΕΠΙΣ [ΚΟ], for episkopos or bishop, indicating that the church also had a hand in the shipment.

The galley was located on the starboard side near the stern, closed off from the rest of the hold by bulkheads. The hearth consisted of unglazed tiles laid over a layer of roughly fitted stone, which also acted as ballast to

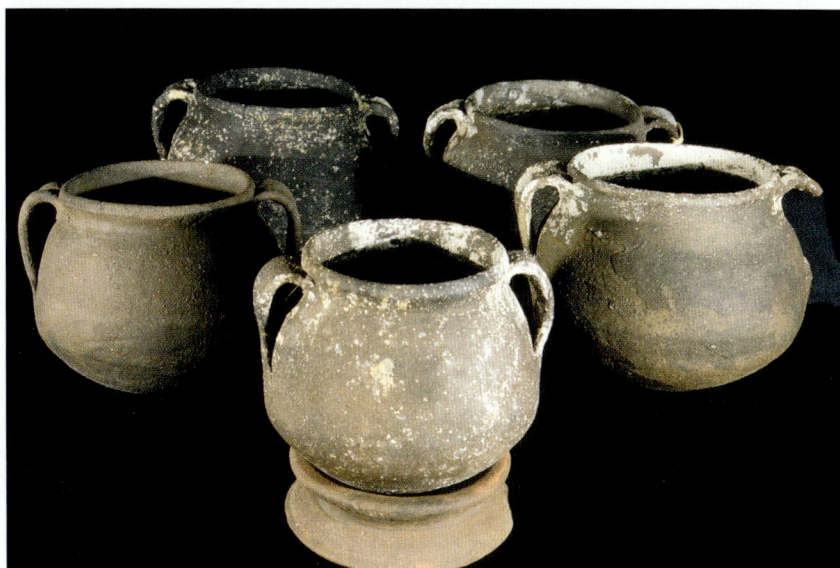

Some of the cooking pots and a collar stand from the galley.

Photo: Don Frey, courtesy of INA

maintain the ship's trim. At least 10 similar cooking or serving pots were found along the forward side of the galley area and one more was found farther aft. These are black, with a nearly spherical body, a flared rim and one or two broad strap handles. Two collar stands, one marked A and the other ΔI were used to keep the pots upright on flat surfaces. At least six pitchers, all of different types and sizes, were found along the starboard side of the galley, with one farther aft. Two had lost their mouths in antiquity and were being used as storage vessels to carry grapes, their necks sealed with rough stoppers and pitch. Two copper jugs, with flat bottoms, tall, narrow necks and strap handles were also found in the galley area.

Farther aft, a set of three very fine glass goblets was found, together with a small, mould-blown glass bottle. These are not typical shipboard equipment and were probably the personal possessions of the captain or a merchant. A single lamp and a bronze steelyard beam with lead counterweight were found just forward of the galley area, and a basket of tools was found in the stern, but no coins, weights or personal effects survived.

Mould-blown glass bottle found in the stern. Photo: Don Frey, courtesy of INA

The ship itself was quite well preserved, with the keel and most of the starboard side of the bottom surviving to above the turn of the bilge. The hull was originally about 15m long and 5m in beam, with flat floors and hollow garboards amidships and a hard bilge. Such a shape offers a good compromise between capacity and sailing performance. The ship was built on a heavy oak keel made of three pieces, with frames of oak in the middle of the hull and pine toward the ends. The planking is primarily of oak, with some chestnut. Light boards of oak and pine were loosely laid over the frames to

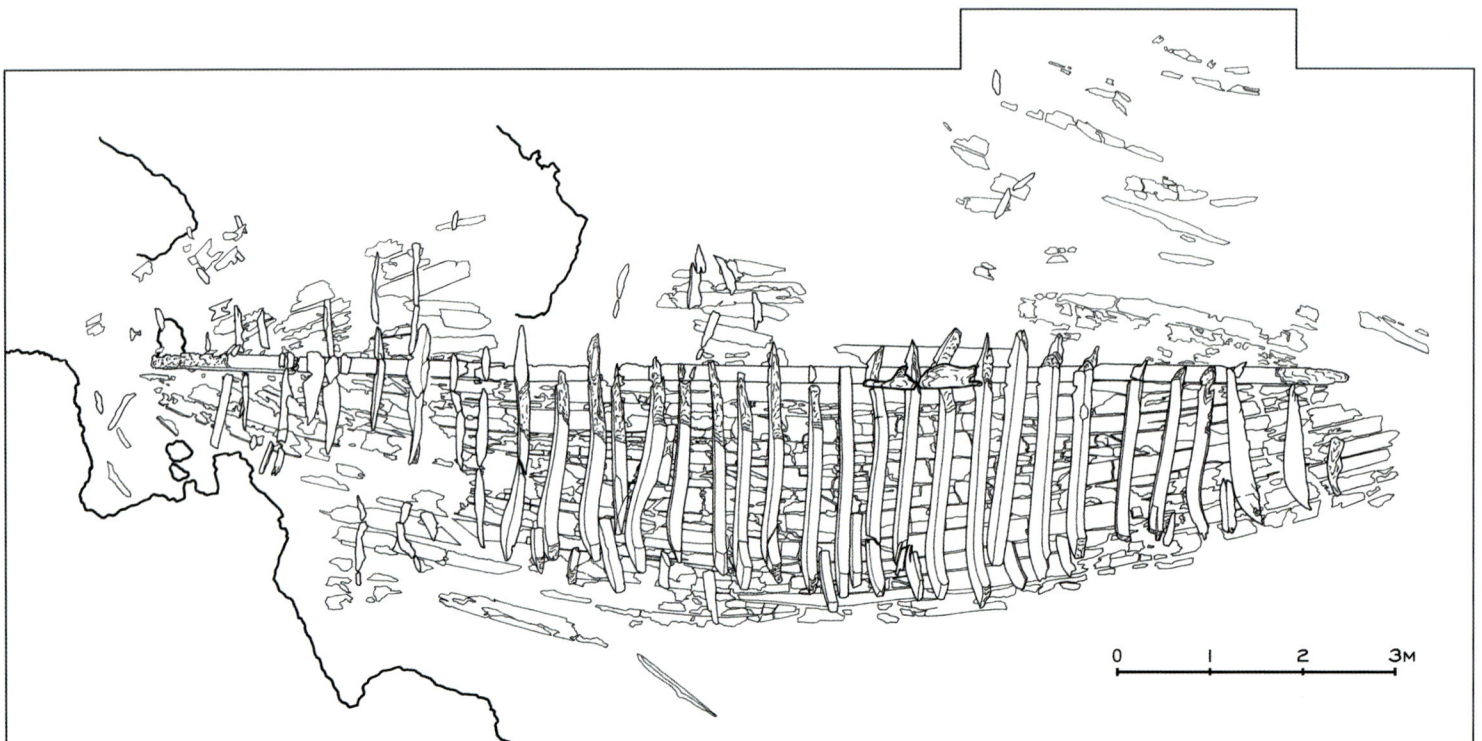

Plan of the wooden hull remains, with the ship's bow to the right. Drawing: Fred Hocker, courtesy of INA

62

protect them from the cargo. The wood was felled in north-western Anatolia or the Balkans in AD 874, according to dendrochronological analysis. This choice of woods is unusual before the High Middle Ages, especially the use of oak planking, but suggests some emphasis on strength and durability.

The construction sequence is particularly notable, as it seems to consist of both conscious, frame-based design and the use of plank shapes in the determination of the hull form. The central oak frames appear to be an initial element in the construction, and their shape and placement can be related to a consistent arithmetical progression based on a standard unit of measure, as is also seen in the Serçe Limanı ship of *circa* 1025. The plank edges have small dowels in them, probably for the alignment of the strakes during construction. This is a perplexing feature, as edge dowels do not otherwise appear in Mediterranean ship remains after the Classical period, and edge fastenings or alignment tenons of any sort are usually thought to have gone out of use by the end of the 7th century AD.

This merchant venture came to grief in a remote part of the Byzantine world when the ship smashed into a cliff after dragging its anchors. Amphorae from the upper layers in the hold were found under the hull, indicating that the crew had tried to lighten the ship by jettisoning some of the cargo. The

An amphora lying beneath the hull at the stern (the keel is visible to the right), evidence of an attempt to save the ship by jettisoning cargo.

Photo: Don Frey, courtesy of INA

absence of coins, valuables or identifiable personal items shows that the ship had stayed afloat long enough for the crew to collect their valuables and scramble ashore or into the ship's boat.

Near to the place of wreckage were small garrisons based in harbour towns, and the ship may have been carrying supplies to one of these, or may have sought one as a harbour of refuge. In any case, the Bozburun shipwreck shows that by the late 9th century, it was practical or profitable to ship wine of no great quality a relatively long distance within the Byzantine economic sphere, despite piracy in the Aegean and warfare with Arab states in the region.

Closely spaced frames in the central part of the Bozburun hull. Photo: Don Frey, courtesy of INA

IV. Between the cracks: reading ships' hulls

In many ways, the composition of Late Antique cargoes and produce closely resembled the classical forms of trade pursued throughout the Roman period. The shapes of the main amphorae types may have changed, but consumer tastes and markets for oils, wines and fish sauces had not. Between the 4th and 7th centuries, however, the character of Mediterranean shipping underwent a revolution with the evolution of a new and radical shipbuilding philosophy.

A nautical revolution

For decades, historians have pored over the meaning in ancient texts of nautical terminology describing the appearance of swifter, smaller, more agile vessels like the 'gazelle'. The breakdown in state transportation, and the ever-increasing Islamic threat to the Mediterranean, are usually seen as the catalyst for an upturn in the fortunes of smaller, smarter craft. Thus Leo VI's *Tactica* recommended that "Thou shalt equip small and large vessels according to the character of the hostile peoples. For the barbarian Saracens and the so-called northern Scythians do not use the same sort of ships. The barbarians use larger and slower vessels and the Scythians smaller, lighter and faster boats…"

A merchant vessel painted on to the wall of a monk's cell at Kellia in Egypt in the first half of the 7th century AD.

Drawing: after R. Kasser, *Kellia. Topographie* (Recherches Suisses d'Archéologie Copte, Geneva, 1972), fig. 156

Top: An early 7th-century AD wooden rigging block recovered from the Dor F shipwreck, Israel.

Middle and bottom: An iron pick from the carpenter's chest on the late 6th century AD Dor D shipwreck, Israel, before and after preliminary conservation.

Photos: Sean Kingsley

Maritime communities now concentrated on building smaller, lighter craft to replace the massive super-tankers that plied the seas of *mare nostrum* (such as the Madrague de Giens ship of 400 tonnes capacity that foundered off southern France between 70 and 50 BC with a cargo of 7,000 amphorae). Merchant vessels of more modest proportions were cheaper to build, easier to maintain, and were financially a smaller investment and risk to own. Small ships were thus seen as a powerful factor of democracy because they suited the limited income bracket of many sailors and merchants of humble birth. The prevalence in trade of vessels of 15–20m length, and the rise in the fortunes of the independent merchant entrepreneur, are seen as the key features of Late Antiquity's nautical revolution.

Throughout the late 4th and early 5th centuries, the relationship between the shipping industry and the government was put under great strain. For centuries, the transportation of the *annona civica* wheat tax from Egypt had been designated a *munus* (public duty). As compensation for being restrained from dabbling in more profitable business, shipmasters were exempted from several compulsory municipal services and from paying taxes. Shipmasters in the Alexandrian fleet also received the monetary equivalent of 4% of the grain they transported, and one *solidus* per 1,000 measures of wheat on their vessels (6.5–7 tonnes).

By the late 4th century the tension between state and shipmaster was at breaking point. Laws inscribed in the Theodosian Code, and published across the empire, leave little doubt that the government was having difficulties forcing shippers to live up to their responsibilities. Ship owners and sea captains had clearly had enough of the state's harsh coercion designed to guarantee continuous tax shipments by making the class of professional shipmaster hereditary. Despite severe threats against officials or private individuals interfering with the organisation and transportation of the *annona*, including fines of between 10 and 20lbs of gold, property confiscation and capital punishment, the system seems to have been breaking down fast during the late 4th century.

Between 396 and 409 some shipmasters were illegally selling government taxation goods for personal profit. Others had taken to illegally avoiding compulsory public shipment by registering their ships under the name of a second party, while bribing dignitaries and officials to escape the obligation of grain shipment was common. Other ship owners proved equally cunning, realising that if you cannot beat the system then you should join it. Since their vessels were compelled to transport wheat to Constantinople between designated periods of time, they started to overload government cargoes with their personal commercial consignments.

The state responded by issuing a series of harsh legal edicts, all preserved in the Theodosian Code. In AD 390 the government reminded its citizens that "Shipmasters shall be shipmasters in perpetuity." Five years later, they confirmed that "[no] person shall place a private burden upon a public cargo,

nor shall he dare to compel, by any necessity, the carriers of grain to accept his burden." The need to reissue the same edicts throughout the late 4th and early 5th centuries is clear evidence that merchant communities were continuously and successfully flouting the law.

State interests were not only being eroded in relation to Egypt and shipping wheat to Constantinople. Funny business in the Near East was similarly affecting the government's former monopoly over purple-dye production. In AD 385 the Theodosian Code was forced to ordain that "if any person should dare to usurp the use of a boat that is assigned to the compulsory public service of purple dye collection and to the collection of shellfish, he shall be held liable to the payment of two pounds of gold."

Yet, by the first half of the 5th century such threats were clearly not taken particularly seriously because the same book reports that in AD 436 some 300lbs of purple silk – a king's ransom – were found to have been "coloured in clandestine dyeing operations." The state was so disturbed by this unlawful activity that it took the extraordinary measure of dispatching an army of bureaucrats to investigate this corruption in the dye-works of Phoenicia, including every seventh man from the bureau of secretaries, every sixth man from the bureau of regular taxes, and every fifth man from the bureau of registrars.

Whether centralised control over purple-dye production was ever secured again is uncertain, but this investigation smacks of desperation in a world where even the most highly specialised industry was becoming increasingly commercialised. In theory, this evidence is strong proof of an explosion of entrepreneurial, independent trade, but to what extent do shipwrecks contribute to this picture?

Shipwrecked hulls

Marine archaeology has revolutionised our understanding of the accuracy of these ancient texts by identifying radical changes in ship construction methods on the hulls of numerous Late Antique merchant vessels scattered across the Mediterranean. The two most prominent trends are a gradual change from tenon-built to frame-first hulls and a decline in the size of merchant vessels. Both have been taken to reflect a major social transformation in the organisation of long-distance exchange towards increased shipping privatisation.

The majority of ancient wooden merchant vessels were constructed using a single shipbuilding technology until the early 4th century, when a greater emphasis on a hull's internal skeletal structure started to replace the primary concentration on outer planking for a vessel's main strength. During the Roman period, large freighters were assembled using up to 20,000 square or rectangular small mortises cut deeply into underlying and overlying strakes (outer horizontal planking) and spaced about 10–12cm apart. Tenons were used to interconnect opposite plank edges and these, in turn, were then locked in place with short horizontal wooden pegs.

An iron hammer head and pick with wooden shafts preserved from carpenters' chests on ships wrecked in Dor harbour, Israel, during the early 7th century AD. All ships carried carpenters' chests for patching up deteriorating parts of the vessels.

Photo: Sean Kingsley

The Dor D shipwreck, Israel

Ancient shipwrecks often turn up in large clusters of graveyards, where over the centuries they fell foul of the same maritime hazards of islands, reefs, shoals or adverse winds. Several remarkable ships' graveyards are renowned for the density of cargoes and hulls scattered beneath bewitching waters: Yassi Ada off Turkey, the incredible island of Dramont in the south of France and in the Near East, the wreck-rich bays of Dor in Israel.

The Biblical city of Dor is perched on a huge headland that juts into the Mediterranean Sea 13km north of Caesarea Maritima. Unlike most of the country's linear shoreline, where opportune anchorages are absent, Dor is blessed with a string of offshore islets that functioned as natural breakwaters, saving engineers a fortune in artificial constructions. For this reason, the town became the most important harbour along the coast of Palestine throughout most of antiquity. The southernmost of the site's three main bays is littered with wreckage dating between the Canaanite period (*c.* 1100 BC) and the late Ottoman era and is a marine archaeologist's dream.

The timing of underwater surveys conducted in 1991 by the author and Kurt Raveh of the Dor Maritime Archaeology Project was fortuitous because the sand level overlying the seabed in the South Bay had been eroded to its lowest point in recorded history between May and December. Huge craters appeared in the seabed less than 30m from shore and at depths of less than 3m, and within them lay six unknown shipwrecks (five Byzantine sites of *circa* 575–640 and one Late Ottoman or Early Modern).

The southern harbour in the South Bay at Dor, Israel, framed by offshore islets. View from the Main Bay.

Photo: Sean Kingsley

In 1999, one of these wrecks, named Dor D, was selected for excavation by an international team directed by the author (Somerville College, University of Oxford), Yaacov Kahanov (Recanati Institute for Maritime Studies, Haifa University), Chris Brandon (Nautical Archaeology Society, Portsmouth) and Kurt Raveh. After 346 amorphous stone ballast blocks covering an area of 10.6 x 8.3m were recorded and removed, cyprus wood hull planking (*Cypressus sempervirens*) was exposed from a medium-sized merchant vessel about 15m long and of 5.2-tonne capacity.

The 15 planks examined across an area of 3.3 x 4.4m were strakes from the ship's outer shell. These measured up to 3.2m in length and 22cm in width and had been interconnected with edge-joined mortise and tenons set 17–44cm apart. Unpegged tenons (3.2–3.8cm wide) were loosely fitted inside mortises (4.9–7.7cm wide), so that some had 2cm of open space on either side. They had clearly only served to loosely guide planks into place

Above left: A copper cooking pot found during the excavation of the late 6th-century AD Dor D shipwreck. This was a poor quality utensil, crafted out of several patches of metal with interlocking crenellated seams, that reflects the low status of the merchants on board.

Above right: Divers entering the water to start a shift excavating the late 6th-century AD Dor D shipwreck off Israel.

A brass oil-lamp recovered from wreckage around the Dor D shipwreck; 6th–7th centuries AD.

Photos: Sean Kingsley

before they were fixed to the inner frames. Dor D had thus gone a long way towards the frame-first ship conception when she foundered on the bay's submerged sandbanks in the last quarter of the 6th century AD. About 68% of outer planks were nailed to frames using wooden treenails, while 32% used iron nails. On average, frames were inserted 24cm apart.

Strictly speaking, the Dor D ship was not carrying a primary cargo. The 771 amphora fragments overlying the hull were products of Ashkelon and Gaza in southern Palestine. Elongated amphorae (LR4) accounted for 7% of all the cargo, and bag-shaped types (LR5) for 89% of the total. The bag-shaped jars had clearly been manufactured in a variety of kilns because three distinct shapes and five different types of clay were analysed.

Wooden outer hull planking on the late 6th-century AD Dor D shipwreck, Israel, with strakes and diagonal scarf in the foreground.

An archaeologist recording wooden outer hull planking on the Dor D shipwreck.

Photos: Sean Kingsley

Where did Dor D originate? Her ballast turned out to be non-local and was linked to the serpentine outcrops of the Troodos massif and Ayia Varvara locality of Paphos, Cyprus. Other amphorae (LR1) associated with the galley, and tiles that roofed this kitchen area, were also Cypriot. The ship seems to have been busy returning empty jars for recycling, collected from northern Mediterranean cities, when she hit troubles off the Carmel coast. Although sailing without a cargo is not economically ideal, it was hardly unknown. Indeed, Themistius described ships converging on Constantinople from Asia, Syria and Egypt with imported merchandise from throughout the world that returned only with builders' rubbish.

Not only was Dor D a medium-sized merchant vessel selling empty wine jars, she was also owned by a 'lower-class' sea captain. Instead of superior iron anchors, the ship was relying on at least three single-hole stone anchors (weighing 66kg, 85kg and 109kg), very much the poor man's substitute for the period (see p. 82). Both captain and merchant associated with the final voyage derived from a fairly humble background, thus graphically corroborating Late Antique historical texts.

Whether the Dor D ship had fallen on hard times, or had simply always functioned like this, remains a mystery. However, despite her size, poor cargo, and the low status of her owner, merchant operatives and anchors, she clearly had no problems trading internationally and had a proven Cypriot connection. An Egyptian Aswan-ware bowl amongst the wreckage hints tantalisingly at Dor D's broader sphere of operations in her lifetime before the bad times set in. Perhaps her sorry state pays her an injustice and she was actually headed for Dor to refill jars with the town's famous wines or even to load up with cloth dyed purple in the city's workshops.

Detail of an unpegged tenon protruding from a mortise amongst wooden planking on the late 6th-century AD Dor D shipwreck, Israel. Scale length: 50cm.

Photo: Sean Kingsley

But by the late 4th century, this technology, which had seen constant use since its emergence in the Mediterranean on the Ulu Burun shipwreck of 1400 BC, was being abandoned. The earliest trace of change was the reduction in the size of mortise and tenon joints, which were now spaced more widely apart. Greater emphasis was now attached to securing strakes to frames using first wooden treenails and subsequently iron nails.

The timeframe and character of this 'revolution' are now generally understood thanks to underwater exploration conducted since the early 1960s. Some of our best evidence comes from the wealth of shipwrecks off southern France, where research has led to extensive excavation of early 4th- to mid-5th-century craft.

The scant timbers from the 4th-century Héliopolis A wreck, recorded by Jean-Pierre Joncheray between the Hyères Islands at depths of 35–38m, included a section of keel and garboard planking (first outer line of strakes), where distances between mortise and tenon joints measured between 17 and 24cm. This increase in the distances between joints was a gradual exercise, with limited change 75–100 years later. Two ships that foundered amongst a ships' graveyard off the island of Dramont in southern France confirm this trend.

Dramont F was lost *circa* AD 400, and analysis of her hull has shown that mortise and tenons were set 19–36cm apart. On the far better preserved Dramont E ship, wrecked between 425–455, joints were placed 10–14cm apart along weak areas of planking and 26–31cm apart elsewhere. This general pattern was a Mediterranean-wide phenomenon, and on the late 4th- to early 5th-century Yassi Ada B shipwreck excavated off Turkey, joint distances ranged from 25–32cm. In all these cases individual tenons were still locked in place within mortises by wooden pegs, as on Roman hulls. In other words, mortise and tenon technology continued to comprise the primary form of ships' structural strength.

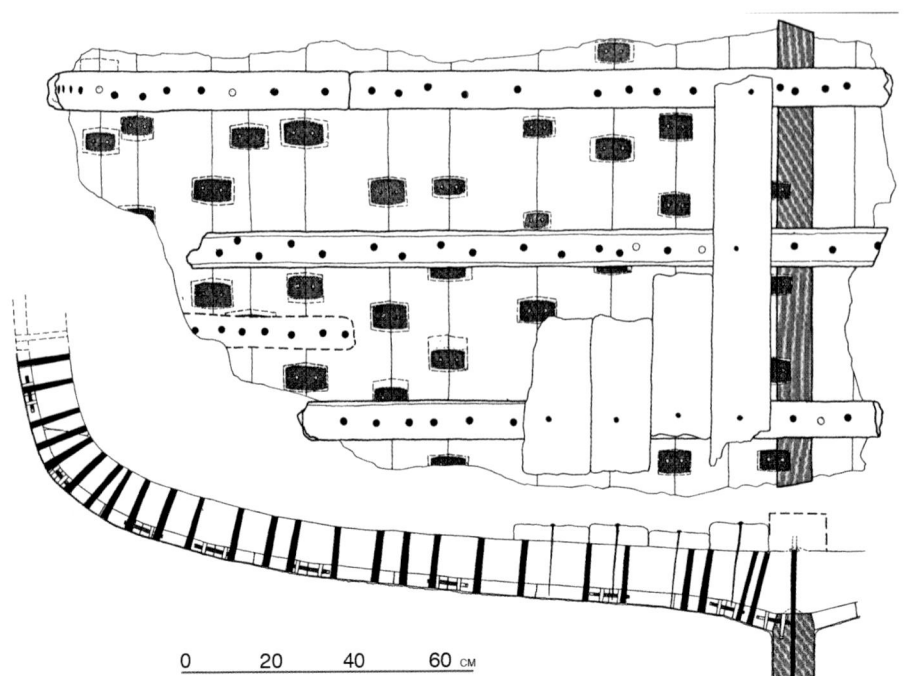

Plan of the wooden hull planking preserved on the Dramont F ship wrecked off southern France *circa* AD 400. Note the staggered character of the mortise and tenons and the relatively wide intervals separating them.

Drawing: after Joncheray 1975, 126

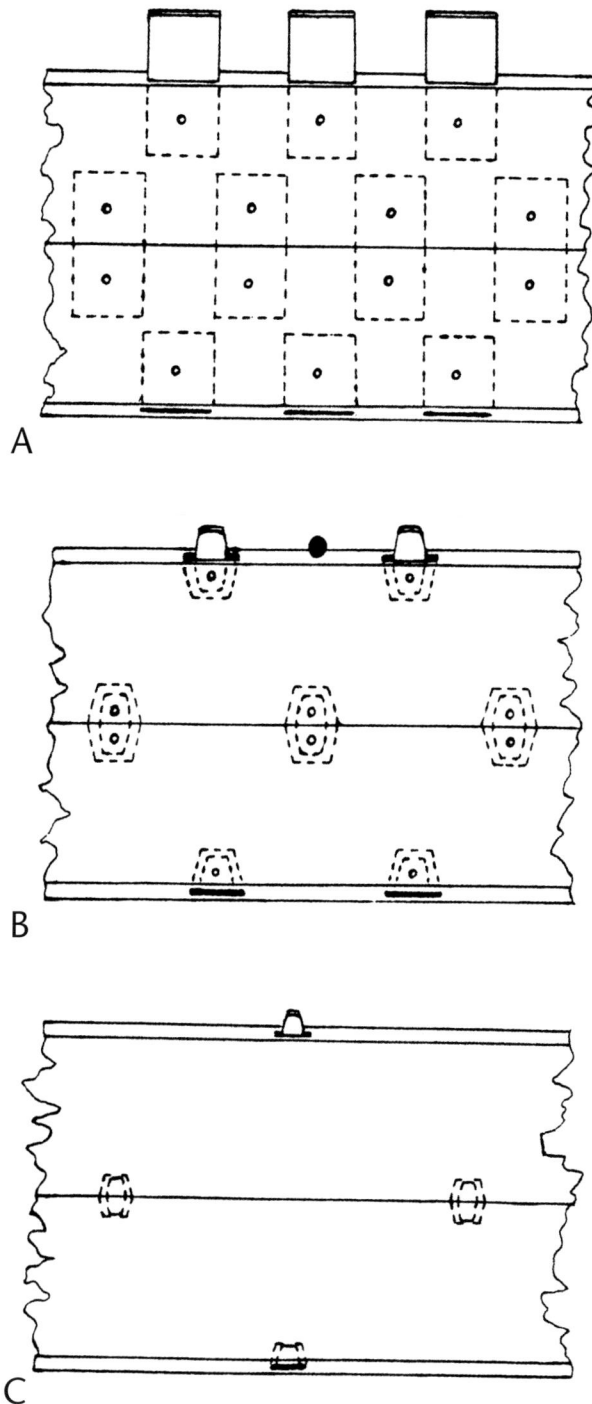

A schematic drawing comparing mortise and tenon distances and character on planking from: a 1st century AD Roman ship (A), the 4th century AD Yassi Ada wreck, Turkey (B), and the Yassi Ada wreck of AD 625/6 (C).

Drawing: courtesy of INA

Some time between the mid-5th century and the late 6th century the second major move away from tenon-built (shell-first) ship construction took place. The excavation of Dor D, a Cypriot merchant vessel involved in the Palestinian wine trade and wrecked off Israel, found that distances between mortise and tenons inserted along outer planks had increased even further to between 17 and 44cm. Much more relevant, however, was the disappearance of the all important wooden peg that, for the preceding 2,000 years of history, had been relied on to securely lock tenons within mortises. Their absence on Dor D could only point to one fact: shipwrights were now no longer relying solely on edge-joinery technology to build craft. Instead, joints were being cut into planks widely, only to loosely hold them in position until a sufficiently high section was linked in preparation for nailing to inner frames. The bond between the iron nails and frames now served as ships' main structural strength.

From this date, the shift towards the kind of modern frame-first ships that were to remain the backbone of Mediterranean seafaring into the late 19th century accelerated. The excavation of Yassi Ada A, wrecked off Turkey *circa* AD 625/6, was a hugely important milestone in the awakening of marine archaeologists' consciousness on this subject. The complete excavation of this 20m-long merchant vessel carrying Syrian and Aegean oils and wines found that small mortise and tenons were scattered along the planks up to the height of the waterline at distances of 35–50cm apart in the stern, 90cm apart in the middle of the hull, and no closer than 2.25m apart between the garboard (first line of outer planking) and keel. As on the Dor D ship 30–50 years earlier, these joints merely served to align the outer planks on top of each other until they were nailed to the inner frames.

The prevalence of this shipbuilding revolution has been confirmed by excavations of the Pantano Longarini ship of 600–650 off south-east Sicily, and of St Gervais B off southern France. On this grain transport of the first quarter of the 7th century (or slightly later), mortise and tenon joints were set at intervals exceeding 1m in the lower part of the hull. Crucially, none at all existed between

The Pantano Longarini shipwreck under excavation. Lost between AD 600 and 650, she was at least 30m long and thus one of the largest known vessels of the period.

Photo: Peter Throckmorton, courtesy of INA

The Pantano Longarini shipwreck, Sicily

In the early 1960s, the marshy wastelands of Pantano Longarini in south-east Sicily were purchased by a farmer keen on reclamation. In the winter of 1963–64, his bulldozers and mechanical equipment were digging deep draining channels and cut into a huge deposit of timber from a ship located 600m away from the modern shoreline. On the assumption that such well preserved wood could only have been modern, local villagers ripped away much of the hull for firewood, and some workmen tried to sell further timber to the local shipyard at Marzamemi. About 15m of planking from the upper starboard of the ship was lost in this way, along with the stem post and an immensely important and rare piece of archaeology: the ship's name plate in the form of five or six Greek letters and a horse head carved in low relief along a 1.2m-long plaque.

Fortunately for marine archaeology, these timbers were brought to the attention of Gerhard Kapitän, who raised the alarm over the destruction of the ancient ship. Independently, and later in conjunction with Peter Throckmorton, the site was excavated with support from the University of Pennsylvania Museum, revealing the upper section of the stern of a large ship with oak frames and cypress wood planking.

The surviving 9.1m-long starboard side of the stern above the waterline showed that this was an unusually heavily framed and roughly finished vessel with iron fastenings throughout. The massive transom timbers included heavy cross-beams passed across the wales in what the excavators described as a 'box-girder' effect. The ship was a large merchant vessel of more than 200–300 tonne capacity and was no less than 30m long (and possibly as much as 40m).

Radio-carbon analysis dates the ship to the politically unstable period of AD 600–650. The vessel must have been heavily laden because she seems to have snapped in two on a sandbar whilst trying to navigate the entrance to the ancient port of Edissa. Heavily pounded timbers evoke the ferocity of the storm that wrecked her. The starboard side broke away and was washed ashore in one piece to be covered by sand. Her cypress planks and pistachio wood tenons used below the water line suggest the ship probably originated in Greece or southern Italy.

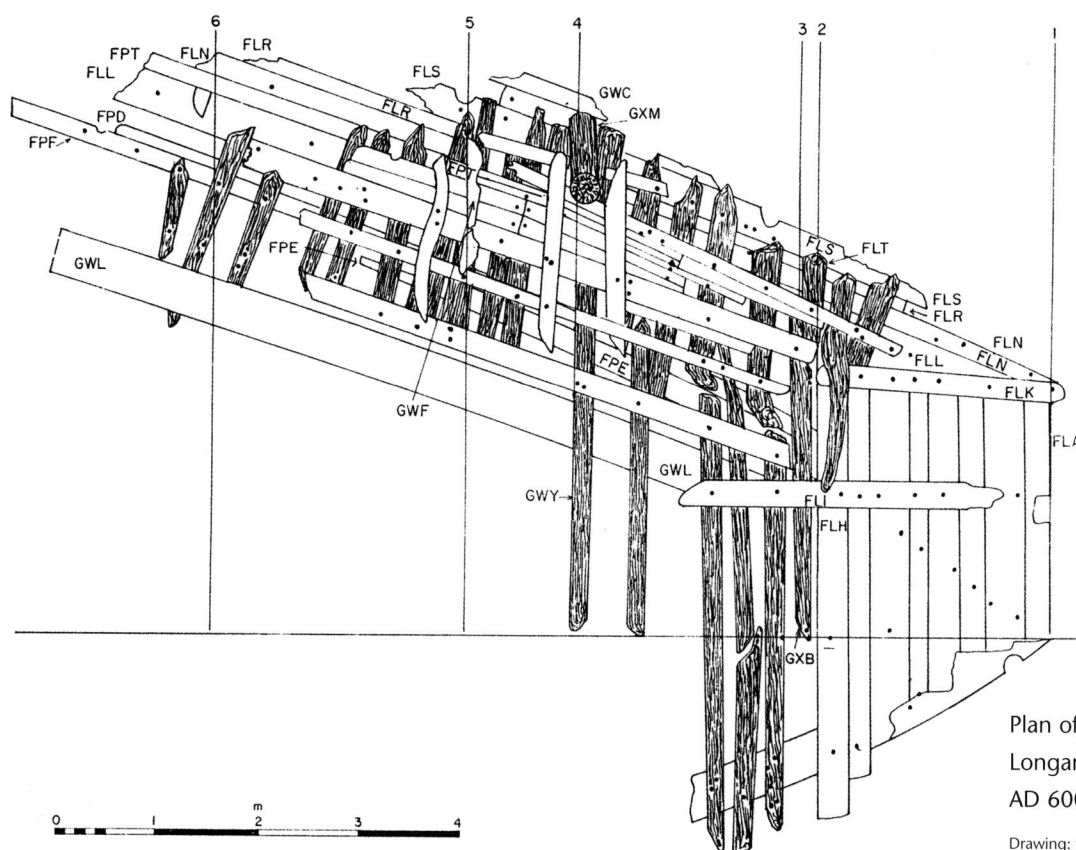

Plan of the hull of the Pantano Longarini shipwreck, Sicily; AD 600–650.

Drawing: from Throckmorton and Throckmorton, 1973, 243–266

the garboards and keel, proving beyond any shadow of a doubt that frames must have been attached to the keel before the strakes. By the time ships foundered in the 9th century AD off Bozburun, Turkey, and Dor, Israel, mortise and tenons were a thing of the past.

At the same time, the main method of securing frames directly to the keel was being reconceived. Instead of an elaborate cluster of mortise and tenons and wooden treenails, massive iron bolts took precedence. Although this method had been used on a minority of Roman hulls, frame-to-keel bolt attachments have been identified on all known Early Byzantine wrecks of the early 4th to mid-5th centuries, including La Luque B, Héliopolis A, Dramont E and F, and Yassi Ada B.

So what lies behind these perplexing facts, figures and measurements? First and foremost, Richard Steffy, the leading expert on classical Mediterranean ship construction from the Institute of Nautical Archaeology at Texas A & M University, has argued that the art of shipbuilding using mortise and tenons was labour-intensive and wasteful of wood. By reducing the quantity of wooden joints used on Late Roman and Early Byzantine merchant vessels, and placing a greater dependency on nailing planks to frames for internal strength, ships could be built more cheaply and quickly.

Once a hull's strength no longer relied on edge-joinery, capital costs could be further reduced by abandoning lead hull sheathing, previously used to protect

Dor's South Bay islets, calm in the sunset, belie the dangers that wrecked at least nine ships here between the 6th and 9th centuries AD.

Photo: Sean Kingsley

Wooden planking and ballast stones uncovered during the excavation of the late 6th-century AD Dor D shipwreck off Israel.

Photo: Sean Kingsley

joints and seams from wood eating organisms and general marine fouling. In its place shipwrights now favoured caulking, a method in which pine-tree pitch and fabric were wedged between plank seams and smeared across hulls. Again, caulking is much cheaper and quicker to apply.

The latest dated ships externally sheathed in lead are Femmina Morta, probably wrecked in the early 4th century (Sicily), Grand Bassin D dated to AD 313, the early 4th century Héliopolis A vessel (both off southern France), and a ship wrecked off Sobra (Croatia), probably around 320–340. Lead patches were recorded on the late 4th- or early 5th-century Yassi Ada B ship, but only to repair damaged sections of hull.

A ship equipped with a lateen sail painted during the first half of the 7th century on the wall of a monk's cell in the monastery of Kellia, Egypt. One of the earliest and most convincing examples of a lateen sail in the Mediterranean.

Drawing: after R. Kasser (ed.), *Survey archéologique de Kellia (Basse-Égypte) 1981* (Mission Suisse d'archéologie Copte de l'Université de Genève 1983), 314

The lateen sail – a Byzantine or Arab innovation?

Another major innovation of Byzantine navigation was the full emergence of the lateen rig. The wonder of this form of rigging was the triangular sail, which replaced the traditional square version. Less efficient generally than square sails, lateen rigs had the benefit of catching the wind on either side of the sail's surface, enabling vessels to ride closer to contrary winds. The genius of the lateen was that sailors no longer had to depend solely on the wind blowing in a specific direction to make good speed.

The question of when this innovation arose, and by whose inspiration, is one of the outstanding debates of naval history. For decades, the lateen sail has traditionally been attributed to the Arabs, who are credited with transmitting it into the Mediterranean from the Indian Ocean. Its common depiction in Arab iconography from the 9th century AD onward has long formed the foundation of this theory. Earlier representations of lateen sails in

Roman art tend to appear only on small boats, but not on large, sea-going merchant vessels.

A crucial new piece of evidence in this puzzle has appeared not beneath the sea, but in a secluded monastic cell at Kellia, located about 80km south-west of Alexandria in Egypt. Excavations conducted by a team from the University of Geneva revealed an impressively detailed colour image of a ship painted on a wall and measuring 70cm in width and 70cm in height. The vessel has squared end-posts and a flat-bottomed hull probably best suited to river transport up the Nile. Two long, V-shaped steering-oars protrude from the stern, and a massive triangular sail dominates the scene. Dating from between 600 and 630, the Kellia ship is the earliest uncontroversial image of a lateen sail, and thus goes a long way to confirming that this form of sail was transmitted into the Mediterranean under Byzantine influence.

Reconstructions of the 4th- and 7th-century AD merchant vessels wrecked off Yassi Ada, Turkey, dovetail with this evidence because both craft apparently used a lateen sail. The recent excavation of the early 9th-century hull of Tantura B at Dor, Israel, points to a similar rig.

Redating the revolution

In the last 10 years the excavation of several exciting shipwrecks in Italy and off Israel has enabled marine archaeology to understand the ebb and flow of this nautical revolution even more clearly. Newly revealed nuances suggest that the move towards frame-first ships was neither chronologically linear, nor contemporary throughout the Mediterranean.

Giulia Boetto's reanalysis of Fiumicino 1, excavated in the silts of the harbour of Portus, Rome, hinted that already by the 4th to 5th centuries some ships were starting to abandon pegged mortises and tenons. This impression has been graphically proven by the discovery of the well preserved 5th-century Ravenna ship, where the mortises were surprisingly cut 80cm apart and were no longer fastened with wooden pegs. Thus, by the 5th century AD the art of the shipwright was a long way along the road to abandoning edge-joinery.

As regards the date of the final abandonment of classical tenon-built ships, what was the social, geographical and chronological context of this revolution? New and immensely important underwater excavations being conducted in the shallow waters opposite the beautiful bays of Dor have revealed startling revelations. In 1995 a joint project codirected by Shelley Wachsmann (Institute of Nautical Archaeology, Texas A & M University) and Yaacov Kahanov (the Leon Recanati Institute for Maritime Studies, University of Haifa) chased a trail of shipwreck debris along the densely sand-blanketed seabed of the South Bay.

After various trials and tribulations, fighting against the weather, their persistence paid off as they discovered a small coaster of 12m length (Tantura A). Despite a rigorous and systematic survey of the surviving timbers, no mortise and tenons were found anywhere along the hull, leading to speculation that the ship must surely post-date the 9th century AD. When the Weizmann Institute returned a radio-carbon date of between AD 415 and 530, the archaeological community was initially incredulous.

The same excavation season resulted in something of an archaeological bonanza. A second Byzantine ship discovered (Dor O), also entirely lacked mortise and tenon joints; its radio-carbon date of AD 553–645 was closely comparable to Tantura A, suggesting that the move towards frame-first ships was certainly complete along the bustling sea-lanes of Palestine by the early 6th century. The final confirmation of this theory appeared in 2000, when further excavations at Dor, directed by Yaacov Kahanov, revealed yet another 6th-century hull without a hint of mortise and tenon technology.

A comparison between these three wrecks from Dor and those of similar date in the Mediterranean (Yassi Ada A, Dor D, Pantano Longarini, St Gervais B), at present suggests that the frame-first shipbuilding nautical revolution originated in the Near East about 250 years before its development elsewhere. If the current economic interpretation of the transition from tenon-built to frame-first ships is correct, then some merchants operating in Palestine may have been more conscious of minimising ship construction costs at a much earlier date than merchants working in other areas of the Mediterranean. A hunger to exploit the great commercial appeal of Palestinian wines may have been a major stimulus behind this development.

Small merchant vessels, small-time commerce?

As real and as influential on society as the shift away from tenon-built to frame-first shipbuilding technology was between the 4th and 7th centuries, describing Mediterranean commerce of the period as being only conducted in small craft darting around ports like fireflies would be inaccurate. Small ships bearing modest cargoes were certainly very common in this period. The early 4th-century vessel wrecked off Randello, Sicily, only held 150–200 amphorae. Dramont F of *circa* AD 400 was only 10–12m long, the 12–14m-long 4th-century Héliopolis A ship had an estimated capacity of only 720 amphorae, and the 13m-long Dramont E wrecked *circa* AD 425–455 could have transported between 700 and 750 amphorae in two layers. The late 6th-century Dor D ship only had a 5.2-tonne capacity, even though when wrecked off Palestine she had clearly been recently trading far and wide from a Cypriot home port.

The 12–15m long Isis ship, discovered at a depth of 800m, 95km north of Tunis, and dated to the last quarter of the 4th century, represents an unsuccessful attempt to shorten the established route between Carthage and Rome. Despite its fate, this wreck reinforces the view that small ships were not coasters by necessity, but were capable of open-sea navigation. Associated cargoes indicate that all the ships mentioned above were long-distance traders. The early 7th-century 15–18m-long St Gervais B had a more respectable 40–50-tonne capacity, as did the fully excavated Yassi Ada A and B 4th- and 7th-century merchant vessels off Turkey, which both measured 20m in length.

Anchors – ships' 'umbilical chords'

The squinting, learned eye of a sea captain experienced in reading the weather patterns of the Mediterranean and the whereabouts of shoals and reefs was naturally an invaluable tool for shippers in Late Antiquity. At all times, however, from calm seas to hostile storms, the most important resource on a merchant vessel was the anchor.

The anchor of choice between the 4th and 10th centuries was made of iron and was cruciform, with the arms attached to the shank at right-angles. During the Roman period wooden anchors with lead stocks were gradually replaced in the first two centuries AD by iron variants with bow-shaped arms. This shape may have persisted in cases into the mid-5th century (if the evidence from the Dramont E shipwreck is reliable). On other craft, such as the far better preserved Dramont F, the transition from bow-shaped to cruciform iron anchors occurred *circa* AD 400, a date that is probably more accurate.

Precisely why ships started to favour this shape is intriguing. Were cross-shaped anchors designed in piety to Christianity? Perhaps in part, although this is unprovable. What is certain is that the gradual decline in the angle of anchor arms in relation to the main shank was a process that dates back to the early Roman period: V-shaped arms gave way to the bow-shaped and

A cruciform encrusted iron anchor from the 6th-century AD Cefalù shipwreck being researched off Sicily by Gianfranco Purpura, University of Palermo.

Photo: Alessandro Purpura

finally the T-shaped cruciform version. By the early 11th century, the arms' angle had lowered even further so that they pointed downward in a Y-shaped configuration. The main reason for this evolution is most probably a gradual realisation that the lower the angle of the arms, the more easily anchors snagged on seabeds could be loosened and recovered, and the less likelihood that they would snap.

Byzantine anchors were carefully welded out of numerous sections of iron, and meticulously cared for in preparation for the day when they might save the lives of a ship and crew. The Rhodian Sea Law took anchor theft very seriously, stipulating that, "A ship is lying in harbour or on a beach and is robbed of its anchors. The thief is caught and confesses. The law lays down that he be flogged and that he make good twice over the damage he has done." Evidence from Dor harbour also shows the extent to which sea captains would go to care for this nautical equipment: a set of four anchors found close to the Tantura A shipwreck were all broken, and had apparently been retained for repairs.

Although the cruciform iron anchor was very much the standard tool of its day, ships owned by impoverished sea captains might be forced to revert to the poor man's substitute, an elementary stone version with a single hole through which the ship's rope was passed. Stone anchors have a long pedigree dating back to the Middle Bronze Age (c. 1800 BC). After the 8th century BC, Greek and Phoenician sailors replaced this style with a composite anchor built mainly of wood, but with a stone stock. From then on the fate of the stone version was sealed. When they subsequently turn up on shipwrecks, they are a strong indication that the ship's owner had fallen on hard times. Such seems to have been the case with the Dor D shipwreck off Israel.

Three single-hole stone anchors associated with the late 6th century AD shipwreck off Dor, Israel, reflect the low status of the vessel's owner. After the 8th century BC, stone anchors like these became very much the poor man's substitute.

Photos: Sean Kingsley

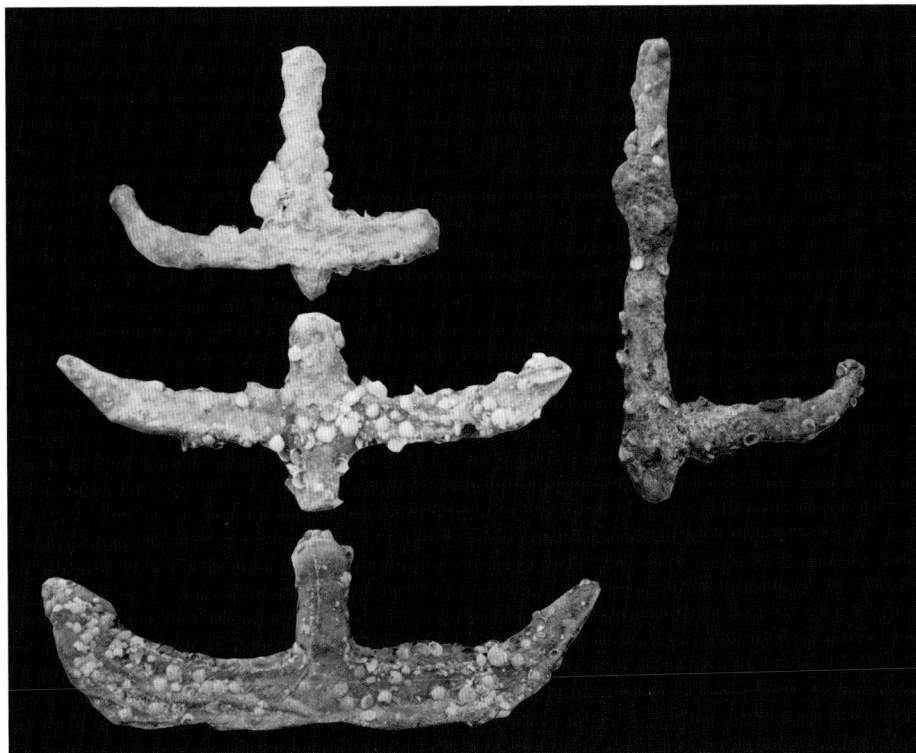

Four broken and encrusted iron anchors from the area of the 6th-century AD Tantura A shipwreck in Dor harbour, Israel. These anchors seem to have been carried for reconstituting into new anchors, reflecting the key importance of this nautical equipment.

Photo: Sean Kingsley

Sounding leads

Mediterranean sailors were conservative by nature, and Late Roman and Early Byzantine mariners continued to rely on many of the same sets of tried and tested nautical equipment that had served their ancestors so reliably. Sounding leads (cast in the metallic medium of lead) were a piece of equipment integral to reliable navigation.

Two particularly unusual examples were on board a merchant vessel wrecked off the Carmel Coast of Israel along with a hoard of early 6th-century coins minted in Constantinople, Nicomedia and Antioch. Both share an elongated bell-shape and have lugs on their apexes designed to take a length of rope that, at appropriate times, would be thrown overboard to determine the depth of water beneath the keel. One is 14cm in height and weighs 3.05kg; the second is 23cm high and 11kg in weight. Like most sounding leads, the Carmel Beach pair have shallow cups in their bases for sampling the seabed composition (mud, sand, rock, seaweed?). This factor was instrumental in determining anchoring practices.

Both Byzantine leads are incised with a Maltese Christian Cross and the letter 'P', the Greek sign for *rho*. Further, one of the weights features an asymmetrical zigzag shaped engraving on the top of its lug that has been interpreted as a heavenly navigational aid. Rather than simple decoration, research conducted by Ehud Galili, Jacob Sharvit and Baruch Rosen suggests that this motif represents the Cassiopeia stellar constellation, which was as familiar and useful for East Mediterranean sailors' charts as Ursa Minor and Ursa Major.

Cassiopeia was known as early as AD 150, when the Greek astronomer Ptolemy listed it alongside 47 other constellations. In Greek mythology, Cassiopeia was the wife of Cepheus and the mother of Andromeda, who was chained to a rock at Jaffa as a sacrifice to a sea monster (before Perseus saved and married her). The same myth was transmitted into Late Antiquity and is depicted on a 4th-century AD mosaic at Paphos in Cyprus. Jaffa was a major anchorage and thus the first port of call for pilgrims travelling to Jerusalem and the Holy Land in Late Antiquity. Reference to Cassiopeia on a sounding lead wrecked off Palestine, within half a day's sail to Jaffa, was thus wholly appropriate.

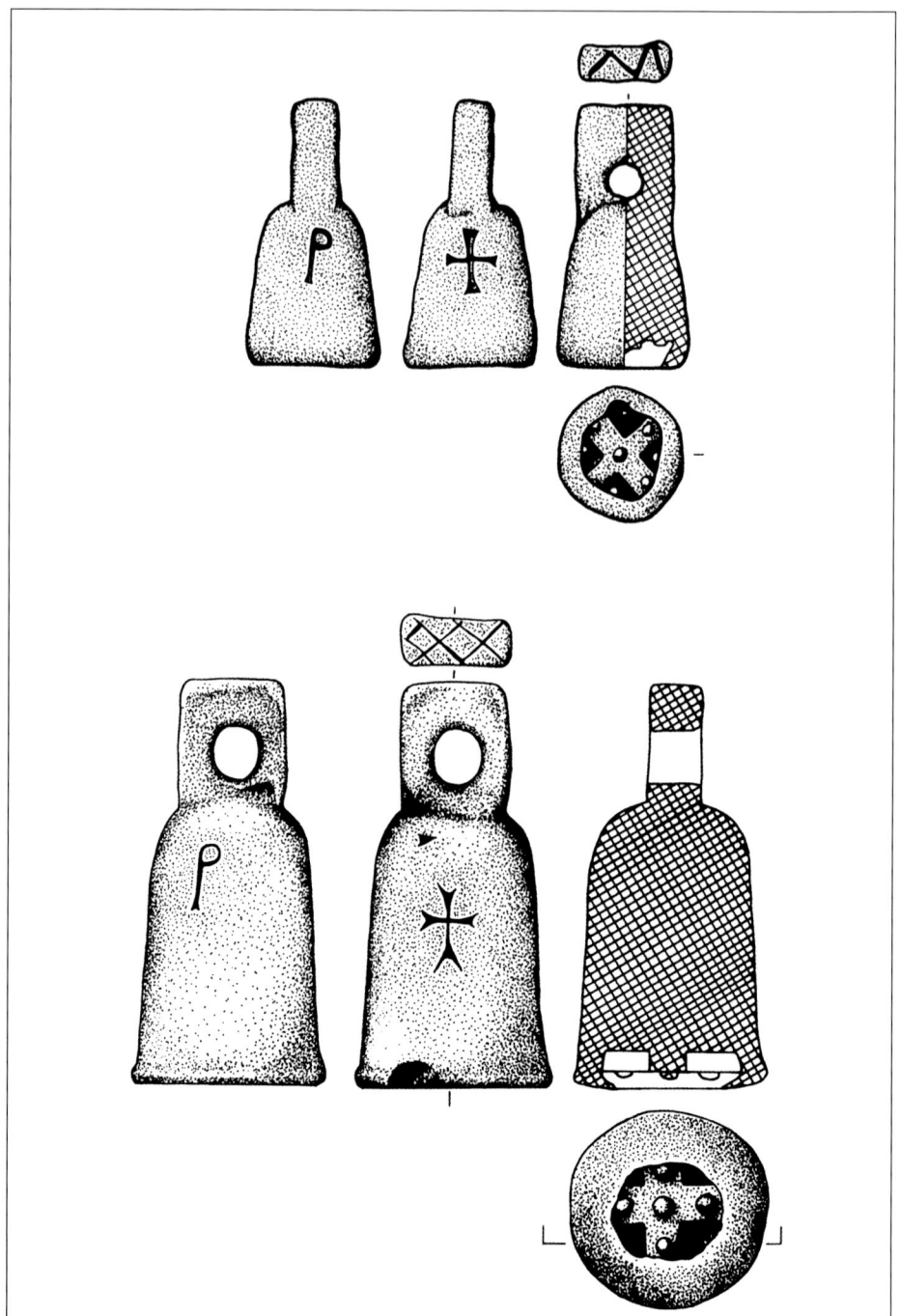

Two lead sounding-weights from a Byzantine shipwreck wrecked off the Carmel Beach, Israel, in the early 6th century AD. The zigzag decoration on the lug of the top weight is believed to represent the Cassiopeia star constellation by which sailors navigated at night.

Drawing: after Galili, Sharvit and Rosen, *International Journal of Nautical Archaeology* 29.1 (2000): 145

While the popularity of small-scale operatives in Late Antiquity was a very real trend, medium-sized and large ships did still ply the sea-lanes. Ancient sources refer to 120-tonne ships in Belisarius' fleet that invaded Vandal North Africa, grain ships with a 20,000 measure burden (about 140 tonnes) were owned by the Church of Alexandria, and John Moschos described a 35,000 *modii* (250-tonne) ship constructed in Palestine. Wrecks recorded off Italy include the 30m-long 7th-century Pantano Longarini ship, which could have accommodated more than 300 tonnes of cargo.

Although small ships seem to have been the preferred choice of Late Antique tradesmen, in reality this was nothing new for the Mediterranean. Vessels transporting less than 1,500 amphorae, or 75 tonnes of cargo, were the most common vessel type throughout antiquity. Just as the massive 'super-ports' of Roman Ostia, Caesarea Maritima and Alexandria were exceptions amongst the hundreds of Mediterranean ports, harbours and anchorages, so ships capable of carrying 500 tonnes or more of cargo were rarities during the Roman Empire. The most common class of vessel had a capacity of 60 tonnes or less. The 1,200-tonne 'super-tankers' used by the Roman grain fleet between Carthage and Rome were also unnecessary in the eastern Mediterranean, because the Alexandria to Constantinople route was shorter and more easily navigable.

The 5ᵗʰ-century AD wreck at the Parco di Teodorico

Stefano Medas

During excavations conducted in preparation for the construction of Theodoric's Park in Ravenna, Italy, the wreck of a Late Antique boat was discovered on 6 November 1998 at a site located 200m north of Theodoric's Mausoleum. The find was embedded in sand about 8.5m beneath the modern level of the land surface at a site corresponding to the former Roman and Late Roman line of the seashore. Archaeological excavation took place between December 1998 and February 1999, when the ship was completely removed. The works were directed by the Soprintendenza per i Beni Archeologici dell'Emilia Romagna (Dr Maria Grazia Maioli) with the cooperation of the Istituto Centrale per il Restauro.

The excavation was undertaken stratigraphically, starting with the internal fill of the hull and proceeding to the underlying outer layer, so enabling the boat's outer hull to be examined. Once timbers were recorded, the wreck was protected by a double-layered protective watertight shell. The first layer consisted of a silicon rubber coating spread directly on to the wood, while the second one was a GPR (glass resin) shell, carefully reinforced by transverse and longitudinal ribs stretched over the first coat in order to obtain a remarkable mechanical resistance sufficient to stabilise the wreck's wooden structure. The entire wreck and cradling were then carried as a single cage unit to the restoration centre in Comacchio (Ferrara) to start preservation treatment.

The Late Roman Ravenna wreck *in situ*. Note the keelson and mast-step at centre, frames protruding vertically at left, deck planking at right and the well preserved interior ceiling planking. Photo: S. Medas, courtesy of the Soprintendenza Archeologica dell'Emilia Romagna

The boat had been abandoned on the seashore, and some objects recovered from the hull – partly remains of shipment, partly boat equipment – date the vessel to the 5th century AD. The wreck is preserved for a total length of 7.22m and a maximum beam of 2.75m. The port side is preserved up to the level of the gunwale. The stern was partly cut off by the developers who unexpectedly found the wreck, while the prow (with bows still largely intact) sunk into the sand and was twisted to the right side. Altogether, the hull is well preserved, besides a certain amount of deformation due to embedding in the sand, an event that also caused longitudinal stretching of the hull. The overall length of the boat can be estimated at about 9m, with a width of 3.1m; the wreck shows a correctly water-lined hull with an almost flat bottom at mid-ship, and sharp extremities.

The internal planking takes up the central part of the hull, corresponding to the length of the keelson, and is connected to the frames with iron nails. The boat was open along this tract, while the original presence of a short deck fore and aft is marked by a series of hollows carved

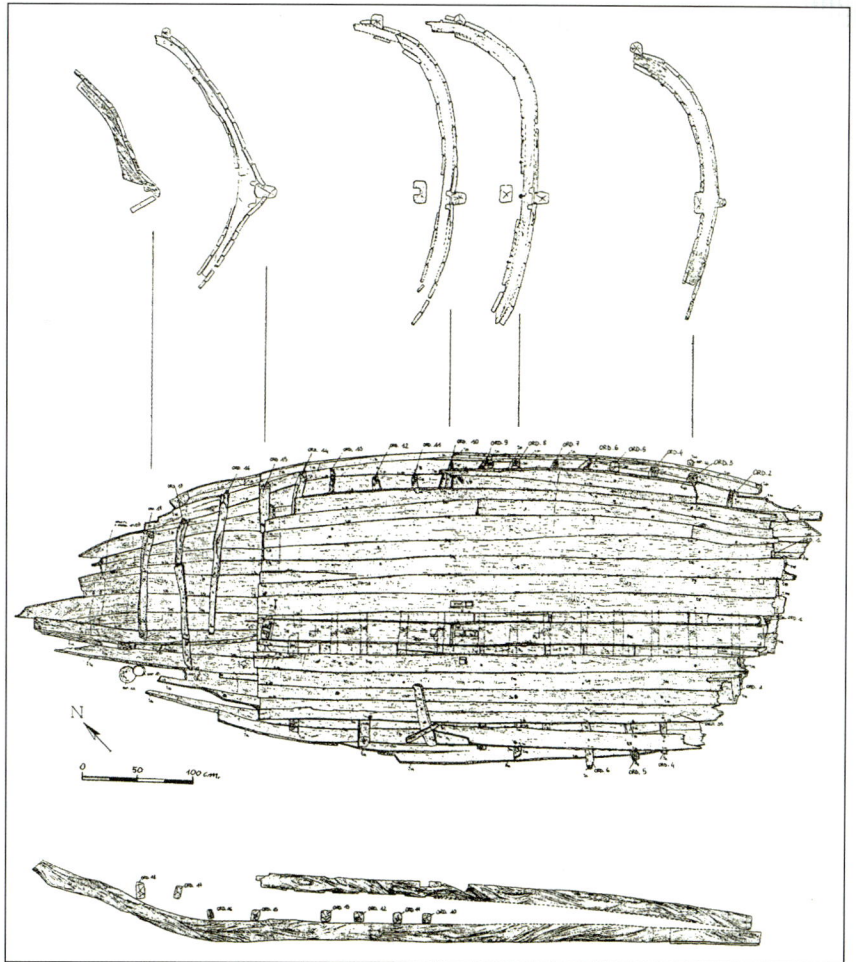

Plan of the Ravenna wreck, with section drawings of the frames (top), and keel and keelson (bottom).

Drawing: Cristina Leoni, La Fenice, courtesy of the Soprintendenza Archeologica dell'Emilia Romagna

into the gunwale in order to accommodate the heads of plank-shaped upright beams. The mast step is carved directly into the keelson and is located some 50cm forward, while its inner angle is shaped with a peculiar slope with the bottom wedged astern, in order to facilitate the mast lowering. The mast itself must have been supported by a thwart secured to the hull at the gunwale level.

The frames are composed of floor timbers, simple high frames without corresponding floor timbers or futtocks. Some floor timbers are nailed down to the keel with iron boat nails. Side planks are nailed to the frames with iron nails and wooden pegs. The presence of mortise and tenon joints was found at least up to the knee level. Tenons are remarkably spaced at 80cm apart from each other, fitted loosely

Close-up view of a tenon within its mortise amongst outer planking.

Photo: S. Medas, courtesy of the Soprintendenza Archeologica dell'Emilia Romagna into much wider mortises, and not fastened in place with pegs. This indicates that the planking of this construction was not self-bearing, constituting a substantial departure from Graeco-Roman ships built according to the mortise and tenon system. So, the hull stiffness was entirely committed to the framing, in this case the main bearing structure. The hull is smeared with pitch.

This wreck is probably one of the last examples of shell-first ship construction during the 5th century AD. While the structure still appears bound to the old classical procedure, the importance given to the framing as the most important strength shows an evolution towards a new technical development, which can be considered almost completely a 'skeleton-bearing' construction concept. More precisely, the building plan may be considered a 'mixed-type'. Recent discoveries indicate that within the Mediterranean region the transition to the frame-based construction of small craft seems to have been completed by the 6th century AD, proven by the Tantura A wreck off Israel. So, the shipbuilding evolution towards 'skeleton-bearing' seems to have started in small hulls, as the Ravenna wreck testifies precisely. Finally, this transitional period towards frame-first (skeleton-first) construction seems to have finished in large vessels by the early 9th century AD.

The Ravenna wreck at the end of the excavation, with the glass resin shell and supports nearing completion.

Photo: S. Medas, courtesy of the Soprintendenza Archeologica dell'Emilia Romagna

A lost fleet of ships in the port of Olbia

Rubens D'Oriano and Edoardo Riccardi

Topography and history

Rubens D'Oriano

From 1999–2001, an area about 380m long and 20m wide was excavated to an average depth of 4m during the construction of a tunnel designed to link the modern port of Olbia in Sardinia with the surrounding suburban network. This coastal zone corresponds to the long-silted ancient port of Olbia. The scientific excavation team was composed of Rubens D'Oriano (Archaeological Director), Edoardo Riccardi (Naval Archaeologist), Giuseppe Pisanu (1999–2000) and Giovanna Pietra (2001).

In the simplest of terms, the area under investigation can be subdivided into a southern section and a northern section, a distinction that was already defined by the presence in ancient times of a natural strip of land protruding from the coast, which separated the town's port into two sections. In the 1st century AD, the southern section was almost completely abandoned due to flooding. This is borne out by what proved to be the richest archaeological context of the entire excavation: an enormous quantity of mud and maritime material including two very rare wooden masts, fragments of two wrecks, beams from a crane and the shafts of four rudders. Since the 2nd century AD, port life was concentrated mainly in the northern sector.

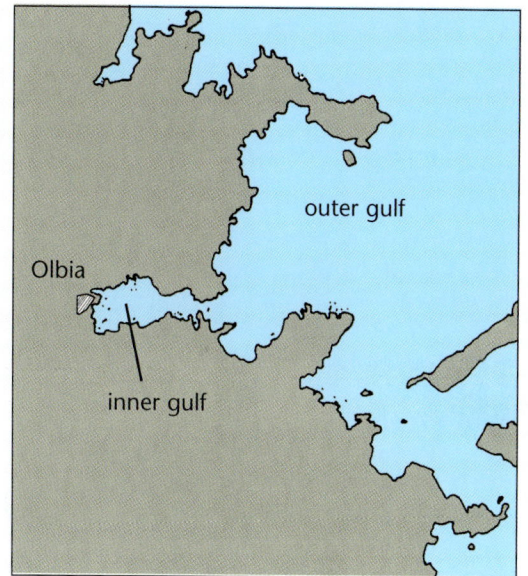

Map of the Gulf of Olbia, showing the location of the port of Olbia.

In the 5th century AD a second disaster occurred, which caused the sinking of at least 11 cargo ships, some of considerable dimensions. This 'fleet' sank in shallow waters at the same depth, with each ship lying parallel to the next at right-angles to the nearby coastline. Therefore, at the moment of their demise the ships had all been moored within the port, probably to long wooden vertical pier stakes, limited remains of which have been recovered.

As for the cause of the sinking, it is certain that in a deep creek like the Gulf of Olbia, which is almost an internal pool, it is impossible that any single meteorological event could have been so destructive as to produce such a monumental catastrophe. If this had been the case, the position of the wrecks would be random rather than uniform.

Olbia, with the tunnel and excavation area in the foreground.

89

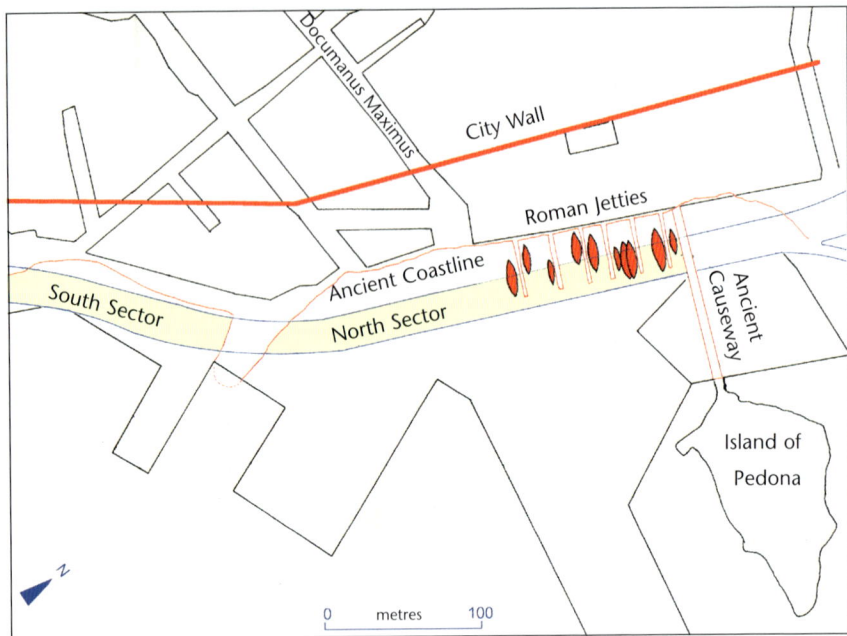

The Roman port, the ancient coastline and the excavation areas.

A more logical explanation, therefore, is human intervention. This act must have had a profound effect on the whole town, since no one subsequently attempted to remove or recover the wrecks. Having sunk in shallow waters, these wrecks would have jeopardised the operation of the port, which had been the source of ancient Olbia's economic subsistence for centuries. Furthermore, land excavations confirm that in the 5th century the town was in deep crisis. Taking into consideration the most destructive historical events of this period, the Vandal raids against Corsica, Tuscany, Sardinia, Sicily, Campania and Rome itself, determining the historic context of the sinking of the vessels and the collapse of the town of Olbia is but a brief step.

The role and importance of Olbia in the early Middle Ages were decidedly inferior in comparison to the Roman period. However, the finds from the port excavations offer invaluable new information – previously unknown – about the town's continued commercial role, albeit on a lesser scale. It was only towards the 13th and 14th centuries that part of the northern sector of the port was filled in. Before this date the harbour was unusable, not so much due to the obstruction of the Late Antique wrecks, but due to the mud which caused the sea bed's level to rise.

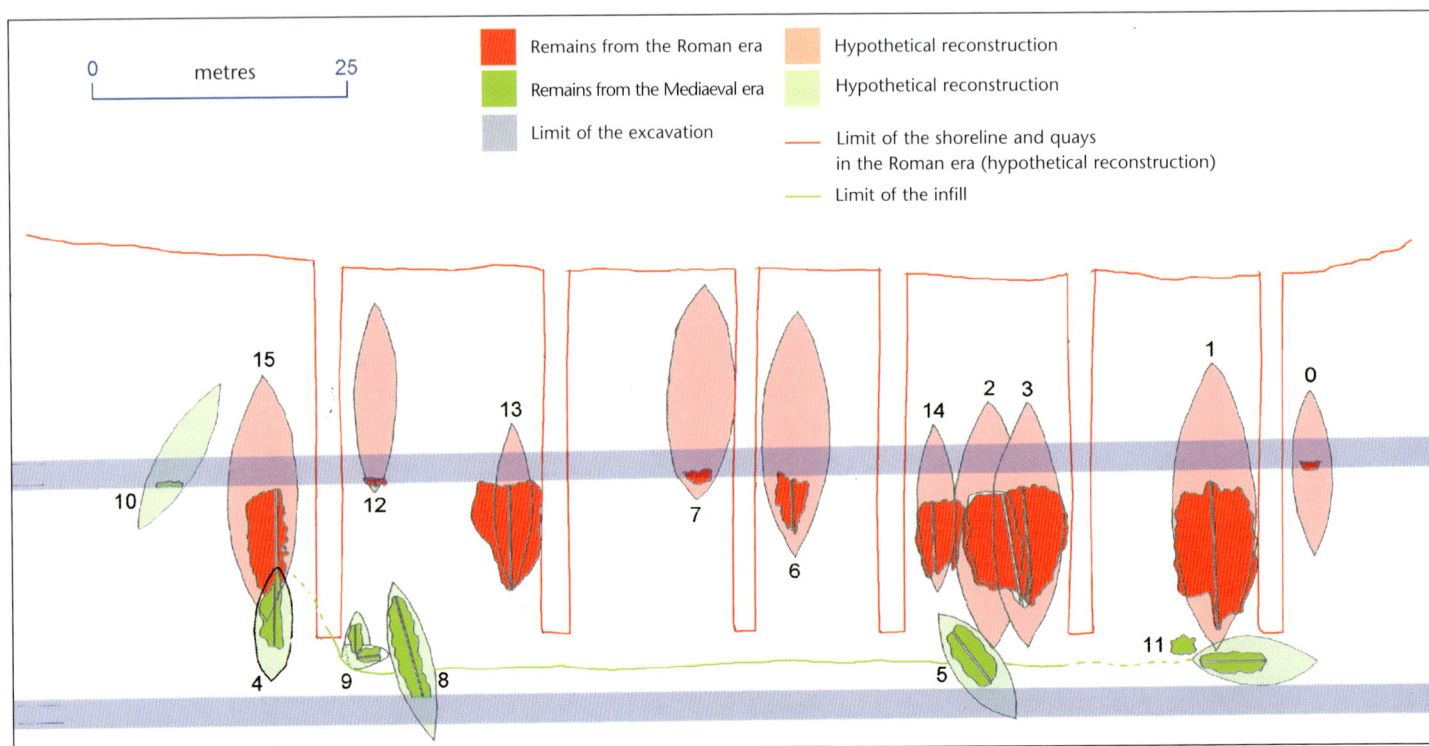

The northern sector of the excavation site. The 5th century fleet are in red, the mediaeval boats in green.

90

A Roman rudder shank preserved in Olbia's Roman shipyard.

The ancient port was then filled in with stones, gravel, shingle and wooden stakes reclaimed from the harbourfront, in order to create a man-made harbour further out into the sea, where the water was deep enough to accomodate ships with a deeper draught. The hulls of three old boats of the 10th and 11th centuries AD were filled with debris and used as the foundation for the new, mediaeval port infrastructure (a method well known, even in antiquity).

This necessity for reclamation was probably related to the new economic vitality that the rise of Pisa brought to international trade in this part of Sardinia. At this time, politics had caused Pisa to develop into a powerful marine republic and Roman Olbia to become capital of the Giudicato di Gallura (one of the four kingdoms into which the island was divided). In the Middle Ages, Olbia was known first as Civita and later as Terranova. The filling in promoted by Pisa is reflected in the writing of the 18th-century editor of the *Veridica Relazione*, who referred to Terranova as "a Roman colony with a large port of which the eastern part was filled in by the Pisans." Abundant pottery excavated in the port of ancient Olbia and manufactured in the productive and commercial centres of Pisa and Tuscany directly verifies the accuracy of this account.

A Roman ship's mast exposed in Olbia's ancient shipyard.

Methodology and results

Edoardo Riccardi

The excavation of the port of Olbia was a rescue project of an urgent nature, compounded by the drying out of sediments in the water-bearing stratum which had been cut through by the company undertaking the construction of the modern tunnel. It was therefore necessary to remove the wrecks quickly. Consequently, the final cleaning and study of the construction features of the ships have been postponed for detailed attention in the laboratory. During the ship dissembling process, however, it was already possible to observe sufficient construction elements to confirm the wrecks' chronology. The vessels were taken apart sensitively at the points where they had originally been fastened, and were immediately placed in tanks of water to await conservation treatment.

The wrecks belong to three different periods: 1st century AD, 5th century AD and the 9th to 14th centuries. The excavation also revealed an area rich in rough wood, partially worked timber and parts of boats awaiting recycling, and carpenters tools, which are presumed to relate to a shipyard situated near the strip of land which separates the northern and southern sectors of the excavation area.

The outstanding level of preservation is evident in the two large sections of masts from the 1st century AD, one preserved along a length of 7.8m and with a diameter of 42cm (belonging to a ship over 30m long). Similarly well preserved and highly rare are five rudder shanks from the same period (one is about 8.5m long). A large beam, which does not derive from a ship, is similar to the transversal beam in the reconstruction of a crane described by Vitruvius.

Reconstruction of the port of Olbia during the Roman period.

Framing timbers on the 5th-century AD shipwreck R3.

The 5th-century shipwrecks

The wrecks of the northern sector R0, R1–R3, R6, R7, R12–R15, RT and of the southern sector R1Sud–R3Sud share common characteristics that are associated with a single disastrous event. Apart from RT, whose remains belong to a small service boat no more than 4m long and crushed between ships R2 and R3, all of the lost ships are commercial craft apparently lacking cargoes or, more accurately, stripped of all reusable content. At the moment of sinking, these would have been in good condition.

Some of the ships show traces of fire damage in the upper areas. All lay parallel in a group and, according to the position of their scarf joints between keels and end posts, all were aligned in the same direction, most probably with their bows pointing towards the shore. Estimated ship dimensions vary from 15m long for R13 to over 30m for R1. Neither the mast step nor the internal structure has been preserved in any of the vessels. The outer shells consist of frames with floor timbers alternating with half frames, which always meet on the keel. The various elements forming the frames are placed head to head and not laid to overlap. Some are directly joined with a simple scarf in order to form a partly constructed frame.

Shipwreck R2 after the dissembly of the internal frames, showing the external planking (strakes).

A 5th-century AD shipwreck (R2) with frames running transversely across the hull.

The edges of the external planking are inter-connected with mortises set very far apart (generally 17–32cm and in some cases at distances of nearly 1m); many tenons are not secured in place with a lock pin, and some mortises are empty. The simple scarf joints interlinking outer strake planking are always reinforced with small red metal nails, and tenons are inserted either straight or at an angle. Caulking is quite common; no ships have lead hull sheeting, but lead patches were frequently used for repairs. There are usually more than two nails connecting a frame to a plank, composed of red metal or hard square wood. The keels have a short rabbet only near the posts. The growing importance given to the skeleton technique (frame-first) is evident. Many of the construction features of wrecks R2, R6 and R15 are so similar that it is not an exaggeration to assume that they were built in the same shipyard, if not even by the same carpenters.

The mediaeval wrecks

Six mediaeval wrecks were investigated, but only three pre-date the 10th century. Three of the ships date to the 10th to 11th centuries (and were used to provide a solid foundation for the filling in of the port in the 13th to 14th centuries):

R5 is the central part of the hull of a medium-sized ship, whose keel consists of a slightly larger timber than the planking. The frames are thin and very high and lack limber holes (for cleaning out the inside of the hull). The ship was found pegged to the seabed with four stakes, set in place before being filled with gravel.

R8 is a galley about 12m long and a little more than 2.5m wide, which preserves the mast step on the keelson and a fragment of an outer strake plank with a rowlock. Two small wales run externally along the entire side of the keel and join at the bows.

R9 exists in two sections that were intentionally separated by sawing and placed in a perpendicular position before being filled with gravel and sunk near the stakes to form the right angle of the mediaeval quay. The ship lacks a keel and the central timber is linked to two massive posts, which have a rabbet. The stern is round. The absence of the keel in these three wrecks permits us to assume that they were boats destined for navigation only in the internal, sheltered part of the Gulf of Olbia.

Apart from the wrecks, the excavation of the ancient port has permitted the recovery of an extraordinary number of implements of Roman date: objects related to the fishing industry, including hooks of every dimension, weights of stone, ceramic and lead for nets and lines, a grapnel anchor, spools for nets, as well as working tools, including sail needles, awls, carpenters' hammers, lead hammers, spokes made from deer and stag horns, deadeye rigging blocks, and clots of paint and resin which preserve the shape of their now decomposed containers. The working tools, in particular, come mainly from the shipyard area.

Finally, five stone anchors have been found, two of which are still associated with organic remains. This type of anchor is traditionally dated between the Late Bronze Age and the Greek period. The wooden plugs and the suspension rope of one anchor cut with three holes have been subjected to radio-carbon analysis, which has yielded an unexpected date in the 3rd–4th century. The analysis of the wooden arm of anchor number three has confirmed this chronology.

English translation: Shirley Backer

Photos: Egidio Trainito, Enrico Grixoni

Plans: Gianfranco Puggioni, Virgilio Gavini

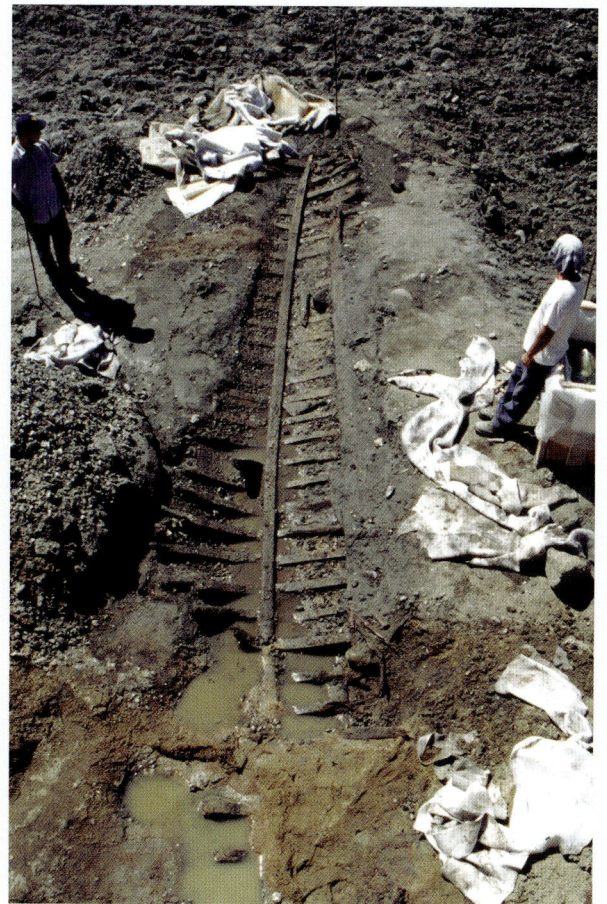

Above left: wreck R9, 10th–11th century.

Above right: wreck R8, a galley of the 10th–11th century.

Left: stone anchors from Olbia, 3rd–4th centuries AD.

The Late Antique shipwrecks of Tantura Lagoon

Yaacov Kahanov

Tantura Lagoon is located on the Mediterranean coast of Israel, 30km south of Haifa. The lagoon is partially protected from the sea by a series of small islands, which are separated from the shore by a narrow, shallow navigation channel. Commercial coasters used to moor in the lagoon, but now it is only used by fishing boats. Napoleon stopped in Tantura on his retreat from Acco and used its anchorage for small boats. The lagoon is south of the ancient Dor promontory, the present Tel Dor, which has been extensively excavated under the direction of Ephraim Stern. At the southern edge of Tel Dor there are the remains of the Crusader fort of Merle, also known as Khirbet-el-Burj. Dor is mentioned in the Bible and Hellenistic sources. The city is apparently mentioned in an Egyptian inscription dated to the 13th century BC, but its most famous ancient record is from the *Golenischeff Papyrus*, also known as the *Wen-Amon* account, dated to *circa* 1100 BC.

The location of Dor, the protected anchorages along the Tel to the north and south, and evidence of marine activities, brought archaeologists to search and excavate the area. One issue to be resolved is the location of the ancient harbour. In addition to land excavation and evidence of 4,000 years of occupation since the Middle Bronze Age IIA, underwater archaeology has revealed evidence of maritime activities since the second half of the second millennium BC.

Surveys have been carried out continuously for more than 30 years in the lagoon. Significant discoveries have been made dating from the Byzantine and Arab periods, which illuminate the evolution of ship construction

Aerial view of the southern entrance to Tantura Lagoon, Israel. Photo: Ari Baltinester

in Late Antiquity. With this rich background, Shelley Wachsmann initiated underwater excavation in 1994. Two wrecks were thoroughly studied, and evidence for five more was found. Tantura A and Tantura B are the results of the combined INA-RIMS 1994–1996 Project.

One problem with the lagoon is that the large quantity of ceramics of all periods found in it is not deposited stratigraphically, since it has been subject to wave-action. Therefore, ceramic analyses must be treated with caution.

Tantura A

A significant part of this wreck, the preserved timbers of which spread over 9m, was exposed over two seasons of excavation. The wood included remnants of the keel, a post, strakes, frames, nail and bolt attachments, and caulking in seams.

The keel was preserved over 5.2m. It had a rectangular cross-section, 11cm sided and 18cm moulded. The keel had two 26cm scarfs, one of which served to attach it to an

A general view of the hull of Tantura A. Photo: Shelley Wachsmann

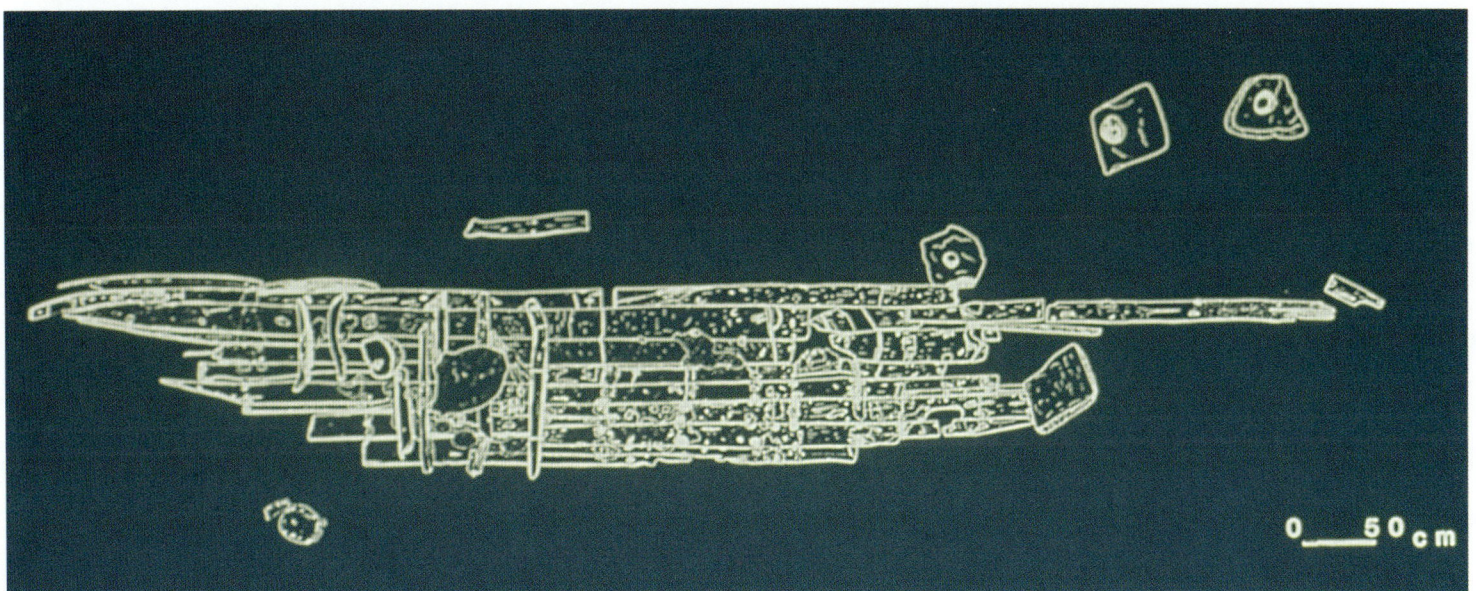

Site plan of the Tantura A shipwreck. Drawing: Patricia Sibella

endpost. The endpost was a naturally curved pine timber, which rose at an angle of about 55°. No convincing evidence has yet been found to indicate whether this was the bow or stern.

On one side of the keel, fragments of eight frames were preserved and evidence for an additional 17 frames, whose timbers did not survive, was found. They were 9cm sided, 9.5cm moulded, with room and space of 32.4cm. The longest remaining framing timber survived to a length of 1.31m. Each frame possessed a 1cm-deep mortise for seating atop the keel. Nail concretions and nail holes confirm that the frames were fastened to the upper surface of the keel by iron nails. Due to the poor condition of preservation of the frames the framing pattern could not be ascertained.

Two strake fragments were found on one side and eight strake remains were preserved on the other, including an 8.78m-long garboard. All strakes were made of pine and were 2.5cm thick. Plank widths varied from 3.8 to 26cm. Planks were butt-scarfed on frame stations to create strakes. Iron nails, driven from the outside at frame stations, were used to fasten the planks to the frames.

No planking edge-joints or treenails were observed anywhere. Caulking was evident in the planking seams in several areas. The estimated dimensions of the vessel were 12m by 4m.

Byzantine-period shards were found 'cemented' to the upper surface of the hull. Usually such a find is conclusive evidence for the ship's date but, as noted, in Tantura Lagoon the conditions are more complicated. Apart from these ceramics, no other finds related to this hull were identified. Based also on carbon 14 tests

Keel and frames on Tantura A. Photo: Shelley Wachsmann

for the wood, the wreck is dated to the 6th century AD. Its frame-based construction is therefore significant, as it moves the transition from strake-oriented hulls to frame-oriented construction by five centuries.

The study of this hull was made by the author and J. G. Royal

Tantura B

While the analysis of the Tantura A wreck addressed the problem of the date when a transition from plank-based to frame-based construction took place in small vessels in the eastern Mediterranean, the Tantura B wreck provided evidence of how the transition took place in slightly larger vessels. The remains of the Tantura B wreck were spread over a 12m x 3m area. Dating to the beginning of the 9th century AD, or the local Arab-Abbasid Period, this vessel exhibited frame-oriented construction.

A 9.8m section of the oak keel survived, and was 10.4cm sided and 9.53cm moulded. It

The endpost and keel of Tantura A. Photo: Shelley Wachsmann

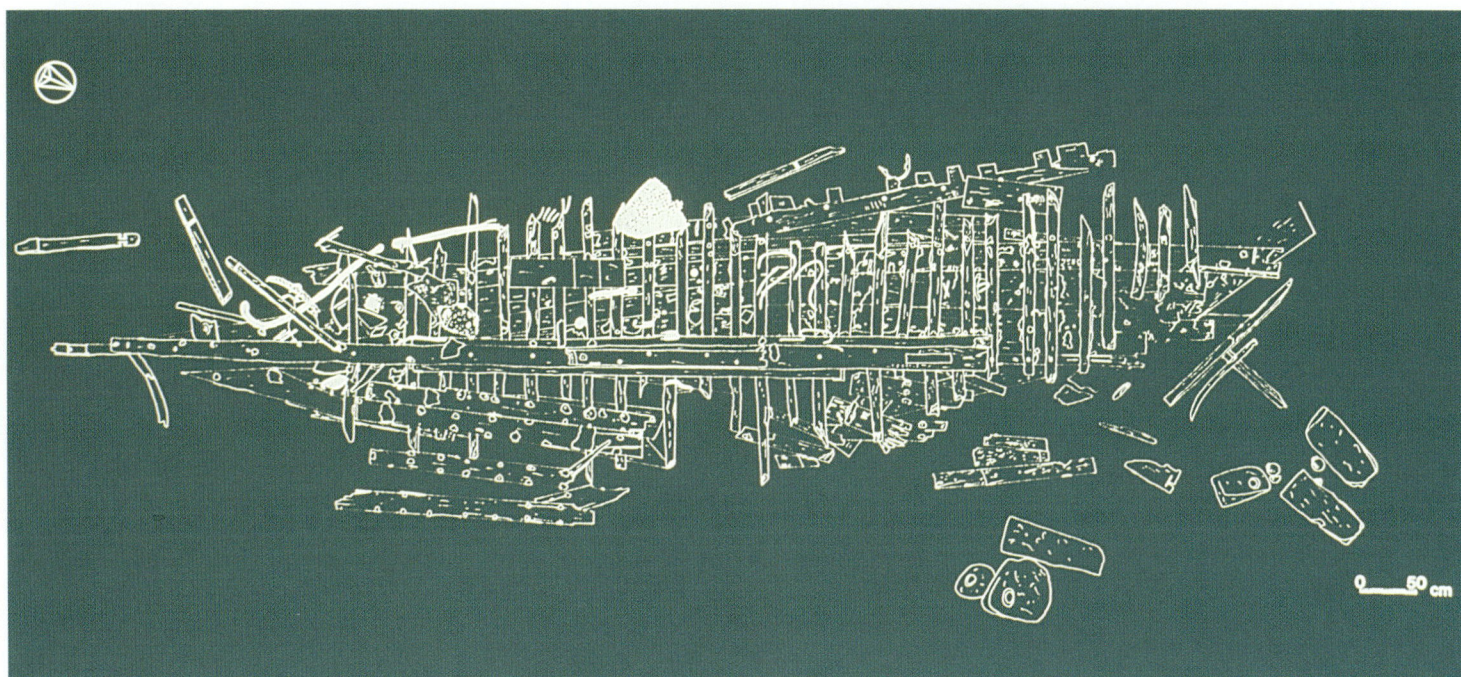

Site plan of the Tantura B shipwreck. Drawing: Patricia Sibella

A general view of the Tantura B shipwreck. Photo: Stephen Breitstein

included two horizontal hook scarfs; one of them probably serving as the post attachment.

A pine keelson, 7.84m long, was 12–20cm sided and 16–18cm moulded. It was recessed on its lower face to receive the frames. The keelson served as a mast-step, having a mortise for the heel of the mast.

Thirty articulated pine frames were preserved, forming a pattern of alternating floor timbers and half-frames. Evidence for 10 additional frames was identified. Some frames, especially those on the western side of the keel, were preserved to the turn of the bilge. Both floor timbers and half-frames were fastened to the keel, although the half-frames were not cross-nailed to each other. The keelson was nailed to the floor timbers with square nails.

Frames were on the average 9cm sided and 9.5cm moulded. The frames at one end of the wreck were flat horizontal, and the angle of deadrise at the other end increased gradually to a maximum of 20°.

Remnants of the first seven strakes of hull planking were preserved to the west of the keel, and the first five strakes to the east. Planks were all made of pine, except strake 6, which was probably oak. Plank widths varied between 4 and 36cm, with thickness ranging from 2.5 to 3.4cm. At 10cm wide and 8.5cm thick, the sixth strake was significantly thicker and narrower and is thought to have been a bilge keel.

Planks were scarfed in a variety of ways, including vertical butt joints, 'L'-shaped joints, and diagonal scarfs. In several instances where it appears that planks were cut too short, caulking was added to fill in the gap. Between one and three rectangular iron nails were used to attach each plank to a frame. Caulking was found in planking seams.

Hull dimensions are estimated at 18–23m total length and about 5m at the beam.

Among the finds were several ceramic vessels including oil lamps, rigging elements, some wooden tools and roundels, one with an Arab inscription.

The hull study was made by the author and J. Hall.

Ongoing excavations at Tantura Lagoon

More shipwrecks are the subject of additional underwater archaeological projects. In one of them, 2001/1, a lot of Byzantine ceramics were found; their being *in situ* is, however, questionable. This wreck carried a cargo of stone. Perhaps this explains the many construction stones found in the lagoon in Byzantine wreck contexts. Research on the Byzantine-period Dor D wreck suggests that ship construction in the second half of the first millennium AD is more complicated than once thought. Simple linear transitions of building methods through time can no longer be supported. The economic and political forces, as well as the geographical and cultural landscapes, which affect technical areas of society such as shipbuilding, have to be considered.

Tantura Lagoon is a study and training field for maritime archaeologists. Thus, the research projects and the training possibilities make it one of the richest future sites of underwater archaeology.

Credit is due to many institutes and people: the local diving club Aqua-Dora, the Center of Nautical and Regional Archaeology at Dor (CONRAD), the Recanati Institute for Maritime Studies at the University of Haifa (RIMS), the Marine Branch of the Israel Antiquities Authority (IAA), the Institute of Nautical Archaeology at Texas A&M University (INA), and The Nautical Archaeology Society of Great Britain (NAS). Of the people working in the lagoon, the contribution of Kurt Raveh has been the longest lasting and most involved.

Tantura Lagoon. Photo: Vaughn Bryant

The four Saracen shipwrecks of Provence

Jean-Pierre Joncheray

There are four shipwrecks off southern France that belong together, and which are particularly important because they relate to a relatively little known historical period in the 10th century AD. They are associated with a maritime culture that has left few traces – the Spanish Muslims known as Saracens. In two of these sites, in particular, excavation took place under difficult conditions: Agay A, which lies off Saint-Raphael at a depth of 50m, and Batéguier in 60m of water off Cannes. The two other Provence wrecks, Plane 3 at Marseille and Nord-Fouras at Saint-Tropez, are much less important because hull structures are no longer preserved. It is worth pointing out that no other Saracen wreck has been discovered anywhere else in the Mediterranean basin, not even along the coast of Spain, which was the cradle of that civilisation. As a result of the excavations, which were conducted over the course of more than 40 years and went through many twists and turns, surprising discoveries were made regarding the unusual techniques employed to construct hulls.

Historically, Christianity and Islam had been in conflict in the western Mediterranean since the 7th century. The two powers were rivals in the struggle to impose their dominion. The conquest of Sicily and the capture of Ceuta, in the 9th century, marked the start of Muslim naval hegemony, but between the end of the 10th century and the beginning of the 12th, Christianity gradually succeeded in imposing its supremacy. In this period of ideological, political and cultural rivalry, the sea nonetheless remained an active commercial arena, as is attested by, among other objects, the presence of African or Spanish Muslim ceramics on Christian soil.

From the 10th century onwards, the Umayyads responded to Viking attacks (such as the sack of Seville in 844) by creating a fleet which little by little became an instrument of conquest. In the 10th century, the golden age of the Umayyad caliphate, Al Andalus in Spain was in de facto control of the whole western Mediterranean

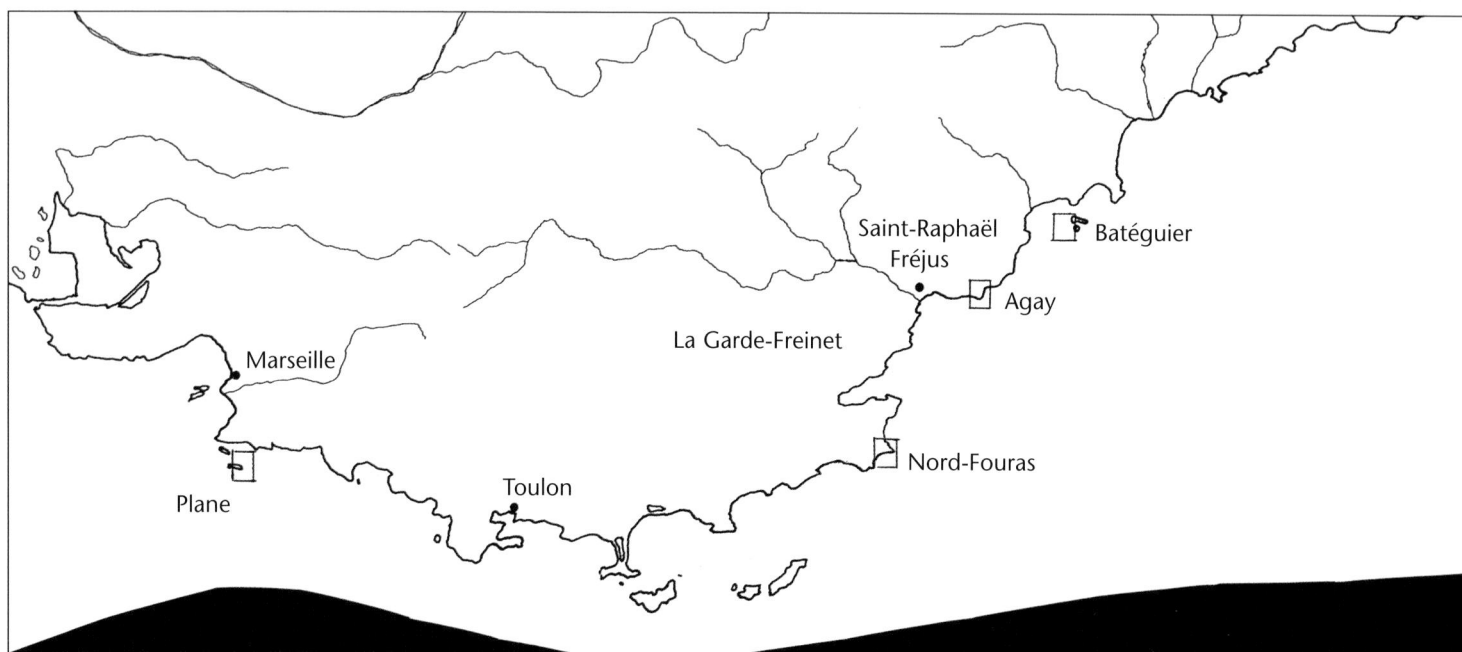

The respective positions of the four Saracen wrecks off southern France. Map courtesy of J.-P. Joncheray

via the bases of its corsair sailors who were established on islands such as the Balearics and Sardinia and on the coasts of the Christian kingdoms. While the historical sources provide a great deal of information about the maritime and commercial activities of the Muslim world in the Mediterranean, they usually have nothing to say on the subject of the ships.

The Agay wreck

Alain Visquis discovered the deep-lying Agay 2 in 1962, and the wreck was at first viewed as post-mediaeval. He worked on the wreck for 17 years, with varying success. In some of those years he was able to draw on the help of the archaeological research ship the Archéonaute. Sometimes, he was supported by a team of over 10 deep-sea divers but, following a severe diving accident, he brought all operations to a halt in 1979. Jean-Pierre Joncheray, who had been taking part in the excavations since 1970, took over in 1996.

Above the keel, the alternating couple/half-couple structure of the frames can be seen on the Agay shipwreck. Photo courtesy of J.-P. Joncheray

The wreck is situated at the entrance to Agay's maritime corridor. The anchorage is sheltered by Cape Dramont from the mistral winds, which blow here from the north-northwest, but it is exposed to eastern and southerly winds. It is unlikely that the ship sank after running aground on a reef. Rather, it may have been wrecked as it was waiting for fair winds, riding at anchor and sheltered from the mistral. However, naval combat or a pirate attack cannot be discounted – as is suggested by the unexpected presence of a second vessel, lying close to and at right angles to the first, with weapons in contact with the hull, and also a large fragment of a hull lying isolated a few hundred metres to the south-east of the wreck.

From an architectural point of view, this wreck can be situated in the middle of the long process of transition between two principles of construction: from shell-first to frame-first (skeleton-first) construction, a process whose main stages can be seen in the 7th-century wrecks Yassi Ada 1 and Saint-Gervais B, at Agay and Batéguier in the 10th century, and Serçe

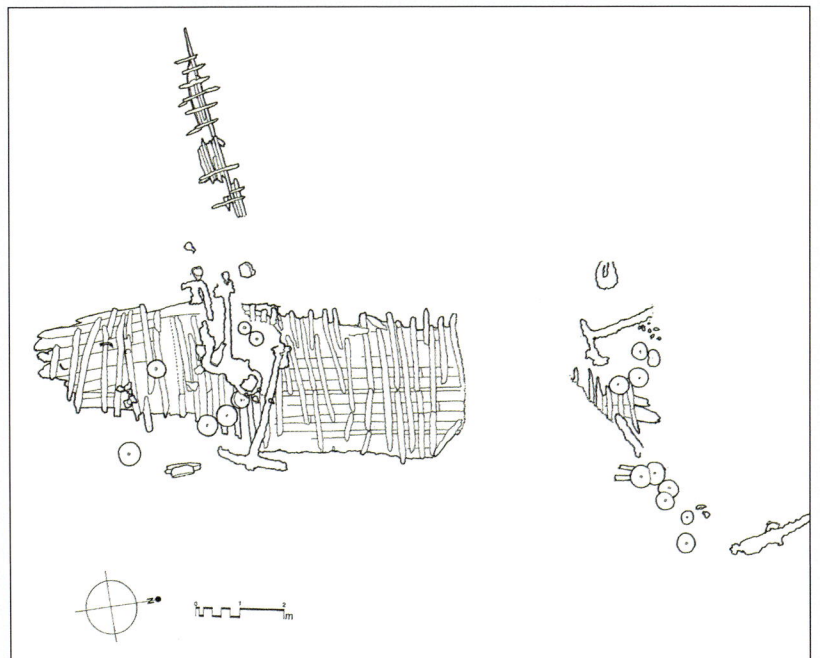

General plan of the Agay shipwreck. Note the remains of a second ship to the west of the main vessel. Drawing: Chris Brandon, courtesy of J.-P. Joncheray

103

Liman in the 11th century. At Agay, the frame construction makes the keel/frame structure fundamental. Furthermore, a minute study of the frames has enabled us to deduce that the Agay vessel was flat-bottomed.

The Batéguier wreck

Jean-Pierre Joncheray discovered Batéguier in 1973 at an even greater depth. In the space of two years, he salvaged over 360 objects and exposed the hull. In 1975, permission to continue the excavation was withdrawn and the site was neglected for over 20 years until 1993, when Henri G. Delauze, President of COMEX (a French company specialising in the manufacture of diving equipment), provided the professional means to carry out a research plan.

The Batéguier is a dangerous reef (recently denoted by the placement of a buoy here), off the town of Cannes on the Côte d'Azur. This reef does not seem to have caused the wreck; rather, it would seem that fire or a naval battle was responsible.

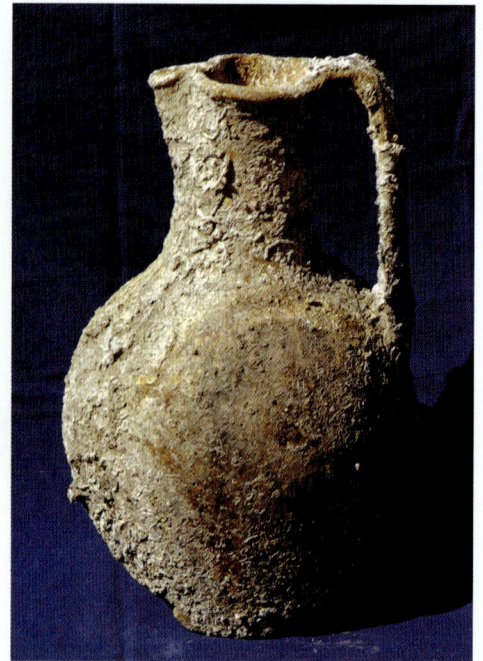

A small jug characteristic of types found on the Saracen wrecks. Photo courtesy of J.-P. Joncheray

Outline of the frames on the Agay shipwreck. Photo courtesy of J.-P. Joncheray

The discovery was characterised by 10 jars of large capacity (over 1,000 litres) intact and grouped together on a flat mud seabed, not forming a prominent tumulus mound. The jars were arranged in a rather strange way: some were half silted up, corresponding to the average sedimentation of the site (50 to 60cm), while others had emerged completely free of the sand, and rolled around at the slightest touch.

The wreck appeared to have a relatively empty central zone, but with sides that were rich in archaeological material: an extensive concentration of pottery (neither very thick nor in any obvious structured order), anchors and ewers to the west, water jugs and other pottery pieces to the east, millstones in the centre, and a hull, in an excellent state of preservation, at least 20 x 6m of which is intact.

The ROV *Super Achille*, used in 1993 on the 60m-deep Batéguier wreck.
Photo courtesy of J.-P. Joncheray

After the latest excavations, the bottom of the hull could be seen resting flat on the keel and preserved to a height of 40cm. A section of the hull measuring 11.35m long and 4.30m wide maximum was uncovered, and is identifiable as one extremity and the centre of a flat-bottomed ship preserved to beyond the turn-of-the-bilge. The frames were flat and L-shaped.

The wreck Plane 3 from the Roches Estéou

The Plane or Calseraigne island is situated in the western part of the Riou Archipelago, to the east of Marseille. The wreck lies at the foot of the Roches Estéou, between 10 and 26m depth. This site is exposed to the wind and the waves. The ship was probably heading from Marseille to Cassis when disaster struck. She must have smashed into the central part of the reef, then drifted and finally sunk at the foot of the rocks. At present, she occupies a sandy basin surrounded by poseidonia algae and pebbles.

The site was discovered by Serge Ximénés and excavated in 1976. The soundings led to the discovery of the first wooden remains, together with anchors and a small number of pottery items.

The Batéguier wreck at the time of its discovery in 1973. Photo courtesy of J.-P. Joncheray

A millstone being recorded amongst granite ballast stones on the Nord-Fouras wreck. Photo courtesy of J.-P. Joncheray

The Nord-Fouras wreck

In 1990, the discovery of a new Saracen wreck was announced, again by Jean-Pierre Joncheray. In reality, for over 20 years, a somewhat vague zone to the north of a small islet with two pointed extremities that lies off Cape Camarat at Saint Tropez was known by the rather obvious name of 'Les Meules' (The Millstones). The wreck lay in a small extended sandy valley, between 15 and 17m long. Only durable vestiges such as millstones and nails are preserved. The evidence available

An assemblage of millstones found on the Nord-Fouras shipwreck. Photo courtesy of J.-P. Joncheray

suggests that the ship came from the south-west, and was bound on a journey from west to east. It should be pointed out that Nord-Fouras is the wreck closest to la Garde-Freinet, a town considered to be the main base of the Saracens in Provence.

The excavation that was undertaken in June 1994, with the scientific collaboration of the specialist Philippe Sénac, uncovered new millstones and a few fragments of pottery. This was a far cry from the wealth of the previous wrecks.

The Saracen material

The four wrecks contained important archaeological material, but in extremely different quantities. While 365 finds were recovered from the Batéguier wreck in the 1975 excavation alone – which leads us to suppose a cargo of at least 1,000 objects – the same cannot be said of the other sites. The Agay ship must have carried 200–300 objects, those of Plane and Nord-Fouras just a few dozen.

On all four wrecks, the bottom of the vessels contained numerous millstones for grinding grain. The ubiquitous pottery pieces are remarkably all of the same age and allow us to deduce that the wrecks were contemporary. Certain pottery items are especially characteristic:

- Two- or three-handled water jugs with a lipless neck in the shape of a truncated cone, extremely long and separated from a belly of generally oval shape by a perforated inside lid.
- Narrow-necked ewers with a trefoil spout at the top. The spherical, broad-bottomed belly is decorated with cross pieces carved in place before firing, running between beading. A long handle runs up the neck.
- Large-volume oval-bellied jars with a funnel-shaped, down-turned lip, and no neck.
- Oil lamps, an item generally little known, especially in Provence. Two varieties have been discovered.
- Round-bottomed amphorae with fluted bellies.

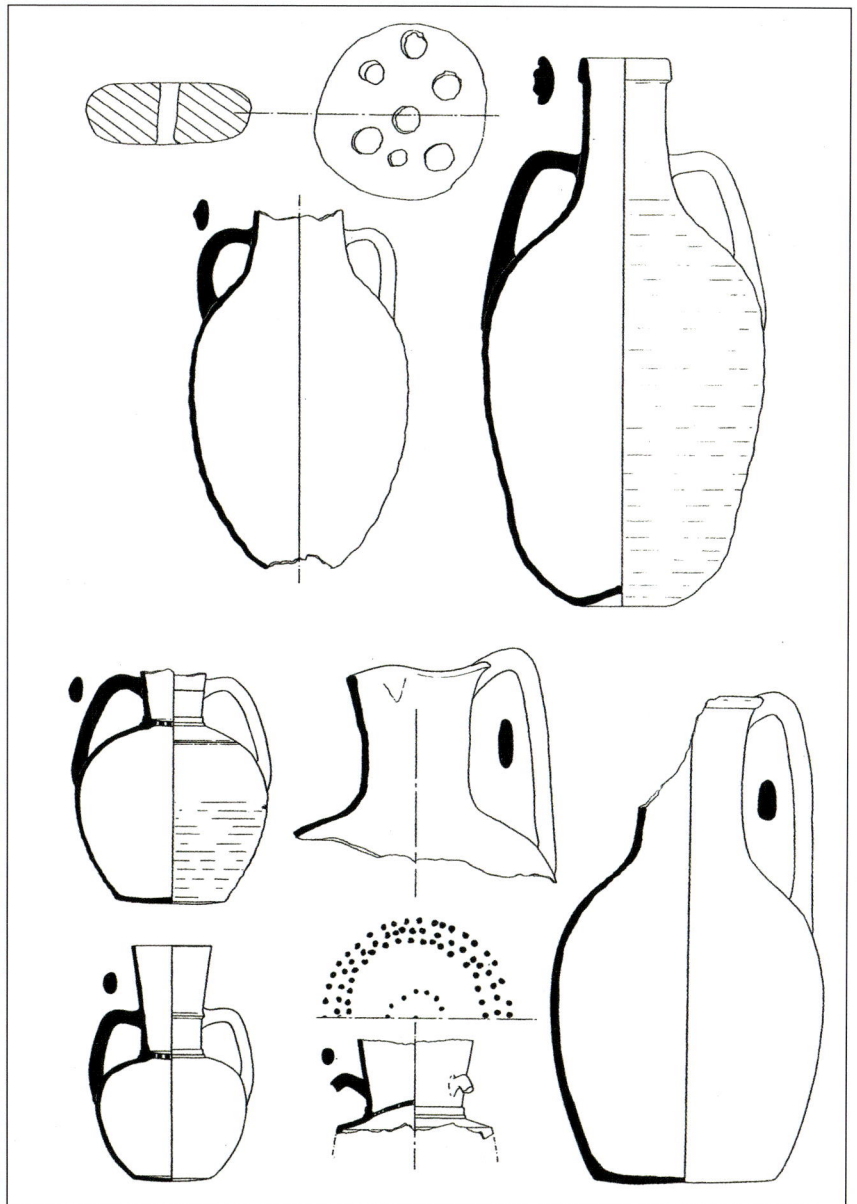

Drawings of some of the Saracen pottery from the Provence shipwrecks.

Drawing courtesy of J.-P. Joncheray

A very rare lamp with seven openings from the Batéguier wreck.

Photo courtesy of J.-P. Joncheray

107

Anne Joncheray and Jean Toulet, alongside the Agay wreck. Photo courtesy of J.-P. Joncheray

V. Phantom shipwrecks

Ships were wrecked for many different reasons throughout antiquity and under various climatic conditions. The abrupt change in the Mediterranean's mood caught out the majority of lost vessels, when the onslaught of a storm would cause waves to crash over decks, inundating hulls and sending cargoes plummeting down to the depths. The same storm might propel a ship shoreward on to the nearest landmass, either a beach or offshore island, breaching its hull. At such times of danger, anchors and sounding leads, relied on to monitor the depth and character of a seabed beneath a keel under normal sailing conditions, were usually rendered useless by the chaos of the sea, which could drive a ship off course. Prayer, rather than seafaring savvy, was the order of the day at times like these.

Yet another danger was lack of wind, which could stall a ship's progress and force sea captains to jettison cargo and spare rigging overboard to lighten a craft's load. Compared to the natural ferocity of the Mediterranean, piracy was a far less worrying evil.

The term shipwreck encompasses archaeological sites with very different preservation levels. Ships wrecked in deep waters exceeding 25m, beyond the pressures of severe currents and surface wave motion, typically form well preserved sites with intact cargoes, wooden hulls, and the original spatial configuration of the ship intact (cargo positions and galley areas). Into this category fall the late 4th- to early 5th-century and early 7th-century AD shipwrecks that foundered off the island of Yassi Ada, Turkey and were excavated at depths of 32–42m.

More important than depth, however, is seabed composition. A vessel wrecked on to a rocky seabed would disintegrate quite rapidly, irrespective of depth, as water pressure and an absence of hull cradling would cause mortise-and-tenoned planking to fall away from inner frames, be consumed by marine-boring organisms, or simply float away. All that survives of these wrecks are durable objects, such as heavy clay amphorae, stone and metal materials. A wreck's upper layers might become covered by a light to heavy layer of encrustation.

Where sand or mud engulfs a seabed, the preservation of organic material can be expected, from significant parts of wooden hulls to rope, rigging blocks, plant and food extracts. Concealed wreckage covered by a layer of sand stabilises due to an absence of oxygen and attack from marine organisms and vegetation. The scale of organic matter preservation is a variable issue, dependent on just how much sediment protects a wreck and how often it is exposed over the centuries from within its protective sediment blanket.

Great storms of antiquity

Since time immemorial, fishermen and folklore have spoken in reverential tones about the 'Great Storm', a climatic episode of monstrous proportions that takes life and limb indiscriminately. Rather than the exaggeration of maritime mythology, scientific readings measured at weather stations show that this natural phenomenon is very real in the modern Mediterranean.

A particularly harrowing Great Storm was recorded by the mediaeval pilgrim Saewulf between 1102 and 1103, while he was staying overnight in the port of Jaffa before starting the journey down to Jerusalem. Although slightly outside Late Antiquity, this narrative is an unusually important and detailed description of the human tragedy that unfolds during such events. The moods of the Mediterranean have remained constant between antiquity and the modern day, so marine archaeologists can be sure that the storm climate that generates extraordinary waves of 5–6m height every seven to eight years off Israel is identical to that of the 4th to 10th centuries.

Following a night's sleep in the port of Jaffa, Saewulf experienced, and later wrote down, the following harrowing description of a Great Storm:

...early in the morning, as we came out from church, we heard the noise of the sea, the cries of the people, and all were running together, and wondering at such things as they had never heard before. We ran, full of fear with the rest, and came to the shore. When we got there we saw the storm running mountains high, and beheld the bodies of men and women without number drowned and miserably lying on the beach. We also saw ships dashed against each other and broken into small pieces.

Who could listen to anything but the roaring of the sea and the crashing of the ships? It was even louder than the cries of the people and the shouting of all the crews. Our ship, however, being very large and strongly built, and several others laden with corn and other merchandise, and with pilgrims outward or homeward bound, still held by their anchors and cables, although they were sorely tossed about by the waves. Oh, what fear of evil did they fall into! How was their merchandise thrown away! What eyes of those who beheld them was so hard and stony that it could refrain from tears?

We had not been gazing long, when, by the violence of the waves or the currents, the anchors gave way, the cables were broken, and the ships were given up to the fierceness of the waves, all hope of escape being cut off. They were now lifted up on high, now drawn down to the depths, and quickly were thrown up out of the deep upon the sand or upon the rocks. There they were miserably dashed from side to side, and gradually torn to pieces by the tempest. The fierceness of the storm would not suffer them to return sound to the sea, and the steepness of the beach would not allow them to reach the shore in safety.

But what boots it to tell how lamentably sailors and pilgrims, when all hope was gone, still clung, some to the ships, some to the masts, some to the spars, some to the cross-timbers? What more shall I say? Some, stupefied with terror, were drowned; some, as they were clinging, were decapitated by the timbers of their own ship. This may seem incredible to many, yet I saw it. Some, washed off from the decks of their ships, were carried out again to the deep. Some, who knew how to swim, voluntarily committed themselves to the waves, and thus many of them perished. Very few, who had confidence in their own strength, arrived safe on shore.

Thus, out of 30 very large ships, some of which are commonly called Dormundi [Byzantine dromones], others Gulafri, and other Catti, all laden with pilgrims or merchandise, scarcely seven remained unwrecked by the time I had left the shore. More than a thousand persons of either sex perished that day. A greater misery on one day no eye ever saw. But from all these [dangers] our Lord delivered me by His grace.

A fine example of a microclimate is the 7th-century St Gervais shipwreck excavated in 2.5m of water off Fos, southern France. Whilst sand preserved the hull, a layer of pitch that had spilled out of amphorae glued in position a rich archaeological layer of organic material. Within this matrix were preserved a cargo of corn, a wooden barrel, and a very rare find in the form of the ship's wooden pump housing. Variable geological and marine conditions make every shipwreck unique, often leaving the content of a wreck as a great surprise to the marine archaeologist.

The southern anchorage of the port city of Dor in Israel offers an insightful case study into the impact of local conditions on preservation. The eight 6th- to 7th-century shipwrecks are scattered in less than 3m of water in the southern bay, where they must have been susceptible since antiquity to extreme disturbance from waves in the breaker zone, currents and perhaps even salvage attempts. However, many of these hulls were rapidly enshrouded within dense sand accumulations, where they stabilised for many centuries, sealing their contents together in a strongly anaerobic environment.

From the 1940s until 1964, coastal quarrying for the booming building industry stripped Israel's central beaches of one-third of their total sand reserves. As waves and currents washed offshore sand blankets shoreward to make up for

The inner reaches of Kotor Bay, Montenegro, near the ancient city of Risan. Natural harbours like these along the northern Adriatic coast are rich in Late Antique shipwrecks.

Photo: Sean Kingsley

Becalmed off Sinai

Shipwreck was not the sole cause of the loss of cargoes and ships' equipment in antiquity. If becalmed without wind, or if fearing shipwreck due to an over-loaded hull, jettison was a common resort. J. S. Buckingham reported a terrible passage between Egypt and Akko in Palestine between 26 December and 6 January 1816 on a Syrian *shuktoor* (*Travels in Palestine*, London, 1821, 3–28). This three-masted merchant vessel, with a capacity of 40 tonnes, specialised in the transport of corn and rice between Egypt and Syria. The ship was sailed by a captain and nine-man crew of Syrian Arabs.

On 1 January 1816, off Damietta, Egypt, Buckingham wrote in his journal: *The wind had entirely forsaken us again soon after midnight, and at dawn it was a perfect calm... Long prayers, with many kisses were bestowed on the pictures of the patron saints [St George], who were produced in full assembly...*

On 2 January, the wind was: *Still calm; water reduced to the last small barrel; the third day of our being without any prepared food, from want of fuel... The dawn opened, however, and not a breath of air was yet stirring... The men were evidently terrified at the prospect of approaching death...*

By 5 January, the over-weighted ship was clearly in trouble as the ship's sails failed to respond to the stormy sea conditions. *We proceeded, therefore, to throw over board every thing on the deck, among which were a large iron anchor... two old and rusty six pounders [cannon] with their carriages, a large and heavy wooden cabouse or cooking-house, the bottom of which was brick-masonry... two spare spars, all the furniture of the boat excepting her rudder and two oars... empty water-casks, coils of spare rope, an unshipped capstern, and, in short, every thing that added to the weight of the vessel's decks.*

The crew threw overboard anchors, provisions, merchandise and even Buckingham's luggage. Finally their desperate efforts paid off: *The benefit of our measures were, however, so evident, as to afford us the tranquillizing consolation of having done our duty. The vessel met the sea with a seeming effort to rise above its destructive foam... no lives were yet lost, and, as far as we could perceive around us, when the lightning's glare extended the range of vision, we were still far from the worst of all a seaman's horrors, a lee shore.*

this deficit by filling depleted beaches, large craters were exposed naturally above the destabilised seabed. Revealed within them was a startling concentration of about 200 shipwrecks found every 25–50m along the shoreline. Although their cargoes had largely been destroyed in antiquity during the act of wreckage, or salvaged shortly afterwards, their wooden hulls proved remarkably well preserved despite the preconceptions of marine archaeologists (see Chapter 4). Rapid cover with silt similarly explains the preservation of the wooden ship hulls at Pantano Longarini (Sicily) and Ravenna (Italy).

Invisible cargoes

During the last 50 years of underwater exploration, the majority of ancient wrecks lying in depths of up to 45m have been detected through the surface presence of dense concentrations of cargo, including marble architecture, metallic concretions and, predominantly, amphorae by the tonne. Even the modern use of side-scan sonar to locate ships lost at depths of up to 800m relies on the presence of the same surface features for target detection on electronic screens. Of the 222 Late Antique shipwrecks currently known around the Mediterranean and Black Sea, over 80% owe their discovery to a highly visible, durable cargo of amphorae, metal or stones.

This cosmopolitan collection of shipwrecks has revealed a wealth of fascinating new information about the organisation of maritime trade that has rewritten the history of ancient economies and commerce. Yet alongside these emerging patterns is an equally enigmatic set of anomalies: cargoes that ancient texts tell us must have been common shipments, but which, to date, have entirely eluded detection. Is this because they sailed sea-lanes that still remain unknown to us? Or perhaps they lie in the deepest waters of the ocean, awaiting new strides in technology before we can hunt them down?

What class of produce currently awaits discovery on these phantom shipwrecks? Undoubtedly most mysterious is the absence of cargoes of wheat. Between *circa* AD 330 and 618, about 31,200 tonnes were shipped annually by the Byzantine state between Alexandria and Constantinople (at least 624 shipments). In other words, just under 180,000 shipments for this entire period. However, other than the St Gervais B shipwreck, lost in the mid-7th century AD off southern France, not a seed of grain has cropped up under the sea. Is this because grain transports were better built than the average merchant vessel?

A second gaping anomaly is the absence of cloth amongst the shipwrecks. Circumstantial evidence for shipments of cloth and silk abounds. The ancient 'database' of the wealth of the Late Roman Empire, the *Expositio Totius Mundi et Gentium* of AD 359, describes numerous Near Eastern cities as bustling centres of cloth production. Scythopolis in northern Palestine was just such a town, defined as a large-scale manufacturer of cloth, which was exported throughout the world. Crucibles for mixing dyes and accumulations of dye pigment rising over 1m high have turned up in seven early 7th-century shops in Sardis, Turkey, while 6th-century furnaces and vats from a *tinctoria* (cloth-dyeing workshop) have been excavated in the ancient city Jerash in Jordan.

A mid-5th century dye factory located next to a synagogue on the shore at Gaza is an intriguing discovery, where scientific analysis of samples of reddish brown and violet crushed dyes found on its floors provenanced the raw materials to local sources in the Negev desert, Sinai, but also to the distant shores of Italy and Greece, clear evidence of high-level capital investment. Just how extensive was this trade? During a five-day period in the 3rd century, Egyptian papyri record how the city of Oxyrhynchos exported no less than 2,000 garments. Elsewhere, the massive, silent dumps of murex shells (from which precious purple dye was extracted) lie scattered along the shores of Tyre, Sidon and Aperlae, and tell a similar story of big business.

If parading in purple cloth was the ultimate expression of wealth and prestige, owning garments sewn from the newly discovered and still rare silk was not far behind as a highly desirable luxury product. During the second quarter of the 5th century, mulberry bush cultivation stabilised in China after 100 years of internal warfare which had crippled trade. Prized raw silk known as *metaxa* was obtained by Sasanian, Axumite and Byzantine merchants from India and the Far East. Sri Lanka, known to the Byzantines as Taprobane, was the main entrepôt between the western and eastern Indian Ocean during Late Antiquity, and into its ports flowed silk, aloes, cloves and sandalwood on Indian and Chinese merchant vessels.

After shipment up the Red Sea into the Mediterranean, raw silk was dyed and woven into cloth in Egypt and most famously Syria, apparently known to the Chinese as Da Qin. It was this finished product that was dispatched as a diplomatic gift by the Emperor Theodosius II to Attila the Hun *circa* 449, along with Indian gems. The Visigoth king, Theodoric II, was similarly praised in the mid-5th century for the purple silk curtains that adorned his palace. In return for the silk, China coveted precious metals, jade, pearls, coral, agate, glass, brooches and Sasanian silver. Byzantine amphorae found in the port of Zanzibar and coins of 450–640 in India and Sri Lanka attest to the accuracy of this far-flung luxury trade.

The historian Procopius claimed that the silk industry was revolutionised in 552, when Nestorian monks smuggled silkworms across Asia and into the Byzantine Empire. A few years later, silkworms were being raised successfully in rural Syria, ending the need to risk life, limb and ships in long-distance import. Subsequently, Byzantine silk was exported beyond the borders of the empire, and has turned up in excavations as far west as the royal graves of Bedburg-Morken-Harff in Germany.

Other phantom cargoes that remain invisible amongst the register of Late Antique shipwrecks can be identified from mid-5th to mid-6th century inscriptions of trade tax tariffs from Anazarbos in Cilicia (south-eastern Turkey). This document lists saffron, *garum* (fish sauce), ropes, gourds, pulses, garlic, fried fish, wine, salt, grafted plants, raw silk, tin, lead, slaves and cattle. Of these, only *garum* and wine have been excavated from Mediterranean shipwrecks. A similar trade inscription from Cagliari, dating to the reign of the Emperor Maurice (582–602), mentions palms, sheep, vegetables, summer produce, wine, wheat and birds. Even more elusive are the luxury products listed in a horoscope of 475 that records a ship destined for Athens taking on a cargo of camels in North African Cyrenaica, which was supplemented by precious fabrics and silver goods in Alexandria. Another horoscope of 479 refers to high-value shipments of small birds, papyrus, bronze objects and a medicine chest. (Horoscopes were drawn up to reassure merchants awaiting deliveries abroad.)

Right: site plan of the surviving wooden timbers and North African amphorae on the 4th-century AD Héliopolis A ship, wrecked off southern France.

Drawing: Chris Brandon in J.-P. Joncheray, *Cahiers d'Archéologie Subaquatique* 13 (1997), 142–3

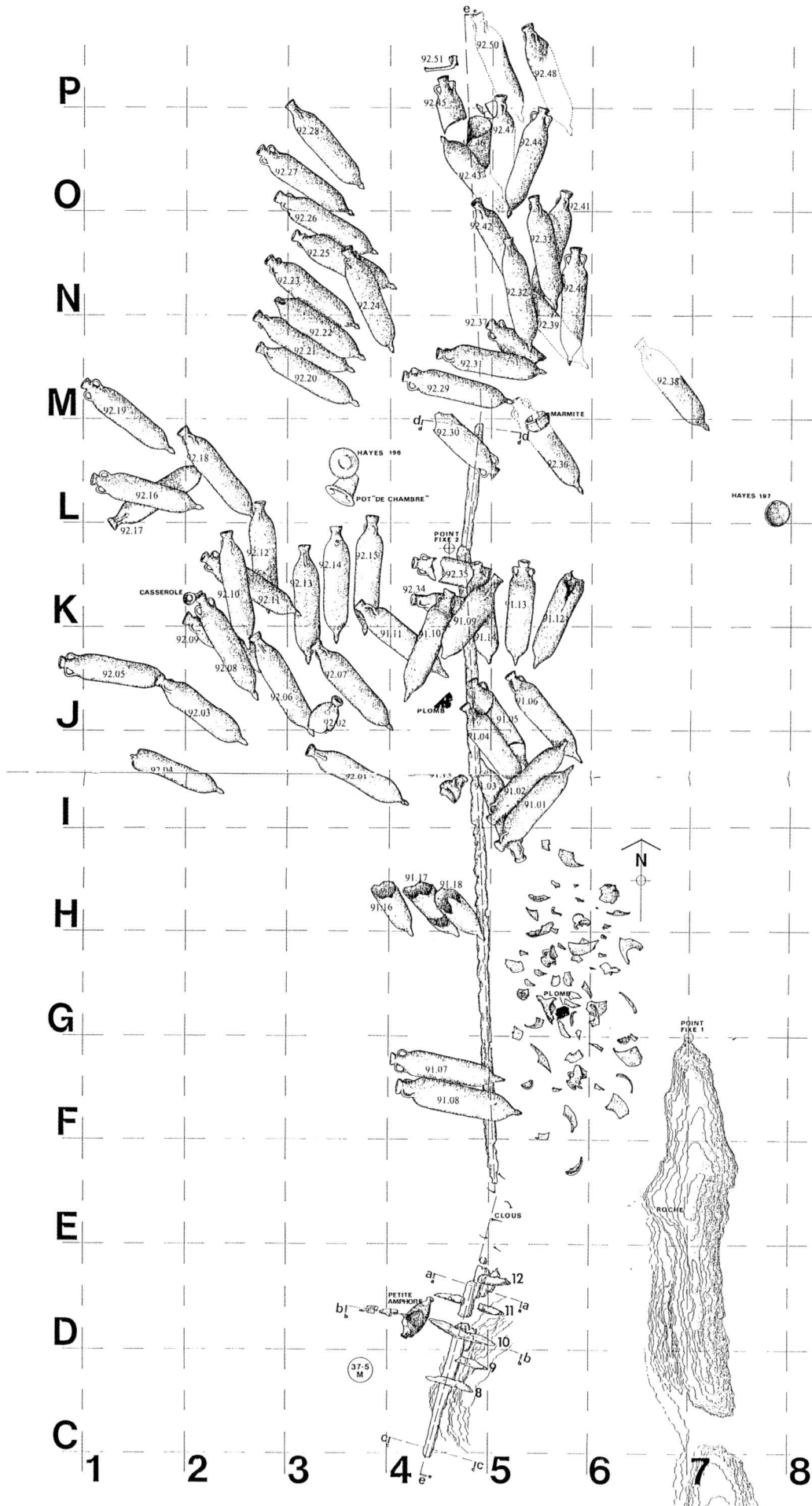

The formation of shipwreck sites

Marine archaeologists use the science of site-formation analysis to study patterns in how wrecks form and are preserved. This helps predict what type of information can be extracted from a shipwreck before a survey or excavation starts, and also assists different countries in cultural resource management of their ancient heritage.

Well preserved shipwrecks are called 'coherent wrecks'. These retain a high degree of the original ship's configuration. Amphorae will largely remain intact in the parts of the hull where they were last stowed, and the location of the galley structure will be visible through the presence of roof-tiles, floor bricks, cooking equipment and the private belongings of sailors (called the domestic assemblage). Significant sections of wooden hull planking and organic material are to be expected. Examples of coherent wrecks dating from Late Antiquity include Port-Vendres A (France), Yassi Ada A/B, Bozburun (Turkey) and Sobra (Croatia).

At the other end of the spectrum are 'scattered' or 'incoherent wrecks', poorly preserved sites where amphorae are broken and only preserved as fragments. The overall structure of the ship and cargo stowage can no longer be observed; all artefacts (often important material) are jumbled together incoherently. Other than small sections of wooden planking trapped between durable artefacts (anchors, ballast stones), the hull is generally obliterated. Examples of incoherent wrecks include Plemmirio A (Sicily), Favaritx (Minorca), and Cape Andreas and Cape Kiti (Cyprus).

Between these two extremes lies a complicated variety of shipwrecks which are termed 'partly coherent' sites. Cargoes of amphorae are on the whole broken, although large sections of jars can be expected. Otherwise, cargo and the domestic assemblage of sailors' belongings are mixed together on a seabed. The latter should prove well preserved. In some cases, significant parts of cargo can be detected and recovered, but very little hull remains (such as the wrecks of La Palud, France and Randello, Sicily). In others, very little cargo remains, but sections of wooden hulls can be surprisingly intact, pinned down under sealing layers of ballast (as on Tantura A and Dor D).

Levels of shipwreck site-formations very often have little to do with processes of marine geology, but are the result of human interference at the time of wreckage in antiquity or in the modern era. The salvage of cargoes was a lucrative business in Late Antiquity, for which the 7th-century Rhodian Sea Law legislated. Thus, "If gold or silver or anything else is raised from the sea from a depth of eight fathoms [15m], let the salvor receive one-third. If it is raised from a depth of 15 fathoms [28m], let the salvor receive one-half by reason of the danger of the sea. Where things are cast from sea to land and found there or carried to within one cubit of the land [50cm], let the salvor receive one-tenth of what is salved." Hulls bereft of cargo on partly coherent wrecks can often be explained by ancient salvage, especially when sites lie in shallow waters.

Far more worrying and sinister for the marine archaeologist is the constant

A

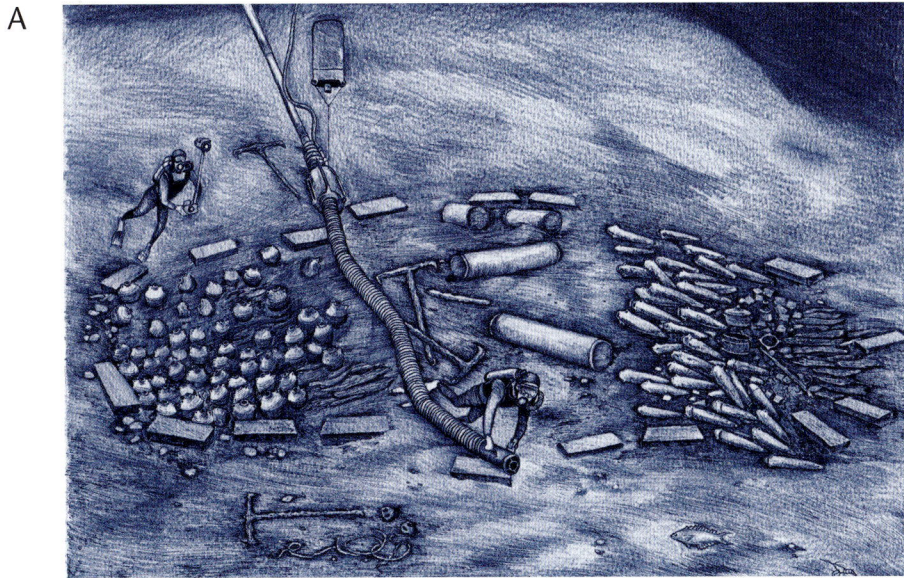

B

C

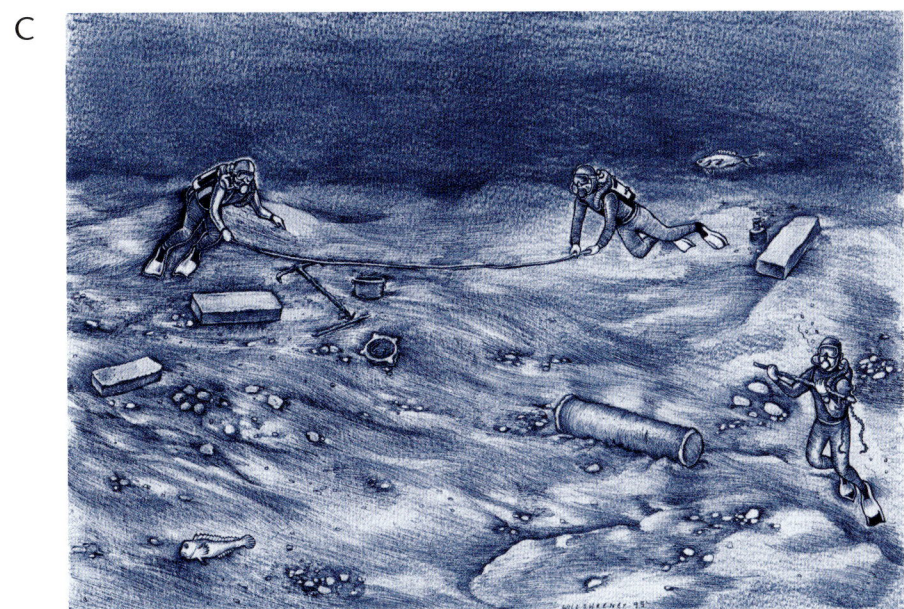

A. An artist's view of a well-preserved, coherent shipwreck of the 6th or 7th century AD. The site-formation retains the overall shape of the vessel and the cargo and domestic assemblage remain in their original stacked positions. The primary cargo is Palestinian wine contained in Gaza/Ashkelon amphorae (LR4 at right) and bag-shaped jars from central Israel (LR5 at left). The ship was also transporting a secondary consignment of two marble columns (centre) and ashlar stone masonry serving as saleable ballast. The domestic assemblage (at far right) included a ceramic casserole, bronze cooking pot, bronze steelyard, marble grinding mortar and a copper flask. Navigation equipment includes three cruciform iron anchors, two rigging blocks and coils of rope. Extensive hull planking survives. Archaeologists excavate sand from the site using an air-lift. The cargo and domestic assemblage depicted are based on Byzantine shipwrecks found in the South Bay, Dor.

B. The same Palestinian shipwreck as a partly coherent site formation. The cargo and domestic assemblage are inter-mixed and their original configuration is lost. Almost all amphorae are broken, but short, disconnected sections of hull planking and some organic matter survive. Durable objects (metal and stone) are still well preserved. Archaeologists plan timbers with a drawing frame positioned vertically over the hull.

C. Byzantine Palestinian shipwreck as an incoherent, scattered site formation. The cargo is only preserved as small sherds trapped under or between stone ballast. Only durable elements of the cargo (marble columns) and domestic assemblage (bronze cooking pot, steelyard, marble mortar and a copper flask) are preserved. No wooden planking or organic material survives. Archaeologists record distances between artefacts.

Drawings: Will Sweeney

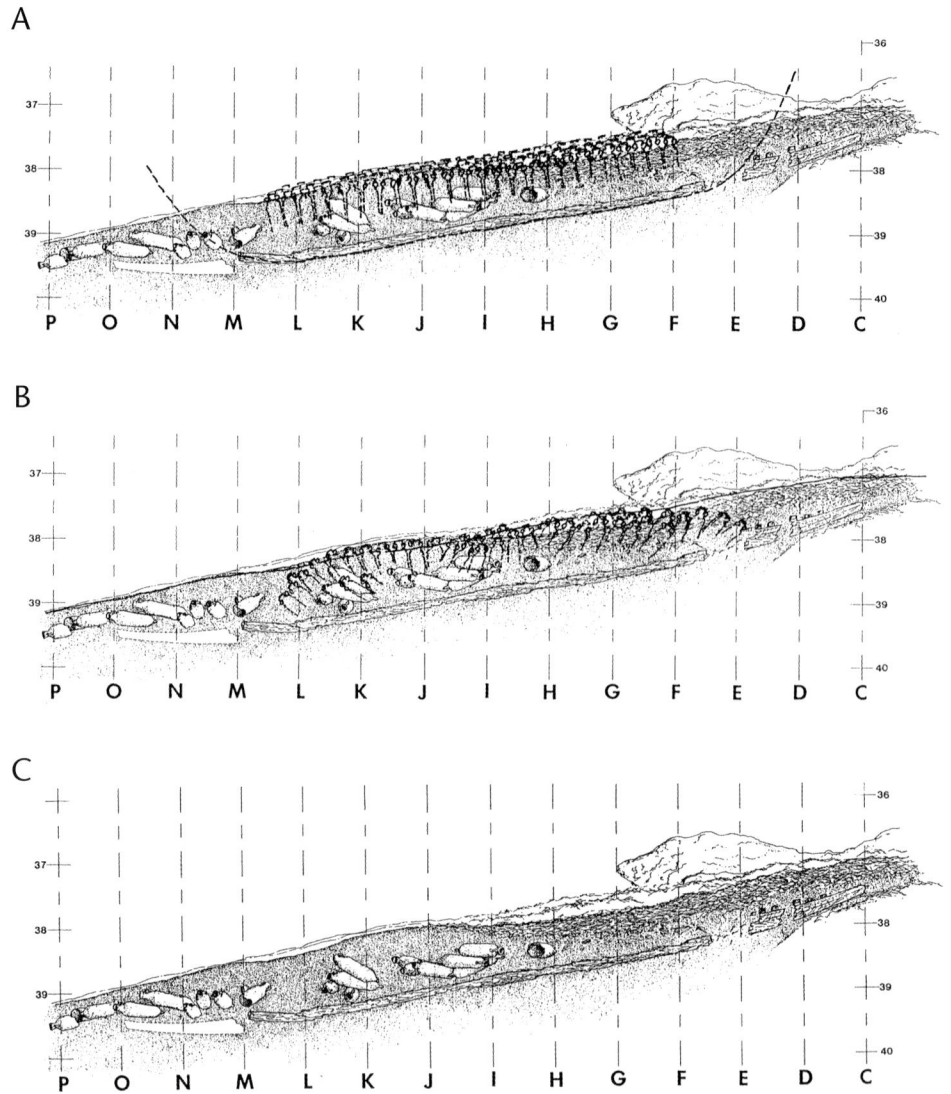

The Héliopolis A shipwreck close to the time of its sinking around AD 400 (A), with a largely intact cargo when first discovered in 1960 (B), and after looting in 1991 (C).

Drawing: after J.-P. Joncheray, *Cahiers d'Archéologie Subaquatique* 13, 1997

battle against treasure hunters. Italy, France and Montenegro have suffered very badly in the last few decades. Research in Israel has suggested that 60% of all existing wreck finds have already been recovered illegally, and that very little of the country's shipwreck heritage will survive underwater in 10–20 years time.

The disturbing scale of looting in some areas of the Mediterranean is exemplified by Héliopolis A, a small ship wrecked off the Hyères Islands of southern France in the 4th century. When first discovered in 1969 at depths of 35–38m, dozens of intact North African amphorae were observed peering out of the sand across the site, perhaps comprising 720 jars in total. Some 22 years later, when the wreck was revisited and excavated between 1991 and 1992, the site had been almost completely looted. Only through the brilliant recording and persistence of a team of marine archaeologists directed by Jean-Pierre Joncheray was the history of this ship reconstructed. With the adoption of the UNESCO Convention on the Protection of the Underwater Cultural Heritage in November 2001, it is hoped that countries will combat shipwreck pillage more effectively.

Phantom warships

The divide of the Roman Empire between the West and East Mediterranean set the stage for various internal bloody insurrections between emperors and usurpers, and for wars with the barbarian hordes. Warships must have been lost by the hundreds throughout Late Antiquity, and Theophanes Confessor recorded how in 745/6 alone, the fleet of the Hagarenes sailed from Alexandria to Cyprus to confront the Byzantine navy in the port of Keramaia, where it sunk all but three of 1,000 warships.

Between the 4th and 6th centuries, the navies of Late Rome, Byzantium and the Umayyad caliphate witnessed the rise of a new and deadly weapon in the history of sea battle. In Late Antiquity the great warships of the classical age, the trireme, disappeared from history. Naval warfare relying on close-quarter fighting using bronze rams was now a strategy of the past, as the latest recorded use of the ram was in a battle between the Goths and Byzantines at Sinigalia near Ancona in AD 551. What did the new wooden warships look like and how competitive were the opposition's different models?

The new tool of maritime warfare *par excellence* in Late Antiquity was the *dromon* ('racer'). The year AD 324 was the watershed for change, when Licinius' 350 triremes were defeated by Constantine's fleet of single banked galleys, heralding the end of the age of this sophisticated, majestic ship upon whose prowess Athens had been founded 800 years previously.

This innovative warship is recorded in greater detail two centuries later, when the historian Procopius described 92 dromons manned by 2,000 men and

Model of a Byzantine warship (*dromon*), in the Aegean Maritime Museum, Mykonos.

Photo: courtesy of the Aegean Maritime Museum, Mykonos

119

500 transport ships used in Belisarius' naval fleet dispatched in AD 533 to retake Vandal North Africa for the Byzantine Empire. Procopius describes the dromon as "single-banked and having decks overhead to reduce to a minimum the chance of the rowers being hit by enemy missiles. Men today call these ships 'dromons' because they are able to sail very swiftly." The dromon seems to have been deliberately adapted for naval warfare along North Africa, because its small size and agility were well suited to the region's shallow waters and small ports.

Archaeologists know precious little about this clever innovation. No contemporary 4th- to 8th-century images of the dromon are preserved, and its anatomy is only described in detail for the first time in AD 900. Over the centuries, three classes of *dromones* evolved. The earliest and most prominent

Conquest of Constantinople by the Crusaders of the 4th Crusade on 13 April 1204 showing the continued use of the Byzantine *dromon. The Conquest of Constantinople*, by Jacopo Robusti, byname Tintoretto (1518–1594). Venice, Palace of the Doge.

Photo: akg-images/Cameraphoto

prototype was a two-banked galley about 45m long, with sails and a minimum of 50 oars in each bank (100 oars in total) rowed by 100 men. By the mid-10th century, the term dromon also referred to the largest warship in operation, manned by up to 300 men (including 200 rowers).

In early dromon construction, wooden planking was attached using nails and wooden pegs, and seams between planks were pitched and caulked with liquid tar. Surprisingly, hulls were sheathed with lead. Although this must have slowed down the dromon's potential speed, such protection was essential to safeguard her wooden shell from flame-throwers. Animal hides were nailed over the most vulnerable sections of hulls for similar reasons.

The potential consequence of building dromons without lead hull sheeting is described in a rare insight into the Arab siege of Constantinople in AD 717. Following the Arab invasion of the Byzantine Empire in AD 636, the Umayyad caliphate quickly realised that without a strong fleet a serious and enduring challenge to the power of Byzantium could never be mounted. Part of the strategy behind the Arab incursion into Cyprus in 653–654 had been to seize the island's rich timber resources for its own shipyards.

By AD 717, however, the Umayyads were still deficient in the art of ship construction. The *Historius Graecus* describes how the ships of the Saracens, "having gone into the sea were shattered against ports, shore, and reefs. The greatest and most strange phenomenon occurred in the Aegean sea in that there a great burning hail fell into the sea and made it boil so much that iron would melt and merge with water and result in a boiling hail, so that the tar which held the ships together was loosened and the ships sunk." Did this happen due to an absence of lead hull-sheeting on the Arab warships? Very possibly.

The Byzantine dromon carried two or three masts, but did not rely on a rowing frame. Instead, banks of oars were pulled through portholes in the hull. The dromon had no true internal decking, only gangways along each side of the ship with a central, longitudinal stiffener timber designed to hold the mast crutches and to function as a catwalk. A light wooden frame built along the gangways held shields to protect the rowers from incoming missiles.

The greatest innovation of naval warfare of the age, however, was what replaced the ram. The new ballistic missile of the Byzantine world was 'Greek Fire', which was a cannon-like siphon that threw a formidable jet of flame at enemy ships. The architect Callinicus of Heliopolis apparently invented Greek Fire during the reign of the Emperor Constantine Pogonatus, *circa* AD 672. This weapon's precise ammunition remains a mystery, although most likely major ingredients included naphtha, petroleum, sulphur or pitch. Greek Fire was notoriously difficult to extinguish, and was best combated with sand or vinegar.

The complex apparatus that administered Greek Fire was a long tube of wood lined with bronze and attached to an air pump. The deadly concoction was poured into the pump box, ignited and pumped out of a muzzle. A 10th-century text explains how "[The dromon] should by all means have forward in the bows

The Byzantine shipwreck of Cefalù

Gianfranco Purpura

A Byzantine wreck, rather long and narrow in shape and of eastern origin, foundered off Cefalù in Sicily around the first half of the 6th century AD and sank in a few metres of water near the shore. The wreck probably came to rest on a projecting reef, where the heavily ballasted vessel was most likely silted up, thereby forming a kind of barrier against the waves. The ship's superstructure will have been destroyed, and the cargo, blown by the wind, scattered around the area. Since the ship foundered in shallow water and near an inhabited area, salvage of the numerous and valuable objects on board was probably attempted.

The shoreline at Cefalù, site of the wreck of a 6th-century Byzantine warship. Photo: Alessandro Purpura

However, where they ended up broken into pieces, buried in sand and mud, it would have no longer been possible to identify them or save them. In fact, Late Antique divers were unable to carry out underwater excavations, even of modest scope. Interestingly, on a Roman wreck transporting fish sauce and studied by Edoardo Riccardi off Sicily, significant underwater salvage work had been attempted in antiquity. The salvagers had even sawed through a floor timber in order to recover wood from the wreck but the more valuable objects scattered around the site under a few metres of water and concealed by a layer of sand were not recovered. The intact cargo and personal belongings on the early 1st-century AD Comacchio wreck, silted up on land near the coast, demonstrate the often surprising potential of shallow sites.

Towards the middle of the 6th century, Sicily was in the hands of the Ostrogoths of Totila, who had invaded the region, and Justinian was attempting to reclaim North Africa and Italy for the Empire: these were territories over which, for some considerable time, no Roman emperor had been in any position to claim the least authority.

Since then, the great tumulus of the ballast stones on the shipwreck, surrounded by sand, have been an irresistible attraction not only for fish, but also for men, who, while fishing, spotted the presence of at least seven contemporary Byzantine iron anchors clustered around this mound. Protruding from the wreckage are what look like the trunks of

A North African amphora neck found on the site of the Cefalù shipwreck. Photo: Alessandro Purpura

trees with their bark still on, located in a regular pattern all along the tumulus (first identified by Alessandro Purpura in 1980).

The idea that this was a shipwreck was confirmed when it was observed that the tree-trunks had been worked (only at intersections), at the level of a beam that must have been a wale, between the remains of the upper deck beams and the floor timbers. Similar partly finished timbers were recorded on the 7th-century Byzantine wreck at Yassi Ada in Turkey, where specific external timbers were left undressed to reduce labour costs.

The uncovering of the fore of the ship – a cleat with traces of wear left by the mooring rope and parts of the planking – that can be seen today (still buried near the site mound), confirms the existence of the disintegrated elements of a shipwreck that had slowly broken apart and drifted away from its final mooring, marked by an anchor located about 100m away.

An additional circumstance contributed to the concealment of this vast archaeological site over the course of time. In the 18th century, Emanuele Filiberto, Viceroy of Sicily, planned to use the mound formed by the Byzantine vessel as a foundation for the construction of a mole, over which rubble would be thrown. This potentially destructive project was, fortunately, almost immediately

This section of a ship's mast was found half buried near the mound of ballast stones at Cefalù. The proximity of 17th-century remains complicates its attribution. Photo: Alessandro Purpura

Part of a stone pulpit with the remains of inlay formed part of the ship's ballast. Photo: Alessandro Purpura

abandoned. Nevertheless, the limited work undertaken was sufficient to conceal the traces of what seems to have been a warship originating in the Black Sea, that had been involved in an obscure naval victory at the time of Justinian's reconquest of Sicily during the war against the Goths (AD 547–551).

The confirmation of the shipwreck's mid-6th century date is provided by various ceramic objects, intact and homogenous, surrounding the site, including an oil-lamp that showed clear signs of use. The variety and limited quantity of the different types of amphorae present tend to indicate a military vessel, rather than a commercial one. Greek and Latin inscriptions written on the amphorae are mainly proper names, and include 'Iereus', 'Aimes' and 'vinu(m) Silvani'. The presence of high-quality fine-ware pottery, such as a large African red-slip bowl, confirms the impression of wealth created by the objects on board.

In addition to the numerous wooden objects found at the site, were amphorae, iron tools of every kind – adzes, sledgehammers, pickaxes and pitchforks, pieces of sulphur, a small copper ingot and a sounding-lead. Objects originally stored in the ship's poop – such as cooking pots, frying pans, and fireproof bricks blackened by flames – were found to the eastern edge of the site. A *foculus*, an onboard portable stove used for cooking and providing hot water, seems to derive from the area of the site mound. To judge from the underwater finds, partly buried *in situ* and partly recovered and now exhibited in the Antiquarium of Imera, the cove saw frequent use as an anchorage from at least the 4th century.

A sword underlines the probable military character of the shipwreck, confirmed by stone cannon-balls and by a mysterious stone object that may have formed part of an ancient catapult. Even more difficult to interpret is an iron

The author examining the remains of a strongbox.

Photo: Alessandro Purpura

pipe, set into a massive wooden beam in a U-shaped cavity. This could be a 15th-century cannon, but objects from that period are absent along this part of the coast. A flame-thrower from a Byzantine dromon has never yet been found. This piece of equipment, fed by bellows, could expel inextinguishable Greek Fire (a sulphur-based mixture) from the prow. Interestingly, fragments of sulphur are present on the site.

Greek Fire was apparently used in the Battle of Crete against the Arab fleet towards the middle of the 7th century AD, but seems to have been preceded by an earlier prototype. Nevertheless, in the absence of any irrefutable evidence, a hypothesis of this object's significance cannot be formulated in relation to the Cefalù shipwreck: an actual discovery has not yet been made, even if one can envisage such an eventuality. Any suggestion that the piping structure on the shipwreck is an early 15th-century cannon is unfounded, although the

A cruciform Byzantine iron anchor from the Cefalù shipwreck.

Photo: Alessandro Purpura

theory that such artillery may have been modelled on more ancient armaments seems justified.

A possible future avenue for research into the history of the Byzantine site at Cefalù involves the composition of the ballast, made up not only of amorphous stones (pink granite, micaceous rock, white marble), but also from high-quality architectural elements, perhaps remains stripped from dilapidated buildings. The architectural finds include part of a small column, a capital, the cornice of an *ambo* (pulpit) inlaid with coloured stones now removed, fragments of flagstones, a marble threshold from Proconnesos and a fragment of the drape from a statue's garment. It might be supposed that the large ship, measuring over 30m long and very finely built, was heavily ballasted with an equal amount of construction material that had been abandoned near the dry-docks of the unknown last port of departure following a disastrous event

The absence of concretions on part of the strongbox fragment indicates an earlier salvage attempt.
Photo: Alessandro Purpura

there, such as an earthquake. Shortly after the despatch of the fleet of 300 dromons during the Justinian reconquest of Sicily, under the command of the former functionary Liberio in 547, Constantinople and the adjacent zones were, indeed, shaken by significant earthquakes (in October 541, August 542, April 546 and in February 548).

A portable stove from the Cefalù shipwreck. Photo: Alessandro Purpura

A Byzantine dromon engulfing an enemy ship with Greek Fire discharged through a flame-thrower positioned in the bows. Prado, Madrid, Spain.

© The Bridgeman Art Library

the flame-thrower [*siphon*], girdled with bronze in the usual fashion, through which the prepared fire mixture is shot at the enemy. Topping a flamethrower of this sort there should be a false walk of planks, also fenced about with planks, on which the fighting personnel will take its stand."

In addition to the flame-thrower fixed on to the bows, personnel on some warships used additional hand-held flame-throwers. Up to 20 mechanical crossbows might be mounted along a ship to fire forged bolts known as 'bluebottles'. Another integral feature of the dromon's armament was the catapult used to sling clay pots of Greek Fire at enemy sails.

The Mainz galleys

Other than an extremely important, 35m-long shipwreck recorded off Cefalù in northern Sicily by Gianfranco Purpura of the University of Palermo, marine archaeology has shed no light on the 700-year tradition of dromon ship construction. The closest examples excavated are a cluster of ships discovered in the winter of 1981–2 along the River Rhine at Mainz, Germany, during the construction of the Hilton Hotel. These are now wonderfully displayed in the purpose-built Museum of Ancient Seafaring at Mainz.

The frontier town of Roman Mainz was developed under the elder Drusus as the legionary fortress of Mogontiacum, later capital of Germania Superior. Rescue excavations directed by G. Rupprecht along the foreshore of the River Main, directly under the shadow of the Late Roman city wall, exposed a Roman river port consisting of two basins surrounded by wooden jetties. Excavations along the foreshore uncovered six Late Roman warships. This flotilla had been assigned to the River Main to guard the entrance to the largest tributary of the Rhine and protect the strategic river entrance from German boats and surprise attacks. This site was not only a naval base, but as the discovery of oak wood shavings and woodworking tools proves, was also a shipbuilder's yard.

These warships eventually failed in their duty, as Mainz was lost to a confederation of Vandals, Suebi and Alans in AD 406. At this time, the naval port was converted into a breaker's yard. None of the ships discovered in 1981–2 were intact. The most serviceable sections of the wooden hulls, masts, rigging, anchors, oars and rudders had been removed for reuse.

The Mainz 1 ship gives a clear picture of how these Late Antique riverine ships looked and operated. The 8.2m-long, 1.8m-wide and 1m-high wreck has seven sets of strake planking preserved on the port side and three rows to starboard. Dendrochronological analysis of the ship shows that timbers were felled around AD 376, with repairs attended to *circa* AD 385 and 394. Mainz 1 was a narrow and quick, carvel-built rowing ship, whose 20–24cm-wide planks lacked mortises and tenons. Recesses recorded inside the ship for benches prove that the ship was rowed. This was confirmed by the ship Mainz 4, dated to AD 393, whose internal ceiling planking still incorporated holes for rowers' thwarts.

The Mainz ships were small, 21m-long sleek and lightweight oared

The wooden hull of a late 4th-century AD galley excavated on the foreshore of the River Rhine at Mainz, Germany, and displayed in the Museum für Antike Schiffahrt, Mainz.

Photo: © Museum für Antike Schiffahrt, Germany

Reconstruction drawing of the bilge-pump found on the early to mid-7th century AD St. Gervais B shipwreck off southern France.

Drawing: after M.-B. Carré and M.-P. Jézégou, *Archaeonautica*, 1984

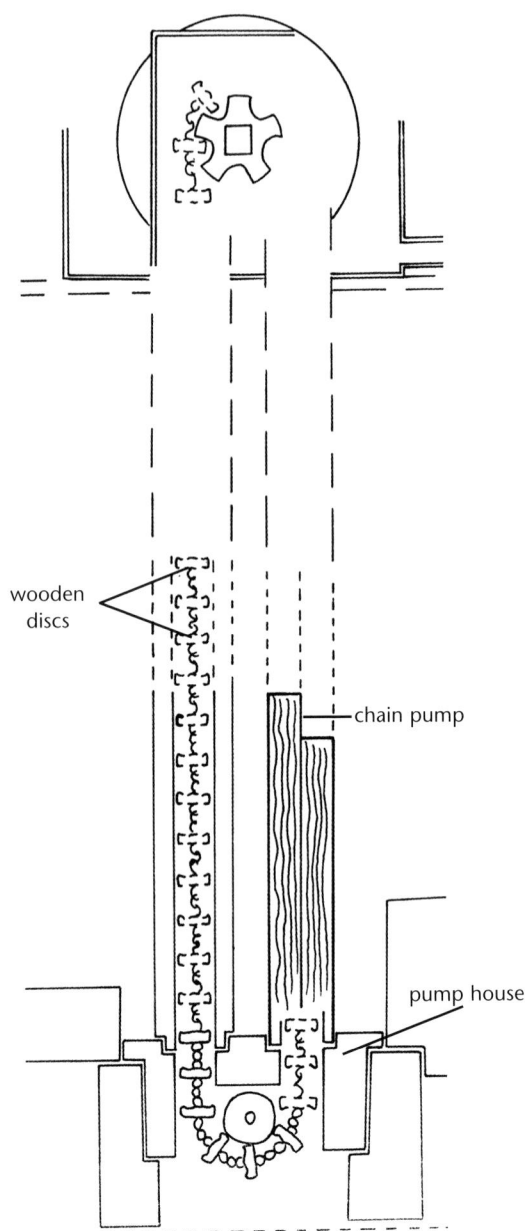

wooden discs

chain pump

pump house

The St Gervais B shipwreck, France

The first and only known shipwreck transporting a primary cargo of corn was discovered in 1978 in 2.5m of water, 200m offshore in the Bay of St Gervais within the port of Fos in southern France. Rescue excavations directed by Marie-Pierre Jézégou from the University of Provence uncovered a remarkably well preserved ship, considering the wreck's shallow resting place. Despite the presence of a half-follis coin on the wreck dating to the reign of Heraclius (AD 611–612), the ship probably foundered later in the 7th century.

A rich layer of organic material was preserved thanks to a secondary cargo of pitch (from coniferous trees) that was used in antiquity as a general sealant, not least for ships' hulls. The recycled North African amphorae containing this resin, probably taken on board in south-west Gaul, had spilled their contents, gluing in place substantial organic remains and protecting them from marine micro-organisms. Covering the back one-third of the wooden hull was the primary cargo of a grain cereal analysed at the ethno-botanical laboratory of the Natural History Museum in London, and identified as *Triticum turgidum*, a free-threshing wheat suited to biscuit baking. St Gervais B held an estimated 3,000 *modii* (21 tonnes) of corn, while the ship's total capacity was 40–50 tonnes.

Other curious finds trapped alongside the hull included the only wooden barrel ever found on a Late Antique shipwreck (32cm in diameter and at least 70cm long, with a 120 litre capacity) and a wooden pump frame that was recovered in an excellent state of preservation. Located low down at the back of the ship, this wooden apparatus was designed to prevent seawater penetrating the hull and damaging the cargo of corn. The pump housing is 55cm long and 18cm wide and pierced vertically with two cylindrical cavities, 9cm in diameter, into which two vertical and hollow wooden cylinders were fixed. Through these ran circular wooden disks attached to a length of rope. When pumped, suction created by the chain pump lifted accumulated water out of the bilge for expulsion overboard. This device could pump 27.5 litres in a single rotation.

The ship's hull was well preserved for a length of 9.5m, a maximum width of 4.5m and to a height of 1m. Unlike the contemporary Yassi Ada shipwreck off Turkey and the slightly earlier Dor D wreck off Israel, this hull was even less reliant on mortise and tenon technology. Unpegged edge-joinery was only used in the structurally vulnerable extremities of the ship, where they were staggered 1m apart. The absence of any edge-joinery between the keel and garboards proves that this ship was largely skeleton-built.

The St Gervais B hull displayed poor design in places. Planks did not fit frames well and in some areas of the hull small pieces of wedged wood were introduced to fill gaps. Another interesting feature was the vessel's mast-step, which rested on stringers nailed to the floors. The ship had a

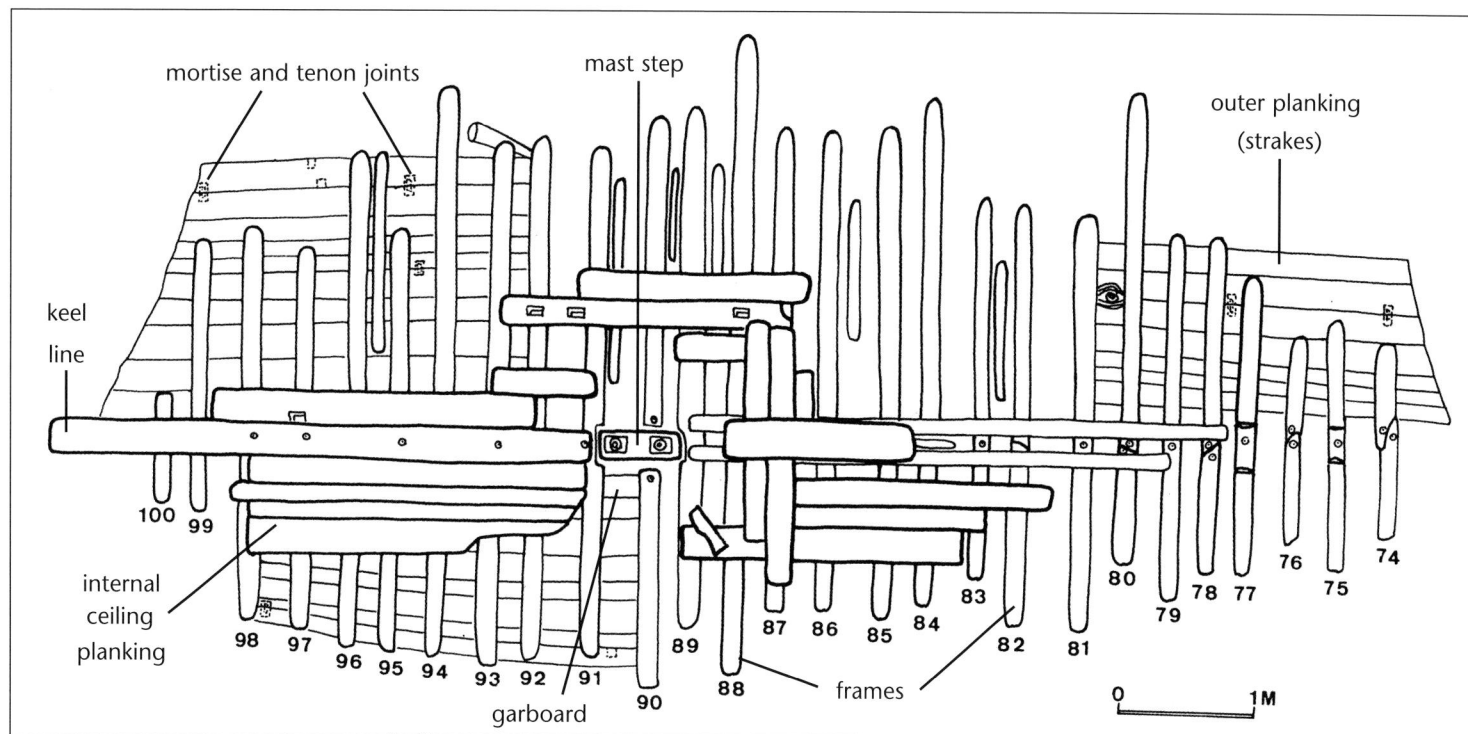

Plan of the wooden hull planking on the St. Gervais B wrecked off southern France in the early to mid-7th century AD.

Drawing: after M.-P. Jézégou, *Archaeonautica* 4, 1984

deep, pointed cross-section with a fine bow and a full stern and is of a shape otherwise unrecorded in Late Antiquity.

In many ways this corn-carrying ship is a mysterious missing link. Although the ship was probably of local design, the presence of North African amphorae, bowls and a lamp hints at the vessel's inter-regional trading orbit. The galley also contained a Palestinian amphora, possibly belonging to one of Syria's infamous merchants who dominated trade at this time.

warships propelled by 30 oarsmen, known in Late Antiquity as the *navis Iusoria*. Their outer planks were slender, 25mm thick, and connected to frames with clenched iron nails. Like the dromon, these craft had no decks, no ram attachments, and included racks for holding shields. However, although they were built shell-first, apparently with outer planks assembled with wooden pegs before the insertion of frames, any similarity with the dromon ends there. The Mainz warships were flat-bottomed ships designed specifically for riverine transport, whose carvel form of construction was of Celtic (European) heritage. Rather than adhering to Mediterranean units of naval construction, these ships were built using the Romano-German standard of the foot (1ft = 33cm). As fascinating as these craft are to naval historians and archaeologists, their shipbuilding tradition tells us precious little about the Mediterranean dromon.

As the discovery of dozens of exciting shipwrecks continues across the Mediterranean year after year, the absence of types of ships and cargoes that ancient texts confirm were highly important and very common in Late Antiquity is a sobering reminder of how much still awaits detection. One day they will hopefully emerge from their secret graves, but not necessarily. Cloth and silk do not fare well under the sea; and without a heavy veneer of ballast or cargo the mysterious wooden hulls of the Byzantine dromon are likely to have been quickly torn apart by currents and waves and scattered to the four corners of the Mediterranean. With 95% of our planet's depths still uncharted, and with great advances in technology, however, marine archaeologists can live in hope. One day the phantom shipwrecks of Late Antiquity may be forced to give up their secrets.

A full-scale reconstruction of a 4th-century Late Roman troop transporter in the Museum für Antike Schiffahrt, Germany, based on hulls excavated at Mainz.

Photo: © Museum für Antike Schiffahrt, Germany

VI. Ports: beacons of hope in seas of trouble

Rome had always prided itself on its gleaming marble cities studded across the empire, symbols of civilisation. Closely linked to this vision was the Empire's desire to tame the seas through a sophisticated chain of artificial ports, whose welcoming lighthouses perpetually flickered across the Mediterranean and the annexed provinces. From the timber-lined docks of Londinium to the monumental, ordered harbours of Ostia, Alexandria and Caesarea Maritima, no expense was spared in using the finest raw materials and state-of-the-art technology, particularly large wooden chests sunk using hydraulic concrete (*pozzolana*) imported from the Bay of Naples.

The transformation of the ports of Late Antiquity was in many ways more radical than the changes that affected the ships of the period. Inexplicably, some of the great maritime gateways of the old empire simply crumbled into ruins. This pattern can be traced at most major ports to which modern marine archaeology has turned its gaze. Thus, following the 4th-century earthquake of Alexandria, the port's quays and breakwaters were left to wrack and ruin. King Herod's late 1st-century BC port of Caesarea in Palestine suffered a similar fate, subsiding beneath the waves perhaps as early as the 2nd century AD, to become a civic embarrassment. Since there is no shadow of a doubt that both cities remained thriving urban landscapes in Late Antiquity as capitals of their provinces, or that both ports still processed huge volumes of trade, how can we explain this bizarre state of affairs?

Ships in the harbour of the port of Classe, Ravenna, on a 6th-century wall mosaic at the Church of Sant' Apollinare Nuovo.

Decline and fall in the ports of Late Antiquity

Caesarea – a port unfit for an empire?

Sebastos, the Roman port of Caesarea Maritima, was the largest artificial harbour constructed in Palestine until the 19th century and represents Roman technology at its most brilliant. Other than through Franck Goddio's intensive research beneath the harbour of Alexandria, the seasonal excavations conducted at Caesarea since 1960 have painted the most detailed picture available of the anatomy of a large-scale Roman port. Research missions have included excavations directed by the Link Expedition (1960), the Underwater Exploration Society of Israel (1960s), the Caesarea Ancient Harbour Excavation Project (CAHEP), and the Combined Caesarea Expeditions (CCE), which continued annually until 2002 under the exemplary direction of the late Professor Avner Raban (Recanati Institute for Maritime Studies, University of Haifa).

The earliest section of the port was conceived around a small natural bay located opposite a single islet that was enclosed by an artificial sea wall and a round tower to create a segment of the *limen kleistos* (closed port) of Straton's Tower around 275 BC. The natural bay was later excavated under King Herod's initiative to create the inner harbour, a rectangular space 100m long and 40m wide, enclosed by a 2.6m-wide and 1.65m-high rubble-and-concrete quay equipped with mooring-stones. The build-up of excess silt was combated using a flushing channel over 1.4m wide. (When opened, flushing channels force a strong flow of seawater across strategic points of harbours, creating a current flow that washes sediment overlying a seabed out of the harbour mouth.)

The construction of the Herodian harbour, which was inaugurated in 9 BC, offered the great architectural minds of the age a huge challenge owing to the

Aerial view of the Roman city of Caesarea Maritima in Israel, looking north across the theatre and hippodrome towards the main breakwaters of the port of Sebastos.

© Hanan Isachar/CORBIS

A Roman quay and bollard in the inner harbour of Caesarea Maritima, Israel.

Photo: Sean Kingsley

site's absence of major offshore islets, whose physical stability would be a natural foundation on which to start building a breakwater. The first phase of the ingenious plan involved constructing a string of strategic offshore artificial islands along the proposed line of the south and north breakwaters. Three of these have been excavated by Professor Raban and his team along the main mole. Their method of construction required assembling wooden 'settling-barges' on land, measuring up to 14m long and 7m wide, following a methodology described by Vitruvius. These were towed into position at sea and filled with hydraulic cement, which solidified when in contact with water, forcing the wooden boxes to sink on to a pre-prepared layer of stone rubble that prevented currents undercutting and eventually tilting the structure. Once the artificial islands were in position, additional settling-barges were sunk in a line until a complete segment of breakwater was formed. This foundation served as the base for building the port's superstructure of quays, warehouses and promenades.

Remnants of wooden casing preserved on the outer surfaces of vertical-sided concrete blocks have been examined in detail at Caesarea. Samples of the wooden planking collected by CAHEP have provided radio-carbon readings of 1,970 years BP (Before Present), leaving little doubt that they are related to the original Herodian master-plan. The construction of the wooden 'settling-barges'

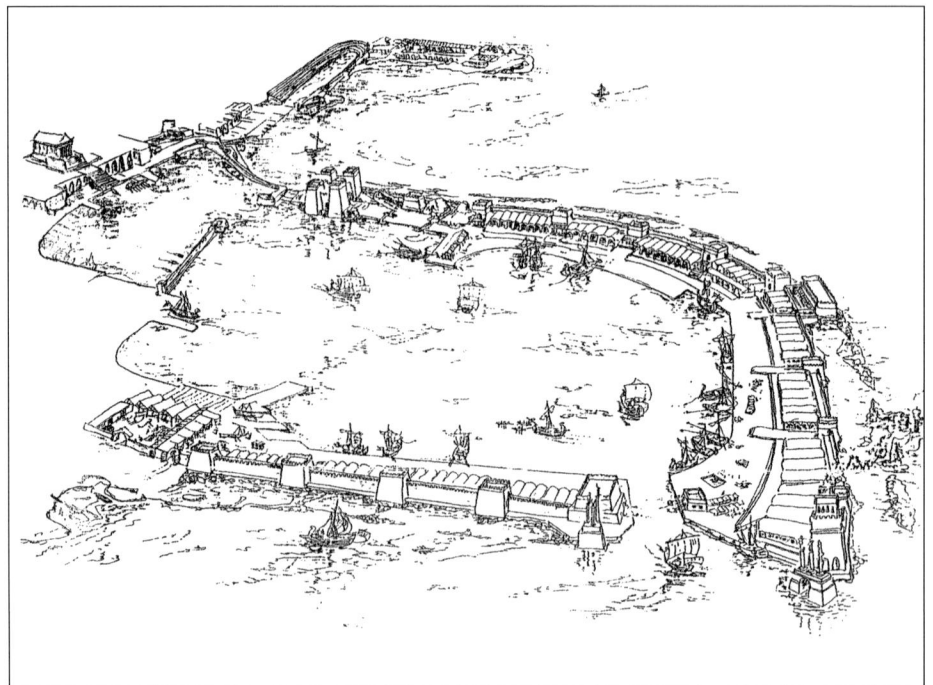

Artist's reconstruction of the port of Caesarea Maritima in the late 1ˢᵗ century BC and 1ˢᵗ century AD, showing the breakwaters covered with warehouses

From A. Raban, 'The Heritage of Ancient Harbour Engineering and the Levant'. In V. Karageorghis and D. Michaelides (ed.), *Proceedings of the International Symposium Cyprus and the Sea*, Nicosia, 1995, p. 183

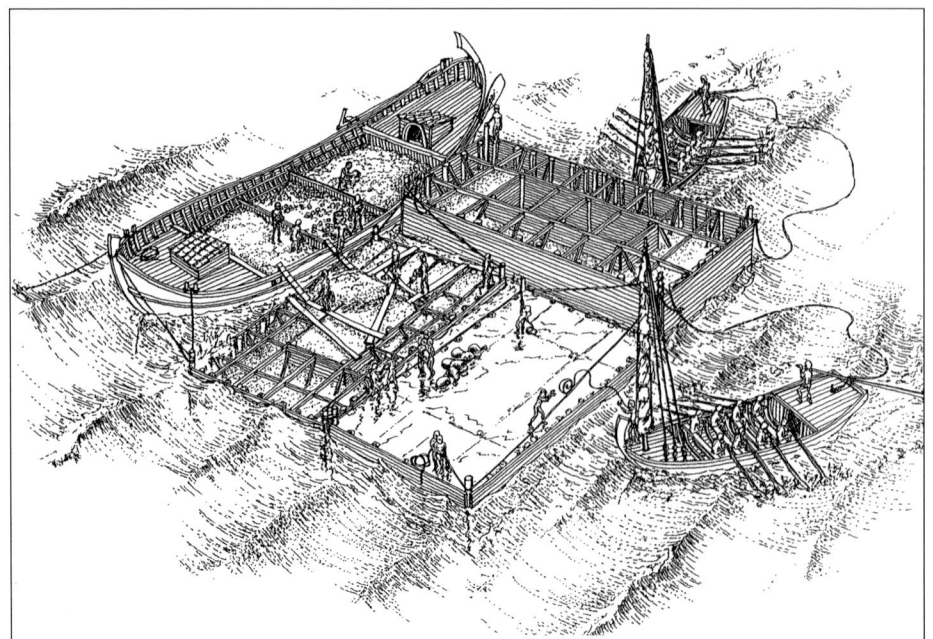

Artist's reconstruction of the breakwaters of Caesarea being built during the late 1ˢᵗ century BC using wooden caissons filled with hydraulic concrete and then allowed to sink.

Drawing: Chris Brandon from Raban, 1995, op. cit., p. 177

An archaeologist uncovers the cargo of the mid-6th century AD La Palud shipwreck, southern France. The ship contained some Palestinian amphorae that would have passed through the port of Caesarea in Late Antiquity.

Photo: Philippe Foliot, CNRS-CCJ, Aix-en-Provence

has particularly impressed archaeologists and naval historians. Planking used to build their outer shells was skilfully assembled, exploiting the shell-first Mediterranean shipbuilding technique whereby horizontal lines of planks were joined to overlying strakes by mortises and tenons, locked in place with short wooden pegs. The attention to detail can be seen in the close spacing between mortise and tenons: distances of 7cm between the locking wooden pegs may be compared with the spacing of 13–14cm recorded on a contemporary late 1st-century BC merchant vessel of 35m excavated at north Caesarea. Such close spacing must have required great investment of time to try and guarantee that the settling barges did not rupture under the weight of the hydraulic concrete.

The raw materials used in assembling these settling-barges again underlines the monumental scale of investment. The wood sampled by archaeologists proved non-local and included imports of European oak, pine and poplar. Analysis of the composition of the hydraulic concrete, which was poured into the wooden casings, has established that the volcanic material (*pozzolana*) that produced the hydraulic properties of the concrete was quarried and imported from a source near the Bay of Naples.

The completed harbour of Sebastos encompassed an enclosed area of about 20 hectares within two pincer-like breakwaters. The southern one was about 500m long and 70m wide, the northern 240m long and 60m wide. Potentially weak sections of the breakwater, constantly buffered by the heaviest winter waves, were strengthened by bonding ashlar stone masonry together with iron clamps sealed with molten lead. A freestanding secondary mole (the *prokumatia*), measuring about 130m in length and 40m in width, was built between 20–30m west of the southern breakwater with the single function of minimising the impact of incoming storm waves hitting the main breakwaters, overlying quays and warehouses. The harbour entrance was 85m wide and flanked on either side by colossal statues set on columns, according to the Jewish historian Josephus Flavius. Excavations on the southern side of the harbour entrance have uncovered additional evidence of what is most logically interpreted as a lighthouse.

So how was this great port maintained and renovated in Late Antiquity? The first point to emphasise is that the Byzantine city of Caesarea, metropolis of Palaestina Prima, was scaled up significantly in comparison to the Roman town. New city walls built in the 4th or early 5th century encompassed twice the area of the former Roman fortifications; and the volume of freshwater conveyed to the city was doubled by the construction of a high-level aqueduct. Major structures excavated within the city include a wealthy town house or possible palace (complete with landscaped gardens), the imperial tax office, a synagogue, and bathhouses. Retail trade and industry flourished side by side. Craftsmen specialised in the manufacture of decorated marble *opus sectile* wall panels, and a glass workshop existed under the cool shadow of the city wall. According to the *Expositio Totius Mundi et Gentium*, a Mediterranean-wide manual of the wealth of the empire published in AD 359, Caesarea also specialised in the manufacture and export of cloth died purple. As befitted a coastal city, the fish trade was important. A dense concentration of bones and scales from excavation Area K3 may be related to a fish market, and artificial fishponds have been excavated within the city and in its northern suburb.

Warehouses beneath the destroyed Temple of Augustus facing the Roman port of Caesarea.

Photo: Sean Kingsley

Storage facilities covered more than one complete *insula* (block of buildings) in the south-west zone at Caesarea. Wheat and liquids (wine and oil) were stored in granaries and warehouses. This sprawling mass of storage buildings most probably mainly held local produce, including wine pressed in neighbouring estates, and wheat processed in the large flour-mills located several kilometres north of Caesarea at the mouth of the Crocodile River, which were powered by a 486 hectare water reservoir contained behind a 190m-long and 6m-wide dam. Caesarea was without doubt the very model of a great city in Late Antiquity.

Despite this evidence of grand trade and high capital investment in the architectural fabric of the city, the port itself seems to have been deliberately neglected. As early as 1960 Fritsch and Ben-Dor of the Link Expedition related the submergence of Sebastos' breakwaters by 5–6m beneath the sea to an earthquake of AD 130. However, Professor Raban has recorded subtle traces of 23 ships that grounded, or jettisoned material, on to the dangerous, partly submerged Roman breakwaters. These discrete clusters include two sites of late 2nd to late 3rd century origin. Additional wreckage, containing four lead ingots dating to the late 80s or early 90s of the 1st century AD, has been located overlying remnants of the submerged tower bases that flanked the harbour entrance at the tip of the southern breakwater. In other words, the submergence of the Roman harbour due to tectonic slumping may have occurred within 100 years of the port's inauguration and thus even earlier than the earthquake of AD 130.

And so the skeletal bones of a once great port were ignobly left to the ravages of looters, time and storm waves. Even though the tonnes of imported Syrian, Aegean and North African amphorae excavated across the city prove beyond a shadow of a doubt that the harbour remained Palestine's primary maritime gateway into the mid-7th century AD, the prevailing archaeological picture is of a harbour significantly reduced in size and complexity compared with King Herod's master plan. No attempt seems to have been made to sustain a closed artificial basin.

Oddly, the facts on the ground do not tally with the words of an ancient historian. Procopius of Gaza did record a renovation in Caesarea's harbour in the early 6th century, under the Emperor Anastasius I, that was initiated because the "harbour of the city named after Caesar had disintegrated through age, and lay open to every threat of the sea. Its structures no longer measured up to the category of harbour, but of its former condition it kept its name alone... But by your will the city is rejuvenated, boldly receives ships, and is full of supplies."

This testimony confirms that the Anastasian renovation was an official state project, but where exactly are its physical remains? As with many historians, Procopius seems to have exaggerated and overglorified Anastasius' impact. The only evidence of this building programme found underwater is stone rubble tipped over the submerged northern breakwater to create a mole crossing and closing the original harbour channel and covering the northern end of the southern breakwater. The discovery of large stone blocks overlying rope and wooden beams in the former Roman harbour entrance may be the remains of

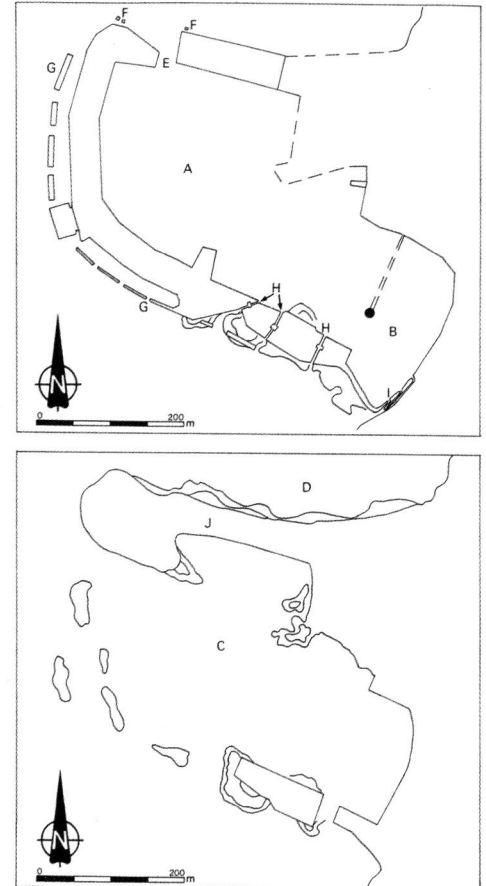

Plan of the port of Caesarea in the Roman period (top) and in Late Antiquity (below). A. Roman harbour basin; B. inner harbour; C. partly sheltered harbour basin in Late Antiquity; D. secondary anchorage in Late Antiquity; E. Roman harbour mouth; F. Roman statue bases; G. Roman *prokumatia* (free-standing secondary mole); H. Roman flushing channels; J. the Anastasian renovation of the breakwater.

Drawing: Sean Kingsley after Holum and Raban (ed.), *Caesarea Maritima. A Retrospective after Two Millennia* (Leiden, 1996)

cradles used to manoeuvre the stones into position. Professor Raban's excavations also hint that the renovation may have included the dredging of the harbour floor and the removal of some old, submerged walls, which had become dangerous to port traffic.

A complementary picture of port decline has been traced within the Inner Basin, which may have started to silt up from AD 70. Certainly, by the first half of the 3rd century the southern sea-wall protecting this basin was breached, the anti-silting flushing channel was blocked, and large quantities of sand, shingle, organic domestic refuse and pottery were deposited across the harbour floor. A source of great city pride in the Roman period, in Late Antiquity Caesarea's cosmopolitan citizens had become used to a ruined port in their midst and must have settled for more natural ways of transferring merchandise from ship to shore.

Dor – ruler of the seas?

A few hours' camel ride north of Caesarea Maritima (13km), Roman Dor straddled a huge promontory overlooking the best natural port in Palestine. This city of Biblical origin has a very long maritime heritage, proven by numerous underwater surveys conducted since 1976 by Shelley Wachsmann and Kurt Raveh (Israel Department of Antiquities and Museums, 1976–1985), Avner Raban and Ehud Galili (Institute for Maritime Studies, Haifa University), and by the author and Kurt Raveh (Dor Maritime Archaeology Project, 1987–1992). Its waters contain hundreds of Middle and Late Bronze Age stone anchors (1800–1100 BC) and at least 17 shipwrecks of Canaanite, Greek, Roman,

Plan of the Roman harbour in the North Bay, Dor, Israel. 1. Coastal warehouse; 2. Location of two mooring-stones. Solid circles show the locations of Byzantine pottery in the bay.

Drawing: Sean Kingsley

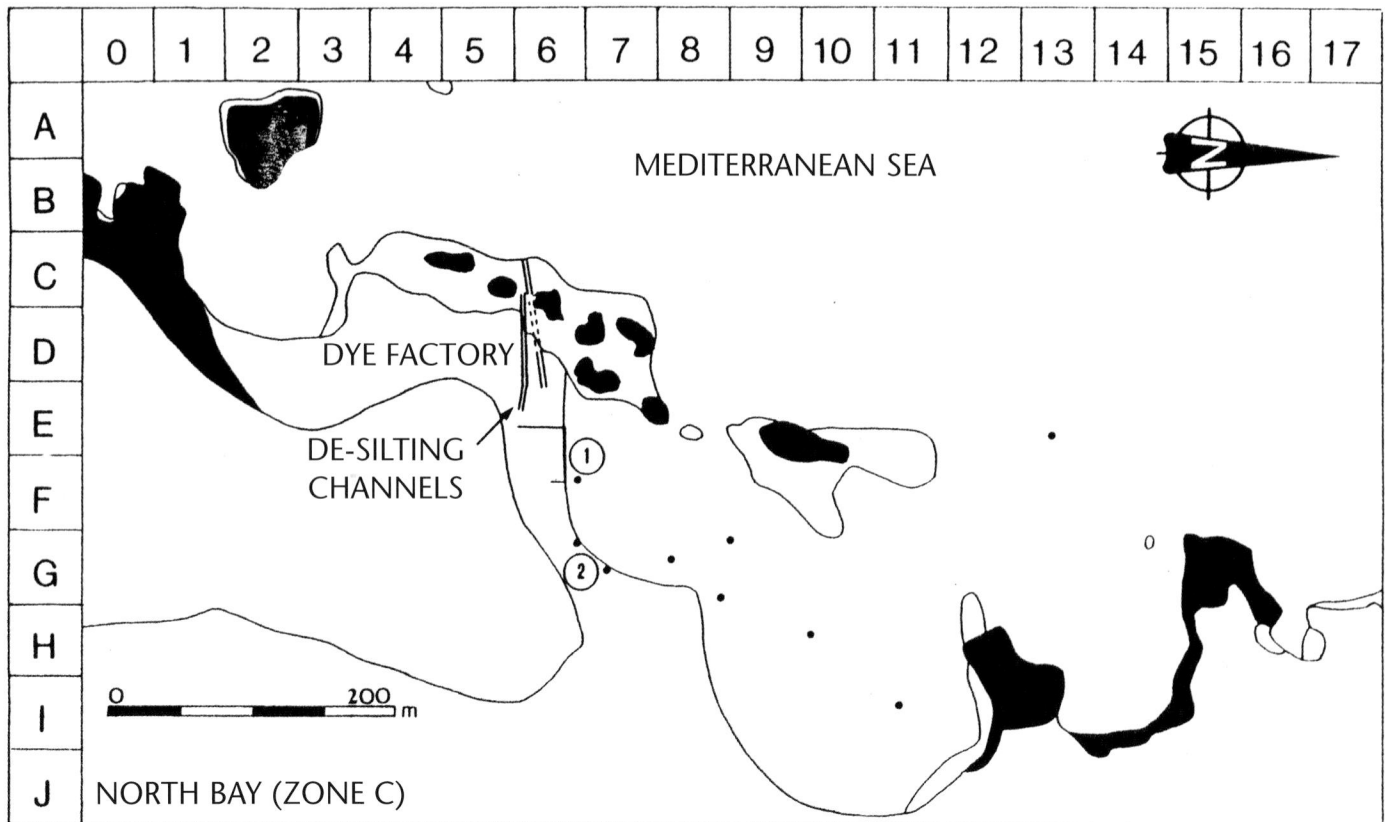

MEDITERRANEAN SEA

DYE FACTORY

DE-SILTING CHANNELS

NORTH BAY (ZONE C)

The North Bay Roman harbour at Dor, Israel. View across a de-silting channel and warehouse towards a quay.

Photo: Sean Kingsley

Byzantine and Ottoman date. Both the Roman and Late Antique cities were renowned for their trading vitality, specialising in purple dye and wine production. A mark of Dor's commercial prowess was acknowledged by coins issued under the Emperors Trajan (AD 98–117) and Julia Domna (AD 193–211), inscribed with the extremely rare title NAYAPXIC, 'Ruler of the Sea'. But for how long did the city retain this maritime mark of distinction?

During the 1st and 2nd centuries AD, the fruits of Dor's fertile hinterland were exported from a partly artificial harbour situated in the North Bay, a 275 x 185m anchorage that exploited a natural limestone reef running parallel to the beach, with an opening to the north. Sheltered in the south-east corner of this bay was a 37 x 35m storeroom and three rock-cut channels cut across the natural reef breakwater to control the flow of seawater into the harbour. When opened, a current could be created artificially within the bay, flushing excess silt out of the harbour entrance.

In 1985, Kurt Raveh recorded a quay extending northward from the storeroom to the centre of the bay, where it turned into the sea and ended at a large structure, possibly a tower or a lighthouse. Two heavy mooring-stones were built into the top horizontal surface of the quay wall. However, as at Caesarea this design was not destined to outlive the Roman period. Following a rise in sea level by 70–80cm, these limited harbourworks seem to have become flooded after the early 3rd century.

What was the response of the city's proud Byzantine traders? In reality, very little: the town's occupants simply abandoned the North Bay and returned to the South Bay, where underwater surveys and excavations have shown that ships had moored behind a 960m-long chain of offshore islets for at least 1,500 years previously. As at Caesarea, archaeology observes a society abandoning a remodelling of the landscape in favour of natural solutions to shipping. The message is clear: an artificial port was a preference in antiquity, not a necessity.

Mooring-stone sitting on the top of a Roman quay in the harbour of the North Bay, Dor.

Photo courtesy of Kurt Raveh

139

Kenchreai – the port of Corinth frozen in time

Kenchreai, the eastern port of the city of Corinth, lies at the bottom of the Isthmus of Corinth on the Saronic Gulf, where it controlled communication with the Aegean, the Black Sea and eastern Mediterranean in the Graeco-Roman world. For decades, the eerie outlines of submerged buildings in shallow waters have been known, evidence of localised coastal subsidence. The Roman harbour was a large, oval artificial installation, whose two breakwater arms enclosed 30,000m^2. Its southern mole was 85m long and the overall harbour's greatest length was 450m. Within its inner reaches the sea descends to depths of 25m, affording excellent anchorages. All around the port was a busy mercantile quarter of commercial fish-tanks and storage facilities.

Behind the warehouses, along the south-western fringe of the harbour pier, is a partly submerged structure notable for its apse, so that in outline it resembles a church. Local villagers have long identified this as the traditional site of the Church of St Phoebe. Yet to archaeologists, this building seemed to promise little because the building's walls had evidently been heavily plundered in antiquity.

When divers from a team directed by Robert L. Scranton and the Universities of Chicago and Indiana for the American School of Classical

The submerged Fountain Court at Kenchreai, the eastern port of Corinth, Greece. This apsidal structure was originally a sanctuary dedicated to the Egyptian goddess Isis before becoming a church in the 4th century AD.

Photo: Robert L. Hohlfelder, Department of History, University of Colorado, Boulder

The Fountain Court at Kenchreai after seawater was pumped out in preparation for excavation in a dry environment.

Photo: Robert L. Hohlfelder, Department of History, University of Colorado, Boulder

Studies at Athens turned their attention to this building in 1963, little more than one course of masonry survived above floor level. Nevertheless, perhaps this 'church' would help clarify the port's trade links and help explain how Greek and Oriental cults coexisted at Kenchreai and how Christianity finally absorbed them.

In view of the church's poor condition, the team's divers were surprised to find a flight of steps descending 1.5m beneath an upper floor to a second, lower floor decorated with a well-preserved geometric mosaic pavement. Even more unexpected was a layer of glass sheet preserved above the mosaic, cut into various shapes including river birds walking among lotus and papyrus plants, as well as a man riding on a crocodile.

In the summer of 1965, this apsidal structure was reopened and excavated dry, by pumping out the shallow water. The mosaic was exposed complete, as well as an octagonal basin that originally supported a fountain. Despite its humble appearance, this building (now dubbed the 'Fountain Court') turned out to be one of the most exciting coastal structures ever excavated within a port. The debris filling the room contained extensive wooden furniture veneered with elaborately incised tortoise shell and carved ivory. More amazing still was the discovery of eight concentrations of glass sheet leaning against three sides of the building.

Further exploration revealed that these sheets were very rare examples of *opus sectile* wall mosaic panels just over 2cm thick, crafted out of glass rather than the more typical medium of marble. Each panel was mounted on a bed of plaster with a base of large rectangular pottery fragments with prefabricated scenes set in glass above, both geometric and floral. Other scenes depicted fishermen, fish, water birds and a winged child holding a duck, rendered in ivory, ruby red, blue and yellow glass. The most startling scenes depict human figures standing on pedestals, one of which is designated in Greek letters as the Greek writer Homer, possibly facing the philosopher Plato. All around the glass were the remains of wooden shipping crates, which had been stored side-on in nine stacks along the floor and walls of the apsidal room. Some stacks contained four packing crates, others at least eight. In total, an estimated 54 crates were discovered with 120 glass panels measuring up to 1.9 x 1.05m.

One glass panel showing a panoramic view of a harbour provides an amazing and neglected resource for studies of port architecture. As in classical Roman ports, it is lined along the shore with colonnaded buildings (almost certainly *horrea*, warehouses). Agile looking ships attest to the bustle of traffic within this port. Given the Nilotic character of the motifs of the glass panel decoration, there can be little doubt that this art work was crafted in and shipped from Egypt. Perhaps the harbour scene was even modelled on (or at the very least inspired by) Alexandria itself.

In light of our knowledge of Late Antique ports, the puzzle is why these expensive art works were simply abandoned in a storage room in one of the key harbour cities of the eastern Mediterranean. Why were they never recovered from a room that was converted into a Christian church and why was the port apparently left to the elements at the same time? Even though the Nilotic scenes and classical allusions depicted on the glass betray a clear influence and probable origin in Roman Egypt, Homer's features are artistically Byzantine, and radio-carbon dating of the packing crates holding the panels has provided a Late Antique date of AD 320 $\pm$ 150.

At the moment of its demise *circa* AD 375, the Fountain Court must have been a hive of building activity as the buildings of Kenchreai's upper precinct were undergoing extensive renovation. As part of the Christianisation of the city, the Fountain Court (previously a sanctuary dedicated to the Egyptian pagan cult of Isis) was being transformed into a church. All over the building's floors were a red polishing abrasive, heaps of marble tesserae for assembling mosaics, blocks of marble bearing saw marks, grinding stones for polishing marble, and wine jars. One day during this extensive facelift, however, disaster struck. A devastating earthquake shook the Peloponnese, rendering the new glass panels in the Kenchreai storeroom useless. The failure to recover the panels and the abrupt end to the renovations speaks volumes about the decline in the fortunes of port cities in Late Antiquity, which again, as at Caesarea and Dor, was to witness ruins in its midst.

Aperlae – the anatomy of an everyday provincial port

While the great cities of Caesarea and Kenchreai were struggling to maintain their subsiding ports, in reality the majority of the Late Antique shipping around the Mediterranean quietly took place with little fuss in small natural harbours possessing very limited port infrastructure. Just such an anchorage was Aperlae, a Lycian settlement to the south of Turkey that was surveyed by Robert Hohlfelder of the University of Colorado and Robert L. Vann from the University of Maryland from 1996–2000.

The town of Aperlae is isolated deep inside Asar Bay, with its urban core clustered improbably on a steep-sided mountain. With no inland means of communication, and no natural springs (only cisterns thirstily capturing winter rain water), this town could never have evolved and flourished without the fruits of the sea. Aperlae's waterfront would have been busy in Late Antiquity, but highly unremarkable.

The source of Aperlae's prosperity may have been small, but it was certainly lucrative: purple dye. Like many settlements of the eastern Mediterranean, this town's waters were blessed with an abundance of snails, whose gland extracts were the favoured source of producing rich purple dye. Deposits of *murex trunculus* shells blanket Aperlae, with the main dump covering 1,600m². Three large cisterns submerged beneath the sea seem to be

A submerged tank in the Byzantine harbour of Aperlae, Turkey, used for storing Murex before the snails were processed into purple dye. The tank is built of clay tiles and plaster.

Photo: Robert L. Hohlfelder, Department of History, University of Colorado, Boulder

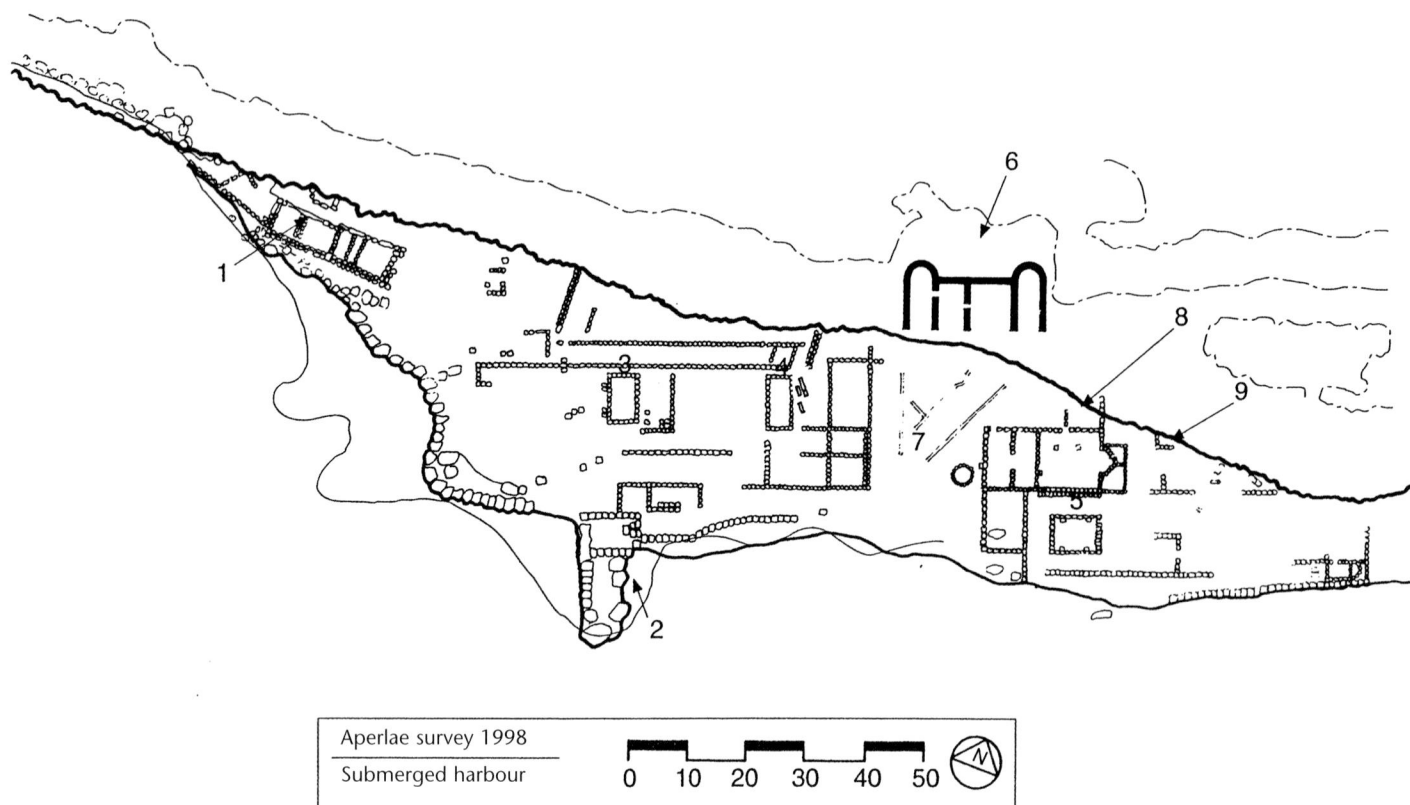

Site plan of the Byzantine harbour of
Aperlae, Turkey.
1: industrial building;
2: jetty;
3–5: *vivaria*;
6: West Bath Complex;
7: open space except for bath drains,
perhaps for storing and repairing boats;
8: church complex;
9: site of large public building.

Drawing: Kathryn H. Barth, from Hohlfelder and Vann,
2000, fig. 8

related to this industry, and it was probably inside these brick and hydraulic mortar *vivaria* with ceramic tile floors that the snails were stored and reared. The harbour zone, today some 2m below sea level, also contained an industrial building and church, where thanks for safe passage by sea could be offered.

The boats serving the town can only have been small coasters that practised cabotage. Cargoes would have been collected and offloaded at Aperlae from a small jetty measuring 22m x 6m from where produce would have been transshipped up the coast to larger, central entrepôts for international shipping. At Aperlae, we could not be further removed from the great ports of Rome, but in many ways we arrive at the commercial heart of the Late Roman and Early Byzantine Empires, where simple, natural ports with minimal man-made installations – traditionally ignored by marine archaeologists in favour of the monumental exceptions – processed the wonders of the world.

The apse of a submerged church in the Byzantine harbour of Aperlae, Turkey.

Photo: Robert L. Hohlfelder, Department of History, University of Colorado, Boulder

Below: Sea-walls and a Lydian sarcophagus along the foreshore of the Byzantine harbour of Aperlae, Turkey.

© Vanni Archive/CORBIS

The technology of artificial ports

Supplementing the frustratingly limited archaeological evidence of artificial harbour-works, historical texts contain short descriptions that fill in some gaps regarding port construction, maintenance, administration and destruction in Late Antiquity. In many cases, the reader is left scratching his head about the meaning of passages, and where detailed accounts of ports are found, archaeologists can only tease so much meaning by reading between the lines.

From a law issued in AD 364 in the Theodosian Code, it is clear that professional guilds still continued to protect people working in seafaring. Here, an edict legislates against 'moonlighters', workers who were not affiliated with the guild of porters (*saccarii*), illegally carting cargoes from ship to shore and into Rome. The government confiscated one-fifth of a cargo from merchants ignoring this law. At Seleucia, the port of Antioch, the *Expositio Totius Mundi et Gentium* describes how the Emperor Constans constructed an immense and reliable artificial port by quarrying the base of a very large coastal mountain and thus bringing the sea inland. This technological wonder awaits discovery.

Most important are the detailed writings of Procopius of Caesarea, who relates how the entire Byzantine fleet could fit into the harbour of Stagnum in North Africa, and that entry into the harbour called Mandracium at Carthage was controlled using iron chains. The construction of maritime installations seems to have been relatively common in the 6th century, when Procopius pilloried the Emperor Justinian, who "saw fit to throw much money into certain buildings along the sea, seeking to put constraint upon the incessant surge of the waves. For he kept moving outward from the beach by piling up stones, being determined to compete with the wash of the sea... seeking to rival the strength of the sea by the sheer power of wealth."

Procopius also makes clear that the basic concepts of Vitruvian 'settling-barge' technology, relied on very heavily in the Roman world, was not a forgotten art amongst the artificial breakwaters of Late Antiquity. At Heraeum and Eutropius on the Bosporus, Justinian thus "prepared great numbers of what are called 'chests' or cribs, of huge size, and threw them out for a great distance from the shore along oblique lines on either side of the harbour, and by constantly setting a layer of other chests in regular courses upon those underneath he erected two very long walls... rising from their foundations deep in the water up to the surface on which the ships float. Then upon these walls he threw rough-cut stones... even when a severe storm comes down in the winter, the whole space between the walls remains calm, a single entrance being left between the breakwaters for the ships to enter the harbour." But what does archaeology contribute to the question of artificial port construction in Late Antiquity?

Constantinople – archaeological oblivion

The port life of Constantinople, capital of the Byzantine Empire, today still remains largely a mystery. A combination of the encroaching modern metropolis and limited key-hole excavation has left archaeologists with a frustrating picture of how the capital's harbours evolved, how they were built and when they went into decline. Almost all of our modern evidence comes from written texts.

The city of Constantinople is blessed with abundant anchorages, being washed on three sides by the Sea of Marmara, the Bosporus and the Golden Horn, so that 11 of the city's 12 urban regions bordered the sea in the 5th century. The capital's greatest natural advantage was the large sheltered anchorage of the Golden Horn, where the commercial port and dockyards (the Prosphorion and Neorion) were located. The Marmara coast, however, seems to have experienced the greatest traffic and it was here that emperors Julian (AD 360–363) and Theodosius I (AD 379–395) built two large artificial harbours. Between these two harbours were the great warehouses of the Horrea Alexandrina and Horreum

Map of Early Byzantine Constantinople with the harbours of Theodosius (1) and Julian (2) to the south along the Sea of Marmara, and the harbours of the Prosphorion (3) and the Neorion (4) to the north along the Golden Horn.

After N. Necipoglu (ed.), *Byzantine Constantinople. Monuments, Topography and Everyday Life* (Brill, Leiden 2001)

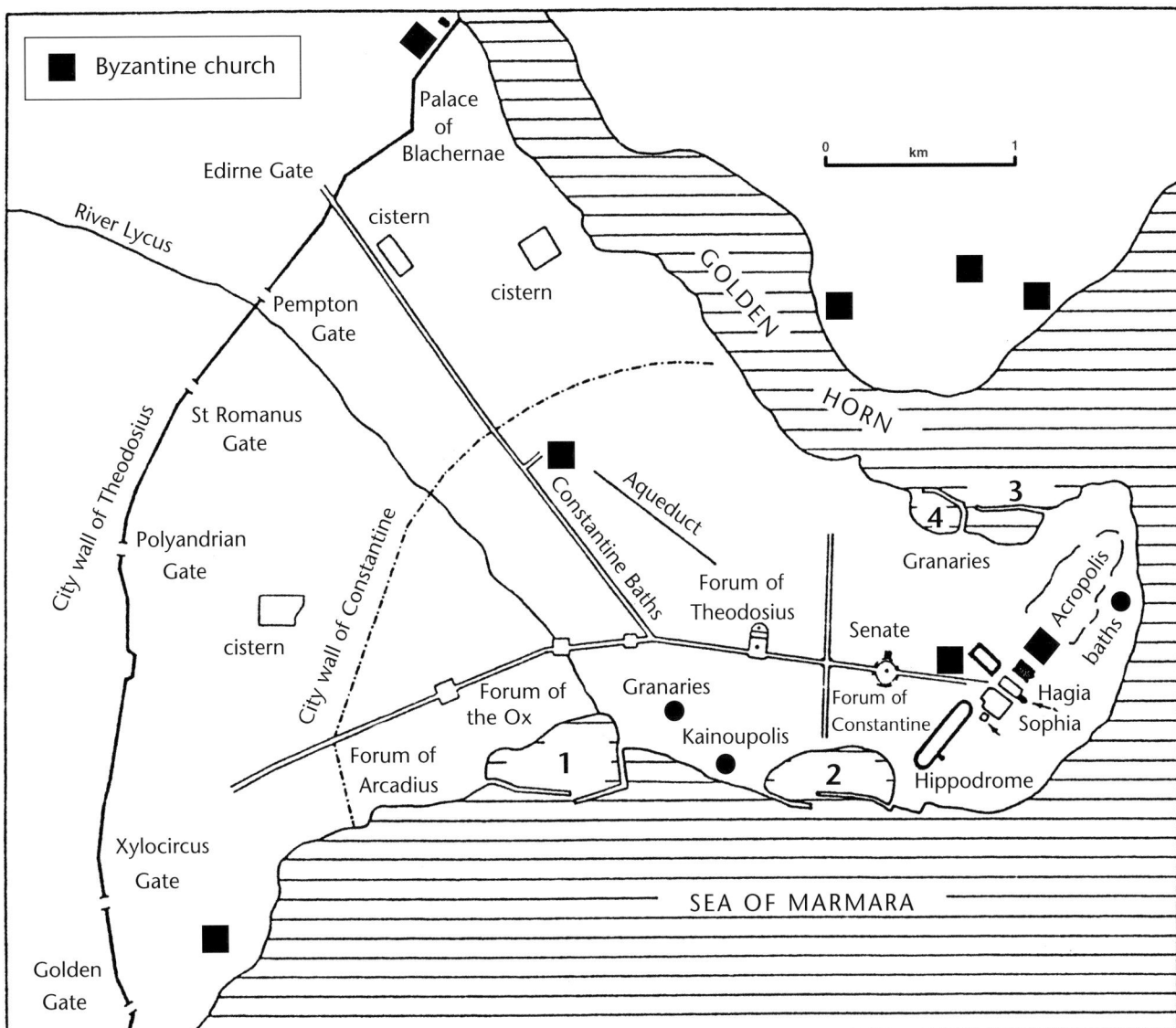

Theodosianum, which handled grain shipments from Egypt. By docking on the Marmara coast, ships avoided the strong currents and headwinds of the Bosporus.

The Harbour of Julian was highly praised by the poet Corippus, who wrote that "One side looks out over the wide sea, the other backwards over the harbour – the harbour formed by the embrace of the arms of the two banks, with walls on top; they make it defy the swift winds, and render the open sea quiet inside the anchorage. They break the waves of the sea with their marble barrier and keep away the waters as they flow back with their narrow neck. The royal pair loved this place; from it they used to watch the waves in the strait and the curving ships carrying all the trade of the world."

Of the four artificial harbours that served the capital, only the Harbour of Julian was maintained during the 5th century, and it remained the centre of the wholesale import market under the Emperor Justinian (AD 527–565). Even though the capital clearly boasted well constructed artificial harbour installations, maintenance was a problem throughout the port's history. The Golden Horn was not flushed out by currents or waves, and even the Harbour of Julian had to be dredged two centuries after its construction. In 556 the harbour near the palace of the Secundianai was similarly emptied and dredged, as was the Neorion in 698.

The acute eye of the marine archaeologist still needs to turn to the waters of Constantinople, if modern urban development has not already caused the large-scale destruction of this grand old city's maritime heritage. The holes in our knowledge about the ports of the capital city of the eastern empire are frustrating. Imagine if we knew nothing of the technology and anatomy of the major ports of Rome. How Constantinople's artificial harbours were built and operated, in reality, remains a complete mystery, shrouded in archaeological oblivion.

The north mole of the Byzantine port of Anthedon, 6th century AD.

Photo: David Blackman

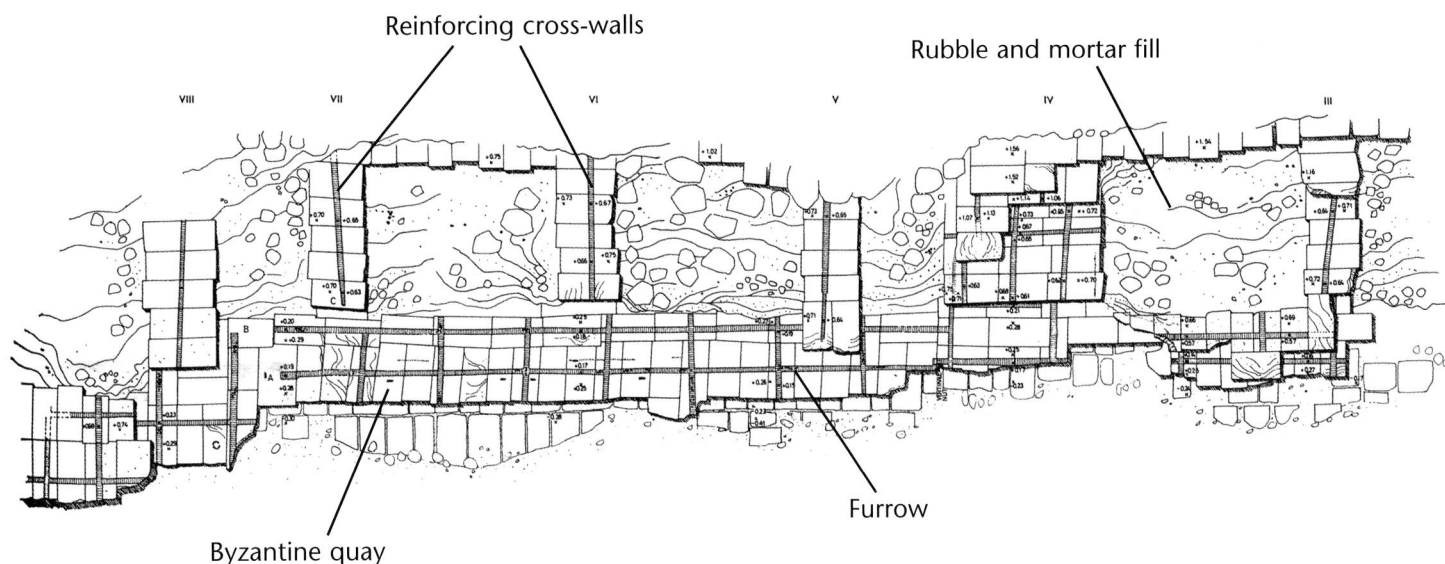

Reinforcing cross-walls

Rubble and mortar fill

Byzantine quay

Furrow

Anthedon, Greece

On each side of a small promontory in Central Greece lie the quiet bays of Anthedon that contain the only recorded remains of a purely artificial Late Antique Mediterranean port. Surveyed in 1966 on land and underwater by David Blackman, J. Schäfer and H. Schläger of the German Archaeological Institute of Athens, the submerged moles preserved to a height of 2m, discovered up to 4.2m beneath the sea, and various quays offer an outstanding opportunity to define just how differently the naval architects of Rome and Constantinople approached port construction.

The harbour basin consists of a huge north mole and a second shorter and thinner mole to the east (poorly preserved). Along the shore sides of each are strewn the remains of quays. The north mole is 165m long and 24m wide at its greatest point and is built of masonry stone blocks measuring between 3.1–3.85m in length. The space between the mole's walls is filled with rubble and hydraulic mortar blending sand, pebbles and broken pottery sherds. This fill is interrupted irregularly by solid stone cross-walls that reinforce the strength of the outer walls. The mole is capped with a stone quay.

The construction style of the south mole is identical to the northern one, with a massive frontal wall and transverse walls filled with a rubble and mortar fill. An astonishing feature of the mole's quay (9.3m wide) is a network of long, shallow furrows (8–9cm wide) filled with mortar, that extend all the way along its length. Mortar seems to have been an essential addition to prevent subsidence and slumping during times of extreme pressure caused by waves, because the quay's masonry seems to have been reused (all the stone blocks vary in height). Thus, the bonding mortar was obligatory to level off the top surface of the quay.

Bird's-eye view down on to the south quay in the Byzantine harbour of Anthedon, Greece; 6th century AD. The quay is buttressed by perpendicular walls creating spaces that were filled with rubble and hydraulic mortar.

Drawing: the German Archaeological Institute of Athens, and courtesy of David Blackman

The technology of breakwater construction at Anthedon is very different to classical port construction that relied on Vitruvian-type wooden caissons and lead and iron clamps to pin stone blocks together. Instead, the stone masonry along the Anthedon moles is bonded with mortar as if on land – a rather crude, land-lubberly form of port construction. Similarly, the 50m-wide harbour mouth seems surprisingly large, as if the kind of care associated with Roman facilities was not extended to Anthedon.

A possible explanation for this construction method may have been a need to build the port as quickly as possible. The harbour was constructed between the 6th and 7th centuries, and all the architecture recorded belongs to a single historical phase. Anthedon was probably designed in the 6th century as part of a wider foreign policy of land defence, to ensure the provision of military supplies to the Byzantine army. The first major eruptions by the Slavs and Huns occurred in 493, 499 and 502, with the first major invasion of Greece in AD 517. A serious Bulgar invasion soon followed in 540. During the last quarter of the 6th century, further Slavic incursions restricted Byzantine control in Greece to a few towns and garrison forts. The rest was annexed as *Sclavinica terra*. Anthedon was probably

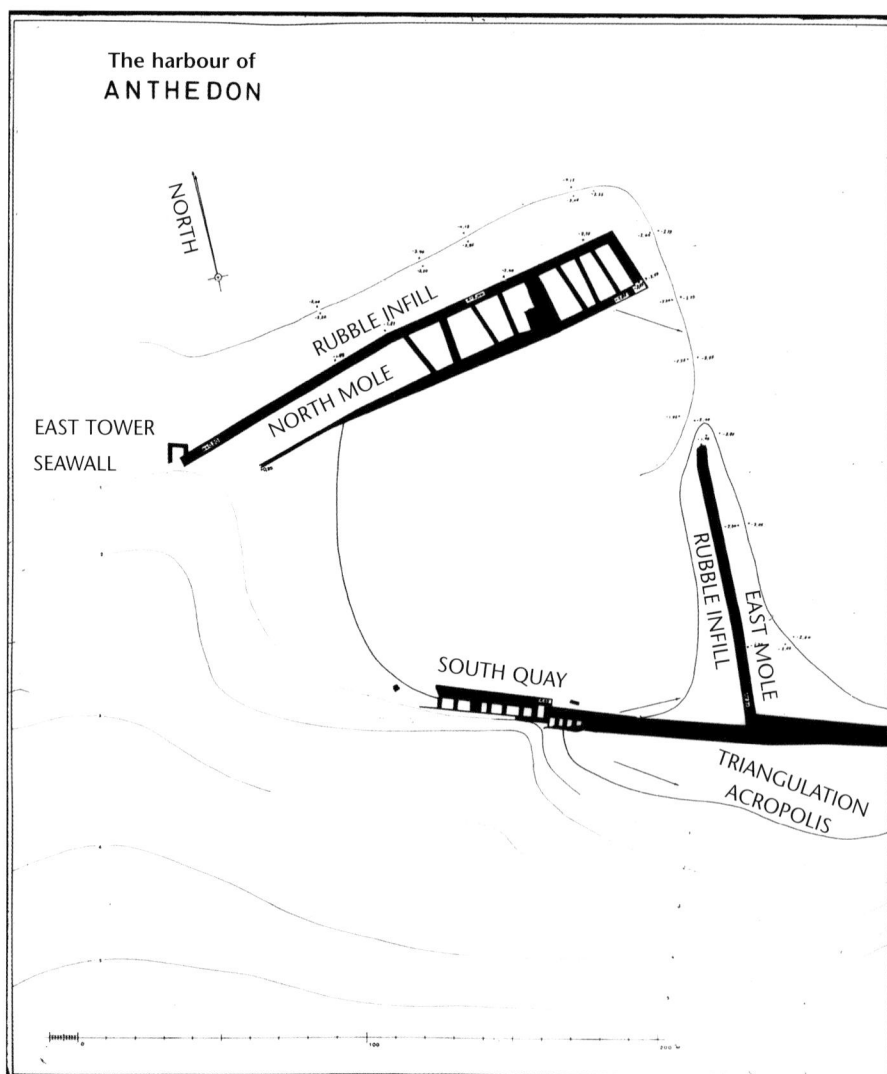

Reconstructed plan of the Byzantine port of Anthedon, 6th century AD.

Drawing: the German Archaeological Institute of Athens, and courtesy of David Blackman

Paving for receiving cargoes along the north mole of the Byzantine port of Anthedon, 6th century AD.

Photo: David Blackman

built soon after AD 540 to strengthen the defence of Greece. The site gave easy access into the interior of Boeotia to which reinforcements and supplies could be sent, and may have served as an important strategic base for the naval fleet.

At some time during the 7th century the breakwaters of Anthedon were abandoned and its short history curtailed. Nevertheless, its architectural legacy lives on to tell us how the Roman and Byzantine Empires' conceptions of port construction, at least in some cases, were worlds apart.

The southern quay in the Byzantine port of Anthedon, 6th century AD.

Photo: David Blackman

Marea – pilgrims' progress

Perhaps the most completely preserved port of Late Antiquity lies not in the Mediterranean but along Lake Mareotis in Egypt. To the west of Alexandria, on the edge of the Libyan desert, is a land known for its great fertility, wineries, oil mills, papyrus factories and abundant pottery kilns. The waters of Lake Mareotis extend up to 70km west of Alexandria, and while the ports of Alexandria, Canopus and Heracleion are today submerged beneath the waves and hard to access, those of Lake Mareotis are brilliantly preserved high and dry, because the lake has dried up to one-fifth of its original size.

Most impressive is the 5th–7th century AD artificial Byzantine harbour of Marea (40km west of Alexandria) that covers an area of 1km along the southern fringe of the lake, and consists of a series of four stone piers jutting at right angles into the water, a causeway, and an enclosed inner port. In one case, a long artificial dike reaches out to a small natural island with a circular, 4m-wide

A stone-built jetty over 100m long in the Byzantine lake port of Marea, Egypt.

Photo: courtesy of Hanna Szymanska and Krzysztof Babraj, the Polish Archaeological Mission at Marea

Byzantine granaries at Marea excavated by Fawzi el- Fakharani.

Photo: courtesy of Hanna Szymanska and Krzysztof Babraj, the Polish Archaeological Mission at Marea

ashlar-built platform identified as a fire beacon. The largest jetty measures 120m in length. The stone seawall is cut by stairs and ramps that offer ease of access down to the water's edge. All of the port is carefully constructed of well cut limestone masonry.

In terms of port architecture, a 5th to 6th century slipway for boat repairs excavated to the west of the port is particularly rare and important as the only known example from Late Antiquity. Here a 20m-long central aisle flanked by perpendicular galleries 7m wide descends diagonally at an incline of 15° into the lake. This dry-dock is built of three courses of headers-and-stretcher masonry, also set obliquely to follow the angle of the lake's shore. A V-shaped trench cut lengthwise along the dry dock served to accommodate ships' keels and to balance vessels within their cradle while repairs were made. The slipway's interior was coated with reddish plaster (as were the jetties).

Marea's waterfront contained a colourful array of urban and commercial buildings, including a fort, cemetery, a double-peristyle church with baptistery, a grain mill, public baths, harbourside shopping arcade and a village with two wineries. Indeed, in the 3rd century AD, Athenaeus praised the region's Mareotic grapes, which were "very good to eat. The wine made from them is

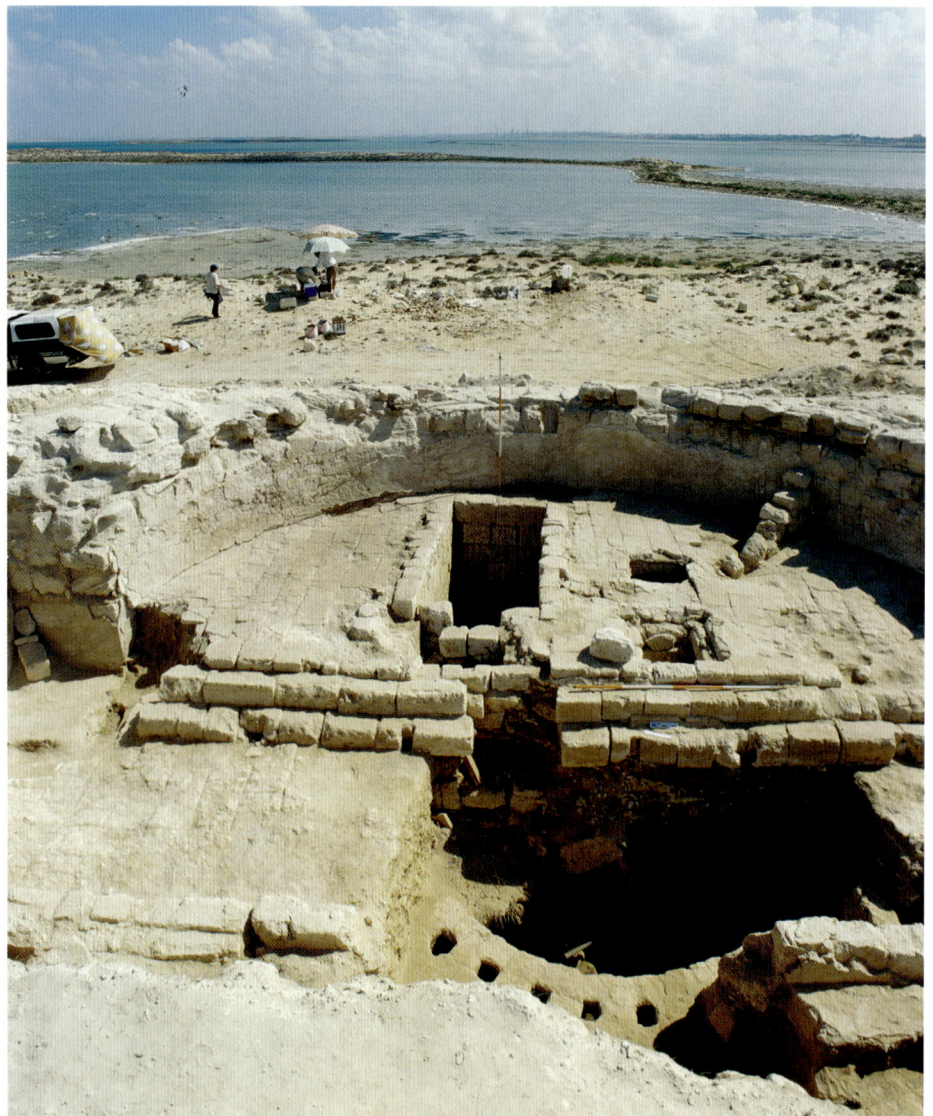

The lake port of Marea with a Byzantine church apse in the foreground (and a Roman pottery kiln uncovered beneath its foundations).

Photo: courtesy of Hanna Szymanska and Krzysztof Babraj, the Polish Archaeological Mission at Marea

A clay flask manufactured around Lake Mareotis, Egypt, and depicting Saint Menas, whose burial shrine at Abu Mena, south of the port of Marea, attracted throngs of pilgrims in Late Antiquity. The British Museum.

© The British Museum – photo: Peter Clayton

excellent; it is white and pleasant. Fragrant, easily assimilated, thin, does not go to the head, and is diuretic." Perhaps centuries of trial and error had improved its taste, because in the Roman era the poet Horace's *Odes* had condemned its produce as heady stuff that induces delusions. Waste scattered across the harbour district suggests that glass was also produced locally.

Marea's attraction for shipping during the Early Byzantine period was greatly enhanced by Christianity: its harbour enjoyed a specific role as the key pilgrim station on the way to the famous shrine and burial place of St Menas, situated 17km south of the town at Abu Mena. The additional role as a military outpost simply enhanced the port's vibrancy. The heavily visited pilgrimage centre of St Menas was a money-spinner, where visitors dug deep to take memories of its holy oils and wines home in locally manufactured clay flasks that archaeologists have dug up throughout the Mediterranean. There is every reason to believe that the Church allocated a healthy part of the lucrative income of this 'pilgrim industry' to Marea for the construction and maintenance of its impressive harbourworks.

Environmental awareness in Late Antiquity

How can we explain the obvious difference between the historians of Late Antiquity, who describe the existence of artificial ports, and the work of marine archaeologists, which has identified a distinct lack of evidence for quays and breakwaters? Even where man-made facilities have been uncovered and recorded, the technology used is always far inferior to that of the Roman Empire.

Part of the problem is a result of our difficulty in dating Byzantine reuse of Roman ports. In many cases, harbour basins simply continued down the centuries, but poor preservation has only left the grand Roman master design visible to the marine archaeologist. The subtle patching and repairs of Late Antiquity are archaeologically invisible.

More specific, however, is the problem of modern perception. Today, we hardly bat an eyelid at television images of the technological brilliance of Rome, of monumental temples, theatres, bathhouses and villas decorated with artistically stunning mosaics and wall paintings, surrounded by gleaming marble statues. Similarly, the scale and huge financial investment injected into massive Roman port projects initiated at Ostia, Alexandria and Caesarea Maritima are exactly what we have come to expect from the great superpower of antiquity.

Yet, these potent pictures of the brilliance of Rome are in many ways anomalies. We now know that there is nothing ordinary in these architectural

Ships moored within the ruined Roman harbour of Tyre, Lebanon, in the mid-19th century offloaded cargo into small lighters that communicated between ship and shore. Similar maritime conditions were common in Late Antiquity.

David Roberts, 1855

Medulin and the Bay of Medulin in Istria, northern Croatia. Natural anchorages like these also contain numerous shipwrecks: 37 Late Antique shipwrecks lie off the coast of Croatia.

Photo: photo archive of the International Archaeological Research Centre of the Zagreb University in Pula Medulin-Brijuni

wonders. Rather, the great artificial ports of the Roman Empire were extraordinary, freaks of an incredibly oversophisticated civilisation. Rather than being built with the single aim of facilitating trade (that otherwise would have been impossible), these super-ports were largely symbols of power, mighty expressions of the wealth of city and empire, and built to signify and promote Rome's world dominance.

If we travelled back in time 2,000 years, we would find that even in the Roman period most harbours were actually humble affairs. The *Periplus Maris Erythraei* (*Nautical Guide to the Erythraeian Sea*), written by an Egyptian merchant in the 1st century AD, describes trade and sea-routes between the Red Sea and India and is the closest surviving equivalent of an ancient manual of nautical terminology.

This document defines a port loosely as a maritime settlement where merchandise is traded, and a harbour simply as the geographical point where a ship can anchor. Neither term was synonymous specifically with artificial maritime structures, and *emporion* (a commercial centre), *epineion* (a satellite harbour of a town), *limen* (a port) or *hormos* (a harbour) were all used to denote natural anchorages in the Roman world, formed by shelter from a natural bay, cove or headland.

The abandonment of the artificial ports of Alexandria, Dor and Caesarea was a reversion to the most common form of maritime communication relied on throughout most of history. So how did shipping operate under such circumstances? First, and most commonly, merchant vessels could anchor offshore, either in an unsheltered roadstead or within a partly sheltered body of water. Communication between ship and shore was conducted using small boats.

Secondly, ships could be beached when not in use, either manually or using mechanical capstans. Modern records of the 19th and 20th centuries show just how vessels of 80–120-tonne capacity were brought to shore in this way. This technique could be facilitated by cutting slipways out of sandy beaches or by using wooden rollers. Finally, it is almost certain that Late Antique seafaring relied on wooden jetties or seasonal moles built from spits of sand, soil and shingle, no traces of which are preserved in the archaeological record.

A highly characteristic feature of Late Antiquity was how society favoured natural solutions over artificial ones. Towns typically recycled old Roman architecture in new buildings, reused marble columns for new art, and felt comfortable with ruins in their midst. The archetypal expression of this ideology is the Arch of Constantine in Rome, dedicated by the Senate to the emperor in AD 315. Rather than being a newly commissioned monument that exploited the finest craftsmen of the day, all of the arch's large imperial narrative reliefs are ancient pieces of art removed from ruined monuments dating to the reigns of the emperors Trajan, Hadrian and Marcus Aurelius. Only the old emperor's heads were reworked to resemble contemporary figures of Constantine and his court.

An artifical jetty built of sand and shingle in Istanbul, 1839. Similar harbourworks from antiquity are never preserved in archaeology.

Drawing: W. Müller-Wiener, *Die Häfen von Byzantion, Konstantinoplis, Istanbul* (Tübingen, 1994, tafel 53)

Similarly, at Caesarea (capital of Palaestina Prima) the town planners actually deliberately repositioned two 500-year-old Roman monumental marble statues into a new Byzantine esplanade as a mark of respect for the city's classical heritage (see p. 6). In the same province, the citizens of Scythopolis in the Galilee left the outer façade of the Roman temple standing for similar reasons. Lack of funds does not explain this behaviour because the cities of the eastern Mediterranean were far wealthier than during any previous period of antiquity.

As with other aspects of Late Antique urbanism, the discontinuity between the Roman and Byzantine Mediterranean ports was largely a result of pragmatism being favoured over monumentality, and not a consequence of economic decline. In this choice the Early Byzantine Empire displayed a far more environmentally friendly ideology than Rome, and in this respect was far more like the modern world than her famous predecessor.

The end of classical port construction

Even though historical texts show that the Early Byzantine Empire could still build large ports the Roman way, with settling barges for breakwater foundations (filled with rubble, but not hydraulic cement), when did classical port construction finally draw to an end?

Following the Arab Invasion, this art seems to have been lost by the 9th century AD. The Arab geographer, Muquaddasi, painted an interesting picture of the construction of the eastern mole of the harbour of Akko in Palestine between AD 868 and 883. Despite summoning all the carpenters and builders living along the coast, nobody could remember how to build an underwater structure. Fortunately, one carpenter recalled an old architect from Jerusalem, Abu Bakr, who was brought out of retirement to direct the work.

This naval architect ordered beams of sycamore wood, which he tied together like a big raft. After this, "…those beams he then caused to be floated on the surface… and upon those beams he raised a structure with stones and lime. After every five courses he strengthened the same by setting in great columns [of marble and granite], until at length they became so weighted that they began to sink down, but this little by little, and finally he knew that they had rested on the sand. Then he ceased building for a whole year that the construction might consolidate itself, after which returning, he began again to build." Abu Bakr was undoubtedly trying to replicate classical settling barges, but hydraulic cement was now unknown and the use of columns sounds a rather desperate and dubious application of this technique.

Meanwhile, further west other evidence confirms that by the 8th century the classical expertise in underwater construction was a lost art. When Anûshirwân initiated maritime construction at al-Barshaliyah in Armenia, the Arab historian al-Baladhuri tells us that "he built the side of it that faced the sea with rock and lead. Its width he made 300 dhirâs, and its height reached the mountain heights. He ordered that stones be carried in boats and dropped into the sea, so that when they appeared above the surface, he could build on them. The wall extended over a distance of three miles in the sea."

These Early Islamic projects are clearly crude by both Roman and Early Byzantine standards, but do appear to have been effective at least in the short term. Should we sneer at the decline in sophistication of port construction in Late Antiquity? To do so would be inappropriately judgmental because, in the final analysis, the genius of the Early Byzantine Empire in the eastern Mediterranean was as great as that of Rome centuries earlier. Ships successfully plied angry seas to deliver masses of basic and luxury cargoes throughout the known world. Historically, the absence of super-ports never impeded their rhythm. Port life may not have looked as pretty or as ordered as in Roman times, but that was a matter of choice and ideology, not one born of necessity.

Base of a gilded drinking glass depicting
Jonah and the whale, of possible Roman
provenance from the 4th century AD.

Conclusion: future frontiers

The modern world generally perceives Late Antiquity either as a time of abrupt cultural decay and fall from cultural sophistication or it judges the period as synonymous with the word 'Byzantine', with inflexible regulations and a labyrinthine bureaucracy.

Even in an age that tends to compress history into easily digestible 'sound-bites', such bad press is ill founded and a picture that modern archaeology has shown to be completely antiquated. Since the Self-Contained Underwater Breathing Apparatus (Scuba) became commercially available in 1948, marine archaeologists have invested thousands of hours scouring seabeds and recording impressive cargoes and complex wooden hulls that have shattered preconceptions about the maritime history of the period.

True, barbarian seas did on several tense occasions run red with blood as civilisations clashed and the political borders of the Roman Empire were divided. Yet most of the citizens of Byzantium, the mediaeval West, and the Umayyad and Abbasid Arab empires never knew what it was like to live under the brilliant glare of Rome, and so never mourned for a lost past. For the consumer of Late Antiquity, fine wines, exotic oils, soft cloth, fragrant herbs and shining marbles were still common currency, obtainable with ease at the local town market. Far-flung provinces were united by a common monetary economy into the 8th century, so that the same coins were useable on the streets of Rome, Vandal Carthage and in the villages of Syria.

The centuries spanning the 4th to mid-7th centuries were an age of unusual economic vitality as the fear of state control over shipping was replaced by unfettered opportunities for a new class of entrepreneur. Although a very wide hierarchy of traders and ship types coexisted, the majority of shipwrecks discovered relate to small- and medium-level trade managed by lower-class merchants and shippers sailing in relatively cheaply constructed merchant vessels.

Hundreds of ships still habitually sailed across the horizon every season to pick up and deliver semi-luxury cargoes, but in craft that were more simply constructed and lacking lead hull-planking. Not because finances were tight, but because of an ideology that was far removed from that of Rome. In fact, archaeologists have proven that historically the bureaucrats of Rome were more controlling and 'Byzantine' than the administrators of Constantinople. If history must judge Late Antiquity, then with its policy of recycling old architecture, adopting natural methods of anchoring in harbours, and of simplifying shipbuilding techniques, the Early Byzantine period was without doubt more environmentally aware and thus more modernistic than Rome or any other civilisation of antiquity.

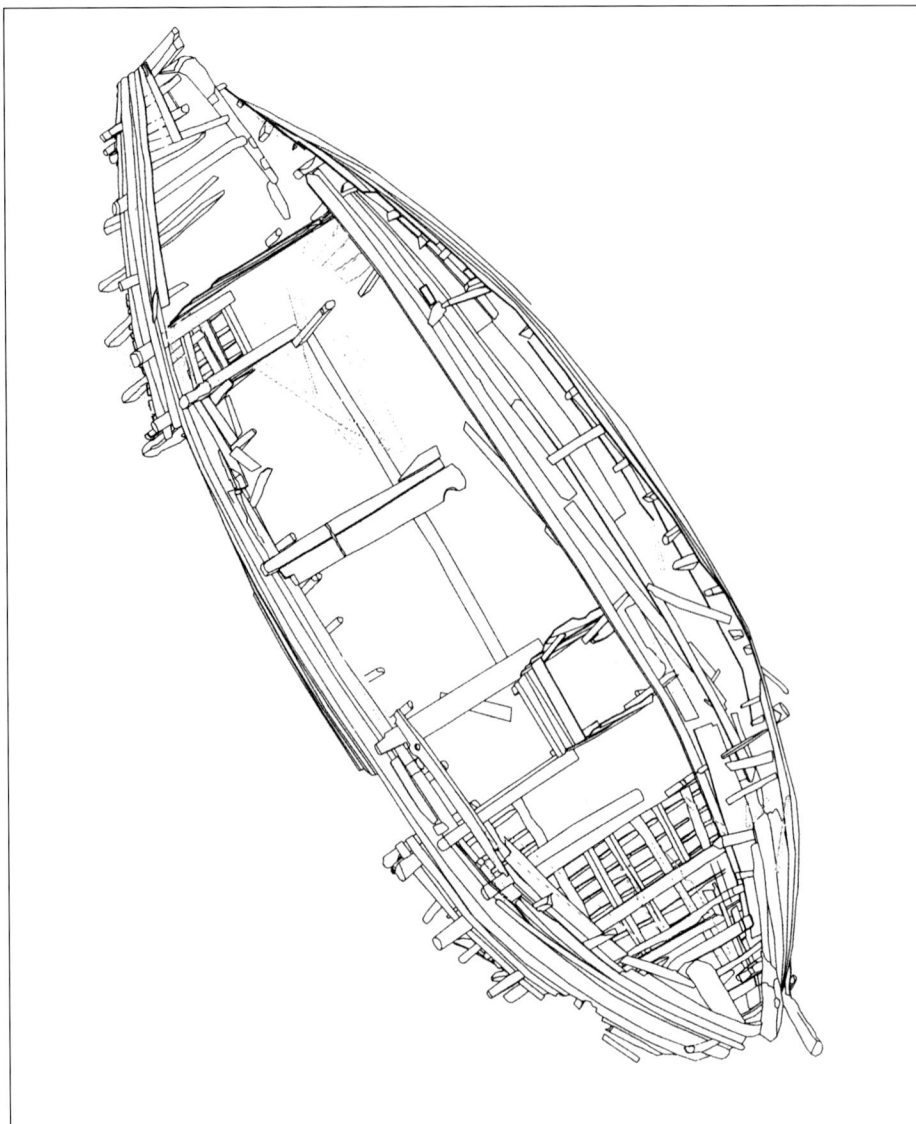

Wreck D in the port of Pisa, Italy, a 14m-long mystery ship awaiting lifting. Possibly an oared galley.

From S. Bruni (ed.), *Le navi antiche di Pisa*, Edizioni Polistampa, 2000, fig. 38

Under the spotlight of the modern media, marine archaeology has obtained an appropriately high profile, so it is easy to forget that mankind still has a huge amount to learn from the depths of the sea. In the last 12 years, remains of 92 shipwrecks have come to light. Just how many more await future generations of explorers?

For the first millennium BC alone, more than 15,000 ships might have been lost in the Mediterranean and Black Sea. Under a booming economy and a highly developed long-distance trade, between AD 320 and 640 some 3,200 ships may have been lost off the Holy Land. Without massaging any statistics, it is clear that thousands of new, exciting sites lie on silent seafloors, so far only visited by unimpressed marine life.

One interesting find soon to reveal its secrets is Wreck D, stranded in the mud of Pisa. This 14m-long oak vessel was exposed in 1999 during construction work by the Italian state railway and remains the subject of intense speculation. Its sides and end-posts are fitted with projecting structures set on large brackets attached above a double parallel series of three beams. The slender prow is sheathed in a form of iron 'ram'.

The ship was found upside-down having turned turtle during a storm and, amazingly, the hatchway leading down into the hold and inner deck are still preserved. This unparalleled type of vessel is yet to be lifted from its silted grave, so its function remains a mystery. Was it an oared galley? Do the absence of mortise and tenon wooden plank joints highlight yet another early example of a frame-first ship of Late Antiquity's nautical revolution? Only time and patience will tell.

In 1950 the planet's population stood at 2.5 billion. Today it has increased to 6.3 billion, and is projected to rise to 9 billion by 2050. As the earth's population level shifts, fewer coastal foreshores and riverine ports like Pisa will survive for exploration. So where does the future of marine archaeology lie?

In the last two decades, robotic technology has entered the marine archaeologist's tool kit. With 95% of the planet's seas still uncharted, ROVs can dive into the abyss beyond 1,000m as the archaeologist watches the depths illuminate from the safety of a research vessel above the waves. The impact on shipwrecks of all periods is huge, and Robert Ballard's discovery in 2000 of four shipwrecks in 90–320m of water on the bottom of the Black Sea has blazed a trail for future exploration.

Meanwhile, advanced research continues. The Deep Water Archaeology Research Group of the Massachusetts Institute of Technology has built a high frequency, sub-bottom profiler, which projects a narrow sonar beam into the seafloor and 'sees' down into the mud. In this way marine archaeologists of the not-too-distant future will be able to generate a three-dimensional model of a wreck by computer without ever physically touching it. Across the Atlantic, the Centre for Maritime Archaeology at the University of Southampton is also working on high resolution, sub-bottom profiling to take images of artefacts buried in up to 30m of marine sediments. Commercial organisations are already excavating ships in 500m of water, with the capability of producing detailed site plans and carefully recovering organic material for sampling.

The future of shipwreck archaeology has arrived, and promises spectacular discoveries that will continue to amaze and thrill us for centuries.

Glossary

Abbasids: Islamic dynasty of Arabic caliphs, AD 750–1517, administered from Baghdad.

ambo: elevated lecturn in an Early Christian church, usually of marble and often elaborately decorated, used for readings of the Gospel.

Ammianus Marcellinus (AD 330–395): the last great Latin historian of the Roman Empire, born in Antioch, Syria.

amphora: two-handled, thick-walled clay vessel used in antiquity to transport foodstuffs.

annona civica: system of free food redistribution (grain, bread, oil, pork and some wine, usually to the poor and specific dignitaries) established in Rome, Constantinople and the major cities of the Roman and Late Roman Mediterranean world. Obtained by taxing the provinces.

annona militaris: system of free food redistribution to the army between the Roman period and Late Antiquity; obtained by taxing the provinces.

Athenaeus: of Naucratis, Egypt, *circa* AD 200. Author of *The Learned Banquet*.

Avars: nomadic warriors who were one of the Roman Empire's main enemies (along with the Slavs) on the Danube frontier in the late 6th and early 7th centuries AD.

ballast: a high-density material, usually of metal or stone (but possibly also sand), positioned in the lower hold of a ship to lower its centre of gravity and improve stability.

Battle of Yarmuk: crucial military encounter between the Byzantine emperor Heraclius and the Muslim army at Yarmuk in Syria on 20 August 636. A crushing victory gave Syria to the Muslims and opened up the Near East for the Arab Conquest whereby the Byzantine Empire lost control of its wealthiest provinces (Syria, Palestine, Egypt).

bilge pump: mechanical device designed to lift leaked water out of the bottom of a ship's hull and prevent inundation.

Byzantines: inhabitants of the Byzantine Empire in the eastern Mediterranean between *circa* AD 330 and 1453; administered from Constantinople.

Callincus of Heliopolis: architect credited with the invention of Greek Fire in the reign of Emperor Constantine Pogonatus, *circa* AD 672.

carvel (ship building): external planks laid edge to edge, without overlapping strakes or mortise and tenon joints. Applies to frame-first technology.

Chorisius (of Gaza, AD 491–518): Greek sophist and rhetorician.

clench nails/clench-built: ship construction technique relying on metal nails or bolts to attach planks or timbers, whereby the projecting end of the nail (after being hammered through two wooden surfaces) is bent back into the wood surface.

Corbita: Roman term for a basic type of merchant vessel with symmetrical, rounded extremities.

cursus publicus: the imperial Roman 'post' system studded with rest-houses and way stations for changing horses.

dendrochronology: dating method based on counting tree-ring sequences.

dromon: Byzantine warship that replaced the trireme as the warship of the ancient world in the early 4th century.

East Mediterranean: geographical term for the lands located between Greece to the west and Egypt to the south.

edge-joinery: horizontal strake interconnection along the outer shell of a ship.

Expositio Totius Mundi et Gentium: mid-4th century AD book describing the wealth of the later Roman Empire.

Euxine Sea: ancient name of the Black Sea, said to be dangerous because of its storms and the inhabitants of its shores. Calling it the 'hospitable sea' was a way of warding off misfortune.

follis: Latin word originally meaning 'purse', used in the Byzantine period for the largest denomination of copper coin, initially worth 40 *nummi*.

frames: transverse wooden ship timbers to which external strakes and internal ceiling planking are attached.

frame-first: method of wooden hull construction whereby internal frames are inserted above the keel transversely to create an internal skeletal structure before the external planking is attached. An innovation of the 6th century AD.

garboard: the first, lowest line of external strake planking attached directly to the keel.

Gibbon, Edward (1737–1794): the supreme historian of the Enlightenment, renowned for publication of the epic work, *The Decline and Fall of the Roman Empire.*

Goths: Germanic people of the later 3rd and 4th centuries AD, who migrated from the Vistula to the Black Sea region in the 1st to 3rd centuries. They launched heavy attacks on Asia Minor and the Balkans in the mid-3rd century. Thereafter, the Goths divided into two cultural groups: the Visigoths and the Ostrogoths. The Ostrogothic kingdom was destroyed by the Byzantines in 20 years of warfare after AD 536.

Greek Fire: highly incendiary liquid projected from 'siphons' on to enemy ships which was almost impossible to extinguish. Allegedly invented by Callinicus of Heliopolis *circa* AD 672.

gunwale: upper edge of a ship's side.

Horace (Quintus Horatius Flaccus, 65–8 BC): Roman poet and author of the *Epodes, Satires, Odes* and *Epistles* under the patronage of Maecenas.

insula: literally 'island'; a block of houses in a Roman city.

kanyr: Late Roman term of container volume in Nubia.

Late Antiquity: historical period bridging the Roman and mediaeval eras, typically the 4th to 8th centuries AD.

lateen (sail): three-cornered sail attached to a yard obliquely crossing a forward-raking mast. Enables craft to sail against the wind. A probable 7th-century innovation.

Lepcis Magna: large Roman city in Tripolitania, western Libya, established as a *municipium* under the Flavian emperors (AD 69–96) and as a *colonia* under Trajan. Renowned as the birthplace of the Emperor Septimius Severus, who adorned the city with numerous rich monuments.

Lombards: Germanic group of the lower Elbe who encroached into the upper

Danube in the 160s AD before establishing independence over Pannonia (Roman province south and west of the Danube) in the early 6th century.

Malalas, John (AD 480–570): resident of Antioch and author of a universal chronicle in Greek, the *Chronographia*.

mansiones: Roman inn houses along road networks.

mare nostrum: literally 'our sea', a term used by Rome to denote its mastery over the Mediterranean Sea.

mortise: a cavity cut into a timber to receive a tenon. Most common on Roman ships along the edges of external strake planking.

navicularii: private shipowners.

The Odyssey: epic poem in 24 cantos recounting the adventures of Ulysses after the taking of Troy.

Nummi (singular *nummus*): Latin term originally meaning 'coin', applied in the Early Byzantine period to the smallest copper coin, 1/40th of a follis.

orthostat: individual piece of stone masonry set vertically.

patera: Latin name for a shallow circular vessel used for drinking or pouring libations.

Periplus Maris Erythraei: nautical guide to the sea-lanes, ports and trade between the Red Sea and India. Written by an Egyptian merchant in the 1st century AD.

pitch: resin derived from evergreen trees, bitumen or tar used to caulk seams between planks and applied across outer hulls for waterproofing. Replaced lead hull sheeting in Late Antiquity.

Pliny (the Elder, 23/4–79): Gaius Plinius Secundus, prominent Roman equestrian, author of the 37-volume *Naturalis Historia*, an encyclopaedia of all contemporary knowledge (animal, vegetable and mineral).

porphyry: Imperial Roman type of purple marble quarried at Mons Porphyrites in the eastern Egyptian desert. Rome's most prized form of architectural stone.

pozzolana: raw material indigenous to the Bay of Naples with hydraulic properties, used in the Roman period for constructing the foundations of moles.

Procopius (of Caesarea): Greek historian born in Palestine *circa* AD 500 and author of the *History of the Wars of Justinian* and *The Secret History*. First-class source for the geography, topography and art of the period, as well as of imperial court life.

Procopius (of Gaza, *circa* AD 465–528): Christian sophist and rhetorician.

radio-carbon dating: system developed by Willard Libby in 1948 to calibrate ancient dates by measuring the decay of carbon in organic archaeological materials.

rake (of a hull): angular profile of the stem and sternpost beyond the ends of the keel.

Rhodian Sea Law: an official seafarers' handbook written and updated between AD 600 and 800, containing legislation advising on the pursuit of private Mediterranean commerce.

ROV: robotic remotely-operated vehicle used by marine archaeologists to access deep-water shipwrecks. Equipped with still cameras and video to broadcast live images of a seabed.

Sasanians: inhabitants of the kingly dynasty of Iran from AD 224–651. At times their empire stretched from Syria to India and from Iberia to the Persian Gulf. Major foe of Rome in the East.

scarf: overlapping joint used to connect two timbers of planks.

***shuktoor*:** Near Eastern term for a specific type of Ottoman merchant vessel.

side-scan sonar: sensor giving an acoustic image of the ocean floor within a band of 50m-150m on either side of the ship. Processing the sonar data produces a mosaic of the surveyed area by juxtaposing geographically positioned bands.

***semissis*:** a one-half *solidus*, a gold coin weighing 2.25g.

***solidus*:** standard Byzantine coin, introduced by Constantine the Great and struck 72 to the Roman pound, thus weighing 24 carats or 4.55g.

sounding lead: bell-shaped object of a lead medium used on ancient ships to navigate dangerous waterways. Thrown overboard to measure the depth between a keel and a seabed; cavities in the base trapped seabed particles to assess its nature and determine navigability and choice of anchor.

spatheia: narrow and tall type of 4th- to 7th-century AD amphora originating in North Africa.

steelyard: Roman and Late Antique weighing device of brass or bronze based on a counterweight system, used on ships to weigh merchandise and guarantee accurate trade transactions.

stem: vertical or upward curving assembly of timbers (joined to the keel) into which the bow planking is attached.

St Jerome (AD 347–420): biblical translator, scholar and ascetic. One of the four Doctors of the Church (with Ambrose, Augustine and Gregory the Great).

St Menas: Roman soldier who converted to Christianity. Died in AD 296 as a martyr after publicly confessing his faith during the annual games in the arena at Cotyaeum in Phrygia. Associated with healing and itinerant trade; buried at Mareotis, Egypt.

strakes: continuous lines of horizontal external ship planking running between the bow and stern.

stringers: longitudinal timbers fixed to the inside surfaces of frames to create ceiling planking.

tenon-built (shell-first): method of ship construction whereby external planking edges are interconnected using mortise and tenons. This traditional Mediterranean shipbuilding technique was used from at least *circa* 1400 BC to AD 650.

Theodoric: King of the Ostrogoths, AD 474–526.

Theodosian Code: collection of about 2,500 imperial laws published in the eastern and western Mediterranean between AD 429 and 438.

Theodosius I (the Great, born AD 346): proclaimed emperor of the Eastern Roman Empire on 19 January 379.

Theodosius II (AD 401–450): son of the Emperor Arcadius, proclaimed emperor in AD 402.

thwart: transverse wooden plank used to seat rowers, support masts or provide lateral strength.

transom timber: athwartship wooden member fixed to the sternpost, shaping and reinforcing a ship's stern.

trunnels (treenails): round length of wood driven through planks and timbers to connect them (such as through a mortise and tenon joint). When submerged in water the treenail expands to create a tight connection.

Umayyads: the first Islamic dynasty (AD 661–750), administered from the capital in Damascus.

***Via Egnatia*:** Roman road built from the Adriatic coast to Byzantium *circa* 130 BC. Main route from Rome to the East.

***vivaria*:** Roman fishpond.

wales: thick reinforcement timber along the side of the vessel for stiffening a ship.

Bibliography

Ashburner, W., *The Rhodian Sea-Law* (Oxford, 1909).

Ballard, R. D., Hiebert, F. T., Coleman, D. E., Ward, C., Smith, J. S., Willis, K., Foley, B., Croff, K., Major, C. and Torre, F., 'Deepwater Archaeology of the Black Sea: the 2000 Season at Sinop, Turkey', *American Journal of Archaeology* 105 (2001), 607-23.

Bass, G. F. and van Doorninck, F. H., 'A Fourth-Century Shipwreck at Yassi Ada', *American Journal of Archaeology* 75 (1971), 27-37.

Bass, G. F. and van Doorninck, F. H. (ed.), *Yassi Ada I. A Seventh-Century Byzantine Shipwreck* (Texas A and M University Press, 1982).

Bowden, W., *Epirus Vetus. The Archaeology of a Late Antique Province* (London, 2003).

Bruni, S. (ed.), *Le navi antiche di Pisa* (Florence, 2000).

Carre, M.-B. and Jézégou, M.-P., 'Pompes à chapelet sur des navires de l'antiquité et du début du Moyen âge', *Archaeonautica* (1984), 115-44.

Casson, L., *Ships and Seamanship in the Ancient World* (Princeton University Press, 1971).

Dolley, R., 'The Warships of the Late Roman Empire', *Journal of Roman Studies* 38 (1948), 47-53.

Galili, E., Sharvit, J. and Rosen, B., 'Symbolic Engravings on Byzantine Sounding Leads from the Carmel Coast of Israel', *International Journal of Nautical Archaeology* 29.1 (2000), 143-150.

Gorin-Rosen, Y., 'The Ancient Glass Industry in Eretz Israel - A Brief Summary', *Michmanim* 16 (2002), 7-18.

Grierson, P., *Byzantine Coinage* (Washington, 1999).

Harris, A., *Byzantium Britain and the West. The Archaeology of Cultural Identity, AD 400-650* (Stroud, 2003).

Hocker, F., 'Lead Hull Sheathing in Antiquity' in H. Tzalas (ed.), *Third International Symposium on Ship Construction in Antiquity, Tropis III* (Thessaloniki. 1995), 197-206.

Hocker, F. M. and Scafuri, M. P., 'The Bozburun Byzantine Shipwreck Excavation: 1996 Campaign', *INA Quarterly* 23 (1996), 3-9.

Höckman, O., 'Late Roman Rhine Vessels from Mainz, Germany', *International Journal of Nautical Archaeology* 22.2 (1993), 125-35.

Hohlfelder, R. L., 'Building Harbours in the Early Byzantine Era: the Persistence of Roman Technology', *Byz. Forsch.* 24 (1997), 367-80.

Hohlfelder, R. L., 'Procopius, *De Aedificiis*, 1.11.18-20: Caesarea Maritima and the Building of Harbours in Late Antiquity', in I. Malkin and R. L. Hohlfelder (eds), *Mediterranean Cities: Historical Perspectives* (London, 1988), 54-62.

Hohlfelder, R. L. and Vann. R. L., 'Cabotage at Aperlae in Ancient Lycia', *International Journal of Nautical Archaeology* 29.1 (2000), 126-35.

Houston, G. W., 'Ports in Perspective: some Comparative Materials on Roman Merchant Ships and Ports', *American Journal of Archaeology* 92 (1988), 553-564.

Jézégou, M.-P., 'L'épave II de l'anse Saint-Gervais à Fos-sur-Mer (Bouches-du-Rhone): un navire du haut Moyen-Age construit sur squelette', in H. Tzalas (ed.), *First International Symposium on Ship Construction in Antiquity, Proceedings* (Piraeus, 1989), 139-146.

Jézégou, M.-P., 'Le mobilier de l'épave Saint-Gervais 2 (VIIe s.) à Fos-sur-Mer (B.-du-Rh)', in M. Bonifay, M.-B. Carre and Y. Rigoir (ed.), *Fouilles à Marseille. Les mobiliers (Ier-VIIe siècles ap. J.-C.)* (Études Massaliètes, Paris, 1998), 343-352.

Joncheray, J.-P., 'L'épave de Bataiguier'. In *Archeologia*, 79, (1975).

Joncheray, J.-P. and A., et al., 'Côte d'Azur : les épaves sarrasines d'Agay et de Cannes', in *Archeologia*, 79 (1975).

Joncheray, J.-P. and Sénac, P., 'Une nouvelle épave sarrasine du haut Moyen-Age', in *Archéologie Islamique*, 5 (1995), 24-34.

Joncheray, J.-P., 'Une épave du bas-empire: Dramont F', *Cahiers d'Archéologie Subaquatique* 4 (1975), 91-132.

Joncheray, J.-P., 'Deux épaves du bas-empire romain. Deuxième partie: l'épave Héliopolis 1', *Cahiers d'Archéologie Subaquatique* 13 (1997), 137-164.

Jurisic, M., *Ancient Shipwrecks of the Adriatic. Maritime Transport during the First and Second Centuries AD* (Oxford, 2000).

Kapitän, G., 'The Church Wreck off Marzamemi', *Archaeology* 22 (1969), 122–133.

Kingsley, S., 'Decline in the Ports of Palestine in Late Antiquity', in L. Lavan (ed.), *Recent Research in Late-Antique Urbanism* (*JRA* Suppl. No. 42, Rhode Island, 2001), 69-88.

Kingsley, S., *A Sixth-Century AD Shipwreck off the Carmel Coast, Israel. Dor D and Holy Land Wine Trade* (Oxford, 2002).

Kingsley, S., *Shipwreck Archaeology of the Holy Land. Processes and Parameters* (London, 2004).

Kingsley, S. and Decker, M. (eds), *Economy and Exchange in the East Mediterranean during Late Antiquity* (Oxford, 2001).

Kingsley, S. and Raveh, K., 'A Reassessment of the Northern Harbour of Dor, Israel', *International Journal of Nautical Archaeology* 23 (1994), 289-95.

Kingsley, S. and Raveh, K., 1996. *The Ancient Harbour and Anchorage at Dor, Israel. Results of the Underwater Surveys*, 1976–1991 (BAR Int. Series 626, Oxford).

Long, L. and Volpe, G., 'Le chargement de l'épave 1 de la Palud (VIe s.) à Port-Cros (Var). Note préliminaire', in M. Bonifay, M.-B. Carre and Y. Rigoir (eds), *Fouilles à Marseille. Les mobiliers (Ier-VIIe siècles ap. J.-C.)* (Études Massaliètes, Paris, 1998), 317-342.

Lopez, R.S., 'The Role of Trade in the Economic Readjustment of Byzantium in the 7th Century', *Dumbarton Oaks Papers* 13 (1959), 69-85.

Magdalino, P., 'The Maritime Neighborhoods of Constantinople: Commercial and Residential Functions, Sixth to Twelfth Centuries', *Dumbarton Oaks Papers* 54 (2000), 290-26.

Maioli M. G., 'Lo scavo del relitto del Parco di Teodorico a Ravenna', in M. Marzari (ed.), *NAVIS, rassegna di studi di archeologia, etnologia e storia navale*, 2, Sottomarina, (2001), 119-135.

Medas, S., 'The Late-Roman "Parco di Teodorico" Wreck, Ravenna, Italy: Preliminary Remarks on the Hull and Shipbuilding', in C Beltrame (ed), *Boats, Ships and Shipyards. Proceedings of the Ninth International Symposium on Boat and Ship Archaeology, Venice 2000* (Oxford, 2003), 42-48.

McCann, A. M. and Oleson J. P., 'Deep Water Shipwrecks off Skerki Bank: the 1997 Survey', *Journal of Roman Archaeology*, Suppl. 56 (2004).

McCann, A. M. and Freed, J., 'Deep Water Archaeology: a Late-Roman Ship from Carthage and an Ancient Trade Route Near Skerki Bank off Northwest Sicily', *Journal of Roman Archaeology*, Suppl. 13 (1994).

McCormick, M., *Origins of the European Economy. Communications and Commerce AD 300–900* (Cambridge University Press, 2002).

Mor, H., 'The Dor (Tantura) 2001/1 Shipwreck. A Preliminary Report'. *RIMS Newsletter* 29 (2002-2003), 15-17.

Parker, A. J., *Ancient Shipwrecks of the Mediterranean and the Roman Provinces* (Oxford, 1992).

Peacock, D. P. S. and Williams, D. F., *Amphorae and the Roman Economy* (London, 1986).

Petruso, K. and Gabel, C., 'A Byzantine Port on Egypt's Northwestern Frontier', *Archaeology* 36 (1983), 62-63, 76-77.

Presle, A. D. de la, 'Inscriptions grecques sur deux balances romaines trouvées à Dor', *Revue Biblique* 4 (1993), 580-88.

Raban, A., 'Sebastos: the Royal Harbour at Caesarea Maritima – a short-lived Giant', *International Journal of Nautical Archaeology* 21 (1992), 111-124.

Raban, A., 'The Inner Harbor Basin of Caesarea: Archaeological Evidence for its Gradual Demise', in A. Raban and K. G. Holum (eds), *Caesarea Maritima. A Retrospective after Two Millennia* (Leiden, 1996), 628-668.

Rodziewicz, M., 'From Alexandria to the West by Land and by Waterways', in J.-Y. Empereur (ed.), *Commerce et artisanat dans l'Alexandrie héllenistique et romaine* (*BCH* Suppl. 33, Paris, 1998), 93-103.

Schläger, H., Blackman, D. J. and Schäfer, J., 1968. 'Der Hafen von Anthedon mit Beiträgen zur Topographie und Geschichte der Stadt', *Archäologischer Anzeiger* (1968), 21-98.

Scranton, R. L., 'Glass Pictures from the Sea', *Archaeology* 20.3 (1967), 163-73.

Scranton, R. L. et al., *Kenchreai. Eastern Port of Corinth, I. Topography and Architecture* (Leiden, 1978).

Stanimirov, S., 'Underwater Archaeological Sites from Ancient and Middle Ages along Bulgarian Black Sea Coast – Classification', *Archaeologia Bulgarica* 7.1 (2003), 1-34.

Steffy, J. R., *Wooden Shipbuilding and the Interpretation of Shipwrecks* (Texas A and M University Press, 1994).

Throckmorton, P. and Throckmorton, J., 1973. 'The Roman Wreck at Pantano Longarini', *International Journal of Nautical Archaeology* 2 (1973), 243-266.

Visquis, A. G. 'Premier inventaire du mobilier de l'épave dite Des Jarres à Agay' *Cahiers d'Archéologie Subaquatique* (1972), 157-172.

Wachsmann, S. and Kahanov, Y., 'The 1995 INA/CMS Joint Expedition to Tantura Lagoon, Israel', *INA Quarterly* 24 (1997), 3-18.

Wachsmann, S., Kahanov, Y. and Hall, J., 'The Tantura B Shipwreck: the 1996 INA/CMS Joint Expedition to Tantura Lagoon', *INA Quarterly* 24 (1997), 3-18.

Ximénés, S., 'Etude préliminaire de l'épave sarrasine du rocher de l'Estéou', *Cahiers d'Archéologie Subaquatique*, V (1976), 139-150.